D0205345

WHAT IS IDENTITY?

WHAT IS IDENTITY?

C. J. F. Williams

CLARENDON PRESS · OXFORD
1989

Oxford University Press, Walton Street, Oxford OX2 6DP
Oxford New York Toronto
Delhi Bombay Calcutta Madras Karachi
Petaling Jaya Singapore Hong Kong Tokyo
Nairobi Dar es Salaam Cape Town
Melbourne Auckland
and associated companies in
Berlin Ibadan

Oxford is a trade mark of Oxford University Press

Published in the United States
by Oxford University Press, New York

British Library Cataloguing in Publication Data
Williams, C. J. F. (Christopher John Fardo, 1930–   )
What is identity?
1. Identity—Philosophical perspectives
I. Title
111
ISBN 0–19–824808–3

Library of Congress Cataloging-in-Publication Data
Williams, Christopher John Fardo.
What is identity? / C.J.F. Williams.
Bibliography: p.   Includes index.
1. Identity.   I. Title.
BC199.I4W55   1989   160—dc20   89–9285
ISBN 0–19–824808–3

Set by Hope Services (Abingdon) Ltd
Printed in Great Britain by
Biddles Ltd., Guildford and King's Lynn

TO
THE SAME MAN

PREFACE

What is Identity? is the last volume in a trilogy which began with *What is Truth?* (Cambridge University Press, 1976) and continued with *What is Existence?* (Oxford: Clarendon Press, 1981). The other two members of the trilogy were largely devoted to the defence of positions held by earlier philosophers: the view of Frege and Russell that existence is not a property of objects, but of concepts or propositional functions, and Ramsey and Prior's so-called prosentential theory of truth. The most original part of *What is Existence?* was the section on the Analogy of Being, i.e. the attempt to explain how the same word can have both a copulative and an existential function. Since this theory was presented in the final chapter of the book, it is not surprising that few readers, to judge from the reviews, persevered long enough to become acquainted with it. The impression left may have been conservative rather than radical.

The present volume, however, has a greater component of originality. To be sure, it begins with an exposition and defence of Wittgenstein's curiously neglected denial that identity is a relation. But it dissents from Wittgenstein's accompanying view that there is no need of a sign of identity. Consideration of intentional contexts seems to make clear that the concept of identity requires verbal expression. What is important, however, is that the expression required is not one that belongs to the category of two-place, first-level predicable, an expression whose purpose is to form a proposition when attached to a pair of names. Rather, it belongs to a category whose function is, roughly speaking, to form a one-place out of a two-place predicable. More of this later. It is already apparent that, like the other members of the trilogy, the theme of this book is that what is required for a proper understanding of concepts like being, identity, and truth is an appreciation of the syntactical categories to which the words which express them properly belong. What sounded like a metaphysical diatribe turns out to be an exercise in syntax.

Those who look for more stirring stuff than disputes over categorial boundaries may be encouraged by the news that consequences are drawn, not only for the philosophies of logic and mathematics, but for the philosophy of mind. The concept misleadingly expressed by the apparently relational predicable '--- is the same as ......' is the self-same concept, I argue, as that expressed by 'herself' and other reflexive pronouns. But there is a concept of *self*, closely allied to that expressed by the first person pronoun, which is different from, though connected with, the concept of identity. These connections are explored in the longest chapter of the book. And there is another chapter which argues that the attempts of certain philosophers of mind to assert identity between mental events and physical events in the brain fail, not merely to attain truth, but to be intelligible. Professor Kripke holds that, since the propositions Identity Theorists are trying to establish are not necessarily true, they are simply false. In maintaining that the sentences in question are strictly meaningless, I hope to have trumped Kripke.

A number of friends and colleagues have given me helpful criticisms of earlier drafts of some or all of these pages. I should like to express particular thanks to John Broome and Simon Orde who commented on all the chapters, and to Roger Teichmann who not only did this but also compiled the index. Others who read and gave me helpful advice on particular sections, for which I am grateful, are Steven Collins, Adam Morton, and John Mayberry. A version of the main argument of Chapter III was published in the *Proceedings of the Aristotelian Society*, vol. 80, 1979–80, under the title 'Is Identity a Relation?', but seems to have provoked no response. My thanks are also due to Peggy Gullidge, who bravely copied the original manuscript on to a word processor. This permitted me to make repeated alterations—even to the extent of transforming my Polish symbols into something more acceptable to the Oxford University Press and its advisors. The advisors, of course, raised more substantial points than this, particularly in the area of philosophy of mathematics; and although I have not always accepted their criticisms, I am most grateful for their expert assistance in this field. The British Academy has once again made a generous grant to cover the cost of typing and making an index, and I wish to express my warm thanks for this. The key to interpreting the coded dedication may be obtained by reading *Thinking about God*, by Brian Davies, OP.

C.J.F.W.

Midsomer Norton, Lady Day, mcmlxxxviii

CONTENTS

ANALYTICAL TABLE OF CONTENTS

CHAPTER I: THE PARADOX OF IDENTITY: PLATO TO RUSSELL

(§ 1) There is a paradox of identity, as of existence. Identity propositions seem either to state trivially that something is the same as itself, or to state falsely that one thing is the same as another. (§ 2) This paradox troubled Plato, Aristotle, and Hume. (§ 3) Frege taught in the first instance that identity propositions state that two names belong to one thing, and later that they can be informative because names can have different sense but the same meaning. The first view is plausible for propositions like 'St John is the same politician as Bolingbroke'. (§ 4) Russell's Theory of Descriptions provides a solution of the paradox. Russell's informal exposition of his theory. (§ 5) A more formal exposition. (§ 6) The logic of identity permits a shortened version of the analysis of identity propositions provided by the Theory of Descriptions. (§ 7) Russell's analysis shows that the paradox of identity, like the paradox of existence, arises from mistaking a second-level for a first-level predicable.

CHAPTER II: WITTGENSTEIN: IDENTITY NOT A RELATION

(§ 1) The Theory of Descriptions itself has the consequence that every informative identity proposition will be representable as being of one or other of two forms which I label (F) and (J). (§ 2) In neither of these forms does the identity sign occur unnegated: i.e., we never have 'x is the same as y', only 'x is different from y'. (§ 3) Wittgenstein suggested an interpretation of quantificational formulae which allows the clauses having the sense 'x is different from y' to be deleted from (F) and (J) without altering their meaning. The truncated formulae which result I label (K) and (L). (§ 4) Wittgenstein's innovation consists, not in expressing identity of object by identity of sign, but in expressing difference of object by difference of sign. No relation is involved in 'No two things φ'. Expressions of the form '$x = x$' are useless, and therefore meaningless. (§ 5) Roger White has pointed out the significance of the fact that in (F) and (J) the argument places of the identity predicable are occupied by bound variables, never by names. He shows the appropriateness of expressing the concept of identity, like that of existence, by the apparatus of quantification. (§ 6) 'The φer is the same as the ψer' is not, on any of these views, the contradictory of 'The φer is different from the ψer'. (§ 7) Wittgenstein's doctrine of identity is required by his theory of a necessary truth, but has independent justification. (§ 8) Hintikka provides a variety of rules for interpreting quantifiers in the manner suggested by Wittgenstein. (§ 9) Hintikka's 'exclusive' interpretations of quantification and the more familiar 'inclusive' interpretation correspond to different ways in which the ordinary-language analogues of quantifiers are used. Linguistic intuitions neither constrain us nor forbid us to adopt an exclusive interpretation of the quantifiers. (§ 10) Hintikka's claim that an exclusive interpretation of the quantifiers can solve Russell's Paradox and other paradoxes of set theory. (§ 11) Hintikka seems to be mistaken in his claim that, as well as its being possible to find a translation in a language with inclusively interpreted quantifiers together with identity for every formula expressible with exclusively interpreted quantifiers, translation is always possible in the opposite direction. This appears to contradict Wittgenstein's claim that in a correct *Begriffsschrift* there is no way of expressing such things as 'Everything is identical with itself' or 'Something is the same as *a*'. (§ 12) Roger White claims that the full import of the doctrine that identity is not a relation lies in just this refusal to allow such sentences to be meaningful. (§ 13) Kripke, like Russell, regards propositions of the form '*x* is the same as *y*', where '*x*' and '*y*' are replaced by proper names, as necessarily true. But Wittgenstein would not allow strings of words of this sort to be propositions at all, and neither he nor Russell would approve of including names and descriptions in a single category of 'rigid designators'.

CHAPTER III: THE NEED FOR A SIGN OF IDENTITY

(§ 1) An argument for the view that (1A) 'Paul thinks that Boscovich was born in Ragusa and that Dubrovnik is a present-day Croatian holiday resort' entails (4A) 'Paul thinks that a town where Boscovich was born is the same as a present-day Croatian holiday resort'. (§ 2) Where does the fallacy in this argument lie? (§ 3) Not in confusing (3A) 'Paul thinks that, for some town *x*, both Boscovich was born in *x* and *x* is a present-day Croatian holiday resort' with (5A) 'For some *x*, Paul thinks that, etc.'. If (5A) is entailed by (1A), so is (3A). (§ 4) A distinction needs to be made between (2) 'Boscovich was born in Dubrovnik and Dubrovnik is a present-day Croatian holiday resort' and (6) 'Dubrovnik was the birthplace of Boscovich and is a present-day Croatian holiday resort'. (§ 5) Two ways of explaining the construction of conjunctive predicables like '—— is old and wise': the explanation in terms of truth and the explanation in terms of satisfaction. (§ 6) Conjunctive predicables as the result of operating (i) on a conjunctive proposition with a name in each conjunct by removing these names to form a two-place predicable, and (ii) operating on this predicable, by an operation which can be expressed in several different ways, to form a one-place predicable. (§ 7) This latter operation (ii) can be generalized to apply to two-place predicables obtained from atomic as well as from molecular propositions. Here it can be expressed by the reflexive pronoun. (§ 8) Geach refuses to generalize the concept of the reflexive pronoun in this way. His reasons for refusing seem to be mistaken. (§ 9) I introduce new symbolism (the Xi-operator) to replace that used by Geach to do the work of the reflexive pronoun partly in order to mark the need to generalize the account of operation (ii). (§ 10) Using this symbolism we are able to represent the difference between (2A) and (6A) as a matter of scope distinction. (§ 11) The fallacious argument presented at the beginning of the chapter forces us to recognize, *pace* Wittgenstein, the need for a sign of identity, while agreeing that the sign we need is not the sign for a relation.

CHAPTER IV: SAME AND SELF

(§ 1) Quine's variable-free notation, and in particular his symbol 'Ref', can help us to form a unified picture of the way in which the concept of identity works. (§ 2) The first of three functions performed by variables: indication of scope. (§ 3) The second function, indication of the direction of a relational expression, can be combined with the first function, scope-indication, by the device of binding variables. (§ 4) An inversion operator reversing the direction of relational expressions can take over the second function of variables, leaving quantifiers shorn of their variables to take over the first function unaided. (§ 5) The third function of variables is to allow a quantifier to operate on more than one argument-place of a polyadic predicable. This is achieved by repetition of a variable in the matrix of the quantified formula. Such repetition still required in the case of n-place predicables for $n > 2$. (§ 6) Quine's two inversion operators enable us to position all repeated variables in final position in open sentences. These operators, together with 'Ref', take care of the third of the functions normally performed by bound variables. (§ 7) Quine's apparatus can be applied to molecular as well as to atomic sentences. (§ 8) The variable-free notation can be used to detect the fallacy in the argument put forward at the beginning of Chapter III. (§ 9) Existential generalization in some cases needs to be split into two operations: reflection and derelativization. This allows us to reject the derivation of (3A) from (2A), on the grounds that 'Paul thinks that' is opaque with respect to reflection although transparent with respect to derelativization. (§ 10) English vernacular equivalents of 'Ref'. (§ 11) Comparisons with other languages, particularly languages which have a middle voice.

(§ 12) If reflection is analogous to the middle, inversion is analogous to the passive voice. (§ 13) Many languages, including an earlier form of English, use just one morpheme to do the work done in modern English by the two morphemes 'same' and 'self'. (§ 14) 'Same' and 'self' express the same concept, although there is another concept of *self*, connected with self-consciousness. This will be studied in Chapter IX. (§ 15) We need a sign for the concept of identity (expressed by 'same' or 'self'), but not for that of difference (expressible by 'other' or 'else'). Wittgenstein was wrong about identity but right about difference.

CHAPTER V: EXTENSIONALISTS AND RELATIVISTS: AN EIRENIC INTERLUDE

(§ 1) Wittgenstein regards '*a* = *a*' as a pseudo-proposition and Russell calls '*a* exists' a 'mere noise or shape, devoid of significance'. (§ 2) But truth-conditions can be laid down for '--- exists' or '--- is the same as ......', taken as first-level predicables, in terms of their extensions. (§ 3) How, on this view, is the meaning of '--- exist' distinguishable from that of any predicable whose extension is the universal class? (§ 4) Can '--- exist' be defined as the only *simple* predicable whose extension is the universal class? (§ 5) Similar questions can be asked about '--- is the same as ......'. (§ 6) Existence and identity, if introduced in this way as first-level concepts, have nothing to do with the words 'exist' and 'same' as they are used in everyday speech. (§ 7) Kripke's manœuvre of replacing *identity* with *schmidentity* examined. (§ 8) Those who hold that identity is relative need to categorize '--- is the same as ......' as a first-level predicable. The relativist theory is incoherent on a Wittgensteinian view of identity. (§ 9) But neither will the extensionalist account of identity give relativists what they want. This removes any hope extensionalists may have had of providing an identity concept of interest to philosophers.

CHAPTER VI: IDENTITY AND INDISCERNIBILITY

(§ 1) The Identity of Indiscernibles is expressible in a Wittgensteinian language which lacks a sign for identity, and does not appear to be logically necessary. (§ 2) The Indiscernibility of Identicals, on the other hand, if stated in a non-trivial form in such a language, splits into two theses which are provable as theorems of the predicate calculus with variables exclusively interpreted. (§ 3) Apparent failure of substitutivity of identicals is to be explained by making appropriate scope distinctions. (§ 4) Contradictory beliefs seem to be attributable to people on a large scale if we allow unlimited substitution of identicals for identicals. (§ 5) Introduction of the Xi-operator allows us to distinguish clearly, by means of scope-distinctions, what it is to hold incompatible beliefs about what is in fact one and the same thing from what it is to hold that one and the same thing has incompatible properties. (§ 6) The same distinctions can be made with the use of the reflection operator. Contexts which are opaque with respect to reflection are transparent with respect to proper names. Reflection makes a difference to the conceptual content of thoughts, but names do not. (§ 7) The role of a proper name is simply to indicate the subject of discourse. Names do not have separately significant parts. (§ 8) One name, one object, and vice versa. 'London', as the name of a city in Ontario, is a different name from 'London' as used to refer to the capital of England. There are two names (at least) spelled 'Cato', whereas 'Dubrovnik' and 'Ragusa' are semantically the same name. (§ 9) Any name of an object will serve to identify a thought about that object, but will not constitute any part of that thought. An expression like '--- thinks that ......' forms an n-place predicable out of an $(n - 1)$-place predicable. 'John thought that Peter struck Malchus' is not of the form 'John thought that p'. (§ 10) This justifies the claim that there is mutual entailment between (1A) and (2A), and makes sense of the Wittgensteinian principle, earlier ignored, 'one object, one name'. (§ 11) The content of (1A) and (2A) is identical, but different from that of (6A). (§ 12) Metalinguistic version of the Principle of the Indiscernibility of Identicals. (§ 13) Summary of the chapter.

CHAPTER VII: ARITHMETICAL EQUATIONS

(§ 1) Arithmetical equations, on the face of it, seem to be identity propositions. (§ 2) Elementary equations, like '$n + m = k$', should be interpreted as formed by attaching three one-place second-level predicables to a three-place third-level predicable: 'the sum of n and m is k' means 'for any φ, for any ψ, if there are at most n things which φ, then if there are at most m things which ψ, there are at most k things which either φ or ψ'. (§ 3) A recursive definition is available for '$n + m = k$' which does not involve the Nominalist assumptions of the last section, but which similarly dispenses with the need to treat identity as a relation. (§ 4) A three-place predicable is inevitable at some stage in the analysis of '$n + m = k$': why not introduce it at once? (§ 5) The specifically Nominalist theory now to be introduced provides evidence of the usefulness of the generalized concept of reflection and of the exclusive interpretation of variables. (§ 6) The term 'quotifier' borrowed from Kneale to stand for expressions like '$4x$' and '$5y$', where '4' and '5' can replace 'n' in propositions of the form $nx\varphi x$ (to be read 'There are at most n things which φ'). A schema is provided for defining quotifiers in terms of quantifiers. (§ 7) Given these definitions, every true proposition of the form $n + m = k$ comes out as logically true. We examine and reject the objection that on these definitions some false propositions of this form will come out as contingently true. (§ 8) This analysis of elementary arithmetical equations agrees with Frege's analysis in being Logicist, but is Nominalist where Frege's analysis was Realist. This is due to the fact that it categorizes 'The sum of --- and ...... is ---' as a third-level predicable. (§ 9) The analysis is extended to cover propositions more complex than '$n + m = k$'. Equations involving more than three numbers are expressible with the help of 'Ref'. (§ 10) Such an analysis also requires that we bind with quantifiers variables whose substitution instances are quotifiers. Gottlieb's anxiety about the possibility of defining in a purely logical vocabulary the 'substitution class' for such variables. (§ 11) The schema provided in (§ 3) gets over Gottlieb's difficulties. My 'maximalist' analysis of quotifiers is tidier and more economical than Gottlieb's 'minimalist' analysis. (§ 12) A rule is given for providing substitution instances in purely logical vocabulary of the schema $nx\varphi x$. (§ 13) This provides only a contextual definition of the term 'substituend for n'. An explicit definition can be given with the help of 'Ref' applied to categories other than names. (§ 14) Formal numerals can then be regarded as mere abbreviations of logical operators. (§ 15) This analysis preserves the structure of natural languages. (§ 16) Analyses provided of '$n \times m = k$' and '$n^m = k$'. (§ 17) This analysis will not work for propositions involving negative, rational, and real numbers. We need in these cases to develop new analyses of the arithmetical operations. One such analysis is sketched for propositions involving negative numbers. (§ 18) None of these developments is likely to involve the reintroduction of ' $=$ ' as a first-level predicable.

CHAPTER VIII: THE IDENTITY OF EVENTS

(§ 1) Specific and numerical identity represent repetition of bound predicative and individual variables, respectively. (§ 2) Reflection, like derelativization, can operate in any category, and itself transcends the categories. (§ 3) Davidson's justification of talk of identity of events: his examples, on examination, prove not to involve the concept of identity at all. (§ 4) A better example found, and its logical form exposed. (§ 5) Preliminary explanation of the notion of a definite description of an event. (§ 6) Failure of Davidson's attempt to cast all designations of events into definite description form. (§ 7) Definite descriptions of events contrasted with direct nominalizations of event-reporting sentences. Direct and indirect designation. (§ 8) Direct nominalizations compared with Kripke's 'rigid designators'. (§ 9) Where Kripke rejects the claim of Mind–Brain Identity Theorists that their favourite propositions are, as they maintain, contingent, we regard the sentences themselves as 'pseudo-propositions'. (§ 10) It will not help the Identity Theorists to regard events as objects and identity as a relation along the lines of our 'Eirenic Interlude'. (§ 11) What the identity proposition *says* must be capable of being *shown* by repetition of some element in a proposition. This requirement cannot be satisfied by the Identity Theorists. (§ 12) If they can explain their view without expressing it in terms of identity, it may after all be acceptable.

CHAPTER IX: PERSONAL IDENTITY

(§ 1) The criteria of personal identity: Bernard Williams's exposition of the tension between 'mentalistic' and 'corporeal' criteria. (§ 2) Are the criteria of personal identity empirical in either of these ways? (§ 3) If not, what is the non-empirical element in the concept of personal identity? We should seek this in Castañeda's account of the indirect reflexive pronoun, which is to be distinguished from the concept of reflection in general. (§ 4) The 'Castañeda reflexive pronoun' (CRP) is the oratio obliqua representative of the first person in oratio recta. (§ 5) Immunity of certain first-person claims to error through misidentification. The subject of such claims is not identified empirically. (§ 6) A positive account is needed of the concept expressed by 'I'. (§ 7) To supply this we need to go back to the CRP. Propositions containing the CRP are not of the form δpa. (§ 8) The difference between 'David thought that he* deserved to die' and 'David thought that David deserved to die', not given by the conditions under which what David believes is true. (§ 9) The proposition containing 'he*' entails the proposition which substitutes 'David' for 'he*'. (§ 10) The relation between 'David believes that he* deserves to die' and 'David believes that he (not the CRP) deserves to die'. (§ 11) Introduction of * which is analogous to Der_0 or $\exists x$. (§ 12) '*' can symbolize 'I' as well as the CRP. (§ 13) If a utters a sentence of the form $*\varphi$ he makes the corresponding proposition of the form $\delta^*\varphi a$ true, and this entails Ref $\delta\varphi a$. It is this relation between it and Ref $\delta\varphi a$ which fixes the sense of $*\varphi$. (§ 14) What David said fixed by the fact that he said it. (§ 15) *Contra* the Wittgensteinians, when Sarah says 'I am worried' she does make an assertion. (§ 16) Just as Der φ's meaning is primarily determined by its being entailed by φa, so the meaning of $*\varphi$ is primarily determined by its logical relation to Ref $\delta\varphi a$. (§ 17) 'Thinking that he* deserves to die' compared with 'saying that he* deserves to die'. (§ 18) David says that he* deserves to die only if what he says does *not* indicate who it is he says deserves to die. Comparison with 'He said it was then time to start the meeting'. $\delta^*\varphi a$ differentiated from Ref $\delta\varphi a$ by this negative condition. (§ 19) A positive account of the use of * to be got from looking at Strawson's P-predicates.

'I am in pain' is, from one point of view, a no-place predicable. (§ 20) The difference between 'I' and 'he*' a matter of scope: * stands for 'I' if it occurs on the extreme left of the sentence containing it. (§ 21) This doctrine supplies the rationale for immunity to error through misidentification. (§ 22) $*\varphi$ & $*\psi$ entails * Ref (φ & ψ), which can be written * Ref Conj $\varphi\psi$. It already involves reflection, and therefore identity. (§ 23) 'a knows that he* is afraid that he* is going to be tortured' is of the form $\delta *$ Ref $\beta\varphi a$. The concept of identity (reflection) is here employed by a without recourse to empirical criteria. This is what gives substance to Swinburne's distinction between meaning and criteria. (§ 24) The connection between the two senses of 'self' is expressible by 'Ref' and '*'.

CHAPTER X: IDENTITY, BEING, AND TRUTH

(§ 1) What we say in ordinary English by using the words 'be', 'same', and 'true' can be said by using quantifiers and variables. (§ 2) The apparatus of quantifiers and variables involves the concept of reflection as well as derelativization. (§ 3) Is derelativization as well as reflection required for the expression of identity propositions? (§ 4) What can be shown and what can be said with respect to identity. (§ 5) 'Der' needed as well as 'Ref' for the reductive analysis of identity *as a relation*. (§ 6) 'Der' and 'Ref' transcend syntactical categories, as do the concepts of being and identity. Truth, on the other hand, can be expressed by 'Der' and 'Ref' only when these are restricted to the category of third-level predicables. (§ 7) Reflection, thus restricted, is the same as correspondence. (§ 8) Natural languages, lacking prosentences, need pseudo-predicables like 'true'. Their category of definite descriptions also fails to distinguish third-level predicables like 'What Percy says' from second-level predicables like 'What the postman brought'. This is a further reason for the emergence of the pseudo-predicable 'true'. (§ 9) Definite descriptions, seeming to name objects, give rise not only to pseudo-properties for these objects, like truth, but also to pseudo-relations between them, like identity. (§ 10) The point about being, identity, and truth made without benefit of logical symbolism.

I

THE PARADOX OF IDENTITY: PLATO TO RUSSELL

§ **1**. There is a paradox of identity which closely parallels the paradox of existence. This latter paradox, which Quine christened 'Plato's Beard', starts from the assumption that, e.g., the proposition 'Unfriendly Italians don't exist', like the proposition 'Unfriendly Italians don't like dogs', ascribes a property to unfriendly Italians. On this assumption, if what it says is true, there is nothing for it to be about. It must, therefore, fail to say anything at all, and its attempt to assert something must be self-stultifying. Since it purports to be about unfriendly Italians, it presupposes that unfriendly Italians exist, which is precisely what it goes on to deny. Negative existential propositions like 'Unfriendly Italians don't exist' are therefore in some sense self-contradictory; and by the same token affirmative existential propositions like 'Unfriendly Italians exist' are tautological or analytic. Affirmations of existence, on this assumption, come out as all necessarily true, and denials of existence as all necessarily false. Hence the paradox.

The paradox of identity similarly proceeds from an assumption —the assumption that a statement of identity asserts a relation. If so, it must assert either that this relation holds between one thing and something else, or that it holds between a thing and itself. If the former, what it asserts must be necessarily false: nothing can be the same thing as something other than it. If the latter, it must be necessarily true and the most trivial of tautologies. But some statements of identity, though false, are only contingently false: the leader of the British Labour Party in 1959 might have been, though in fact he never was, the Prime Minister of the United Kingdom. On the other hand, some statements of identity which are true are neither trivially nor tautologically true: the founder of Eton College was the founder of King's College Cambridge, but those who are not well-informed about medieval history may easily be unaware of the fact. How can we reconcile these features of identity statements?

Wittgenstein gives classical expression to this paradox: 'Roughly speaking, to say of *two* things that they are identical is nonsense, and to say of *one* thing that it is identical with itself is to say nothing at all.'[1]

§ **2.** But we did not have to wait for Wittgenstein. The paradox of identity, like the paradox of existence, was already exploited by Plato. In the *Theaetetus*, arguing for the impossibility of false judgement, Socrates is made to say:

> To put it generally, consider if you have ever set about convincing yourself that any one thing is certainly another thing . . . so long as a man is making a statement or judgement about both things at once and his mind has hold of both, he cannot say or judge that one of them is the other . . . so long, then, as a person is thinking of both, he cannot think of one as the other . . . or if he is thinking of one only and not of the other at all, he will never think that one is the other. (*Plato's Theaetetus*, 190 B–D.)

Again, Aristotle in the entry under 'same' in his philosophical lexicon, *Metaphysics Δ*, says:

> . . . sameness is a kind of oneness, either of the being of more than one thing or when a thing is treated as more than one (as for instance when someone says that a thing is the same as itself, which is to treat it as two things). (*Metaphysics*, Books *Γ*, *Δ*, *E*, tr. with notes by C. Kirwan, Oxford: Clarendon Press, 1971, 1018^a 7–9.)

Aristotle, who is no paradox-monger, does not suggest that thoughts involving identity are impossible. He holds merely that there is an internal tension in such thoughts—in judgments of numerical identity, at least. Judgements of specific identity are the norm: here we are affirming oneness of the being of several, as when we say 'Reagan is what Thatcher is—a populist politician'. In judgements of numerical identity (where they are true) we do not *have* several things, we have to *treat* one thing as two.

Aristotle's 'treating' one thing as two may be compared with Hume's idea of a 'fiction'. But Hume, like Plato, is more ready to regard the notion of identity as involving paradox. He writes:

> First, as to the principle of individuation, we may observe that the view of any one object is not sufficient to convey the idea of identity. For in that

---

[1] Ludwig Wittgenstein, *Tractatus Logico-Philosophicus*, tr. D.F. Pears and B. F. McGuinness, London: Routledge and Kegan Paul, 1966, 5.5303.

proposition, *an object is the same with itself*, if the idea express'd by the word, *object*, were noways distinguish'd from that meant by *itself*: we really shou'd mean nothing, nor wou'd the proposition contain a predicate and a subject, which, however, are imply'd in this affirmation. One single object conveys the idea of unity, not that of identity.

On the other hand, a multiplicity of objects can never convey this idea, however resembling they may be suppos'd. The mind always pronounces the one not to be the other, and considers them as forming two, three, or any determinate number of objects, whose existences are entirely distinct and independent.

Since then both number and unity are incompatible with the relation of identity, it must lie in something that is neither of them. But to tell the truth, at first sight this seems utterly impossible. Betwixt unity and number there can be no medium; no more than betwixt existence and non-existence. After one object is suppos'd to exist, we must either suppose another to exist; in which case we have the idea of number: or we must suppose it not to exist; in which case the first remains at unity. (*Treatise of Human Nature*, ed. Selby-Bigge, 2nd edn. rev. P. H. Nidditch, Oxford: Clarendon Press, 1985, p. 200.)

The 'fiction' to which Hume appeals to overcome this difficulty is that of the idea of an 'unchangeable' object. This is something which is strictly impossible, since in Hume's view we have the idea of time only where we have the idea of change. That something should persist through time unchanged is conceivable only because we conflate the constant idea of the object with the idea of a series of changing objects, principally our own perceptions, each of which coexists with a stretch of the duration of the unchanging object. 'This fiction of the imagination almost universally takes place; and 'tis by means of it, that a single object . . . is able to give us a notion of identity' (ibid., p. 201). The mind, attending to the different times at which the object exists, receives the idea of plurality. Switching, however, to the unchanging object which exists at each of these times, it obtains the idea of unity. These ideas are not, of course, compatible; but Hume's theory of the imagination regularly supposes that self-contradiction is allowed to pass unnoticed because the mind shifts its attention from one element in a complex to another which is incompatible with it, while failing to notice its own operation.

Here then is an idea, which is a medium betwixt unity and number; or more properly speaking, is either of them, according to the view, in which we take it: And this idea we call that of identity. We cannot, in any propriety of speech, say that an object is the same with itself, unless we mean, that the object existent at one time is the same with itself existent at another. By this means we make a difference betwixt the idea meant by the word, *object*, and that meant by *itself*, without going to the length of number, and at the same time without restraining ourselves to a strict and absolute unity. (Ibid. p. 201.)

Hume's solution of the paradox, even if it worked, would work only for statements of identity over time, e.g., 'The dog you just ran over is the dog which bit my child last week'. Plato tried a similar solution of his paradox of false judgement; but unlike Hume, he was aware of its limitations. Where Hume considers only propositions stating identity over time, Plato originally prescribed a treatment applicable only to misperceptions—misfittings of perception to thought. He then realized that this would not explain the possibility of judgements like 'The sum of five and seven is the same as eleven'. The same example—with 'twelve', perhaps, substituted for 'eleven'—would have served to alert Hume to the inadequacy of his analysis. Arithmetical equations do not state that 'the object existent at one time is the same with itself existent at another'. But theories of identity had better make room for the propositions of elementary arithmetic.[2] Hume's theory is a non-starter. It is of interest only as evidence of the perennial perplexity which the paradox of identity has engendered amongst philosophers.

§ 3. Frege addressed himself to this paradox, and produced, in turn, two solutions to it. The first, which he gave in *Begriffsschrift*,[3] is that identity is a relation between names, not between the things they name. If I say 'The flower vase is on top of the piano', I am asserting a relation between the object named by 'the flower vase' and the object named by 'the piano'. But when I say 'St John is the same as Bolingbroke' it might well be supposed that I am saying something about these two names, to wit, that they are names of one and the same politician. As Frege says (ibid., p. 10), 'Elsewhere names are mere proxies for their content, and thus any

---

[2] I try to follow my own advice in ch. VII.

[3] See P. T. Geach and M. Black, *Translations from the Philosophical Writings of Gottlob Frege*, Oxford: Basil Blackwell, 1980, pp. 10–12. Even here Frege emphasizes that we need more than one name only because what he calls the 'content' of the name, i.e. the thing named, can be determined in more than one way.

phrase they occur in just expresses a relation between their various contents; but names at once appear *in propria persona* so soon as they are joined together by the symbol for equality of content; for this signifies the circumstance of two names' having the same content'.

In his later paper, 'On Sense and Meaning',[4] he explicitly repudiates this view.

> . . . this relation would hold between the names or signs only in so far as they named or designated something. It would be mediated by the connexion of each of the two signs with the same designated thing. But this is arbitrary. Nobody can be forbidden to use any arbitrarily producible event or object as a sign for something. In that case the sentence $a = b$ would no longer refer to the subject matter, but only to its mode of designation; we would express no proper knowledge by its means. (Ibid., pp. 56–7.)

Frege goes on to give two examples of 'proper knowledge' which is clearly expressed by means of an identity proposition. One is an example of a priori, one of empirical knowledge. The a priori knowledge is expressed by a sentence 'The point of intersection of a and b is the same as the point of intersection of b and c, where a, b, and c are the lines connecting the vertices of a triangle with the midpoints of the opposite sides'. The empirical knowledge is the astronomical discovery expressed in the sentence 'The morning star is the same as the evening star'.

What Frege means by 'proper knowledge' in the last sentence of the quoted passage is illustrated partly by his examples and partly by his implied contrast. The examples are a matter of geometrical and astronomical knowledge, respectively. The contrast is with some proposition whose truth depends on the arbitrary decision of human beings to call a certain object by certain names. The example I used to illustrate Frege's *Begriffsschrift* doctrine fits this last description fairly closely. The fact that St John was the same man as Bolingbroke is a fact about how certain human beings decided to use certain names: there was no incongruity in my use of the paraphrase ' "St John" and "Bolingbroke" name the same man'.

Frege's revised account of the possibility of informative identity propositions rests on the distinction between sense and meaning in

---

[4] Ibid., pp. 56–78.

his special use of 'meaning (*Bedeutung*)' where the meaning of a name is the object it names. What makes it worthwhile to say that the point of intersection of *a* and *b* is the same as the point of intersection of *b* and *c* is that, though the expressions 'the point of intersection of *a* and *b*' and 'the point of intersection of *b* and *c*' have the same meaning, they have different senses. It is their having the same meaning which makes the proposition true: it is their having different senses which makes it informative. We do not find it difficult at an intuitive level to see what Frege means by 'sense' in this context. (His developed theory is more difficult. Here senses are *objects* which can themselves stand as the meaning or reference of proper names.) Like 'the morning star' and 'the evening star', these expressions are complex. Frege is willing to call complex expressions of this sort proper names: 'The designation of a single object can also consist of several words or other signs. For brevity, let every such designation be called a proper name.' (Ibid., p. 57.) Since complex names inherit their sense from the sense of the expressions which compose them, and the complex names we are concerned with are composed of different expressions, we can readily understand how they can have different senses. 'The morning star' has a different sense from 'The evening star' because 'morning' has a different sense from 'evening'. But what of 'St John' and 'Bolingbroke'? What of proper names which are not complex, having no component parts which themselves have a sense contributing to the sense of the whole. The syllable 'tot' makes no contribution to the sense of 'Aristotle', nor does 'St' contribute to *this* sense of 'St John', who was certainly no saint. What then is the sense of 'Aristotle' or 'St John' or 'Bolingbroke'?

Frege has an answer to this question in the case of 'Aristotle'. In a footnote on p. 58 of 'On Sense and Meaning' he suggests that different people may attach different senses to the name 'Aristotle'. Some may take its sense to be 'the pupil of Plato and teacher of Alexander the Great', some 'the teacher of Alexander the Great who was born at Stagira'. Frege has been understood as implying by this remark that what is supplied by complex expressions like these is a definition of the proper name, 'Aristotle'. On this view, the relation between 'Aristotle' and 'the pupil of Plato and teacher of Alexander the Great' will be the same as that between 'square' and 'equilateral rectangle'. It should be possible for the sense-giving complex expression to be substituted for the simple name in any context without changing the significance of the whole. Thus what people mean who say 'St John is the same as Bolingbroke' might be taken to be 'Queen Anne's last Secretary of State is the same as the author of *The Idea of a Patriot King*'. There would be no more difficulty about understanding how there can be sameness of meaning together with difference of sense in this case than there was in the case of 'The point of intersection of *a* and *b* is the same as the point of intersection of *b* and *c*'.

Those who have doubts about the notion of the sense of a proper name, or about this interpretation of Frege's remarks about the sense of a proper name, may well return to the doctrine of the *Begriffsschrift* for their explanation of identity propositions like 'St John is the same as Bolingbroke', which have simple rather than complex expressions flanking either side of the phrase 'is the same as'. The proposition about points of intersection must certainly be taken to express 'proper knowledge', if this is understood by contrast with 'information about signs or words'. But 'St John is the same as Bolingbroke' gives a strong impression of being a statement about words—names in this case. At least one of the names is likely to be being mentioned here rather than used. We might just as well have said 'St John is sometimes called "Bolingbroke"', or '"St John" is an alternative name for Bolingbroke'. But if this is how we understand identity propositions of this sort, we are once again regarding them as equivalent in sense to propositions in which 'is the same as' is flanked on one side, or on either side, by a complex expression. That is to say, whereas on the previous interpretation we understood 'St John is the same as Bolingbroke' as meaning 'Queen Anne's last Secretary of State is the same man as the author of *The Idea of a Patriot King*', the present suggestion is that we regard it as meaning 'The man we call "St John" is the same as the man we call "Bolingbroke"'. 'Queen Anne's last Secretary of State' and 'The man we call "St John"' are both, in Frege's terminology, complex names.

It is, of course, to context that we must look to determine who it is that is referred to by 'we' in this last description. Even if our pronunciation of 'St John' makes it clear that we are not now concerned with the use of the word to name the author of the Fourth Gospel, there will be many different people who have, or have had, 'St John' as their Christian name or surname. But in practice there will not be much danger of misunderstanding. Context makes clear which copy of which issue of which newspaper I mean when I say 'I've left the newspaper in the bedroom'. In the same way context will make clear that in this case that I am not referring to Norman St John Stevas (who now, it turns out, is the same as Lord St John of Fawsley). Nor, when I speak in this context of 'the man we call "Bolingbroke"', will I be taken to be referring to King Henry IV. Such propositions are rarely simply about names considered as noises or patterns on paper. They are about spoken or written symbols as used in a certain way. Nevertheless, with that proviso, 'St John is the same man as Bolingbroke' can be regarded as an implicitly metalinguistic utterance.

But if it can be regarded as the result of embedding ' "St John" ' and ' "Bolingbroke" ' in the two-place metalinguistic predicable 'The man we call --- is the same as the man we call ......', it is also the result of attaching the phrases 'The man we call "St John"' and 'The man we call "Bolingbroke"' to '--- is the same as ......'. Frege's later rejection of the metalinguistic theory of the *Begriffs-schrift* makes room for informative identity propositions like 'The point of intersection of a and b is the same as the point of intersection of b and c', which are in no way concerned with the use of words; but the old examples as well as the new ones can be regarded as the result of embedding complex names of the kind Russell was to call definite descriptions in the matrix '--- is the same as ......'. The cash value of the claim that in an informative statement of the form 'a is the same as b' the senses of a and b will be different lies in the fact that the replacements for a and b will always be, or be elliptical for, definite descriptions.

Recent writers have talked of the two main theories currently offered to explain identity as (i) the objectual and (ii) the metalinguistic theory.[5] This way of making the distinction is, in my view, a mistake. A theory, like Russell's, which regards as the typical identity proposition one in which '--- is the same as ......' is flanked by definite descriptions can be said to regard such a

---

[5] Thomas V. Morris, *Understanding Identity Statements*, Aberdeen University Press, 1984, sets out this contrast on the first page of his Introduction, and it dictates much of the structure of his book. It can also be found in S. Kripke, 'Naming and Necessity' in D. Davidson and G. Harman (eds.), *Semantics of Natural Language*, 2nd edn., Dordrecht and Boston, Mass.: Reidel, 1972, pp. 309 ff.

proposition as saying something, not about objects, but about propositional functions. 'Something satisfies both φx and ψx', where φx and ψx are unique descriptions, may be given as the form of such propositions. But it would be a grave mistake to regard propositions about propositional functions—propositions which Frege would see as involving second-level functions—as propositions about language. 'Something satisfies both φx and ψx', is no more metalinguistic than ' "x is bald" is sometimes true'. Substitution instances of φx and ψx here can be 'x is called "St John" ' and 'x is called "Bolingbroke" ', but they can also be 'a and b intersect at x' and 'b and c intersect at x'. Talk about language is an unimportant feature of certain particular examples of the form of proposition in question: it is in no way a feature of the form itself. This will become clearer when we turn from Frege's account of identity propositions to that given by Russell.

§ **4.** Russell's Theory of Descriptions was in fact intended to solve *inter alia* certain problems about identity. The form which the paradox of identity takes in 'On Denoting'[6] is the puzzle about George IV. Despite the fact that he wondered whether Scott was the author of *Waverley*, and despite the fact that Scott *was* the author of *Waverley*, George IV was not exercised over the question whether Scott was Scott. The denotation of 'the author of *Waverley*' is the same as the denotation of 'Scott', but Scott's being the author of *Waverley* is a more interesting matter than Scott's being Scott. It is non-trivial, known only to a few, and in every way contingent. That Scott was Scott, on the other hand, is a necessary truth, a useless tautology, and a fact of which even George IV was aware.

In the case of those propositions where 'is the same as' is flanked on either side by a proper name Russell concedes all that is urged by the paradox-mongers. Even if different names appear in this position, if instead of 'Scott is the same as Scott' we take as our example 'Scott is the same as Sir Walter', we have, according to Russell, the same futile statement as is expressed by 'Scott is identical with himself'—provided, that is, both names, both 'Scott' and 'Sir Walter', are here being *used* as names, provided their function is simply to refer, to single out as the subject of discourse

[6] In R. C. Marsh (ed.), *Logic and Knowledge*, London: George Allen and Unwin, 1956, pp. 41–56.

the person who was called 'Sir Walter Scott'. Not that he thinks it very likely that someone who says 'Scott is the same as Sir Walter' is using both names in this way. The overwhelming probability is that the speaker is informing us that by 'Sir Walter' someone was intending to speak of Scott, or that Sir Walter is usually referred to as 'Scott' by those who point out his monument in Princes Street. Indeed Russell regards it as so unlikely that anyone should actually be using a proper name in any context as a proper name—a logically proper name, that he can practically disregard the possibility that paradox may arise from someone's asserting a propositions of the form '$a = a$'.

In Russell's view, almost every use of a proper name is to be understood as an abbreviated definite description. This is necessarily so if the object named is not something with which the speaker is acquainted. The sense of 'Aristotle' would seem to him unquestionably the same as that of some complex expression like 'the pupil of Plato and teacher of Alexander the Great'. And he certainly holds that it is only 'truncated definite descriptions' of this sort—names regarded simply as abbreviations for complex expressions—or overtly complex expressions like 'the author of *Waverley*', that can usefully stand on one side or the other of the identity sign. He puts his position with admirable vigour in his 'Lectures on the Philosophy of Logical Atomism':

> Identity is a rather puzzling thing at first sight. When you say 'Scott is the author of *Waverley*', you are half-tempted to think there are two people, one of whom is Scott and the other the author of *Waverley*, and they happen to be the same. That is obviously absurd, but that is the sort of way one is tempted to deal with identity.
>
> When I say 'Scott is the author of *Waverley*' and that 'is' expresses identity, the reason that identity can be asserted there truly and without tautology is just the fact that the one is a name and the other a description. Or they might both be descriptions. If I say 'The author of *Waverley* is the author of *Marmion*', that, of course, asserts identity between two descriptions. (*Logic and Knowledge*, p. 247.)

Russell is here slipping carelessly from talk about what object or objects the proposition 'Scott is the author of *Waverley*' is *about* to talk about what sort of *expressions* stand on either side of the 'is' which 'expresses identity'. But we get his drift. By 'descriptions' he means complex expressions of the sort Frege was indicating when he said 'The designation of an object can also consist of several words or other signs'. Frege, as we have seen, was prepared to call such complex expressions 'proper names'. Russell will not allow that strings of words like 'the point of intersection of *a* and *b*' or 'the author of *Marmion*' are proper names or designations of objects. (No proper name for Russell can be complex.) Strings of words of this sort do not, in Russell's view, have any meaning at all in isolation. They are 'incomplete symbols'. To understand their function in a sentence we have to take the complete sentence in which they occur and spell out what it means—in modern jargon, state its truth-conditions. Russell does just this. In his earliest exposition of his Theory of Descriptions, in 'On Denoting', he explains the role that 'the author of *Waverley*' has in 'Scott was the author of *Waverley*'. The rule is this: 'speaking generally, suppose we wish to say that the author of *Waverley* had the property φ, what we wish to say is equivalent to "One and only one entity wrote *Waverley*, and that one had the property φ"' (*Logic and Knowledge*, p. 51). He then applies the general rule to the case of our identity proposition:

Every proposition in which 'the author of *Waverley*' occurs being explained as above, the proposition 'Scott was the author of *Waverley*' (i.e. 'Scott was identical with the author of *Waverley*') becomes 'One and only one entity wrote *Waverley*, and Scott was identical with that one'; or, reverting to the wholly explicit form: 'It is not always false of *x* that *x* wrote *Waverley*, that it is always true of *y* that if *y* wrote *Waverley* *y* is identical with *x*, and that Scott is identical with *x*.' (Ibid.)

A little later Russell explains how his theory provides the solution to our paradox:

The usefulness of *identity* is explained by the above theory. No one outside a logic-book ever wishes to say '*x* is *x*', and yet assertions are often made in such forms as 'Scott was the author of *Waverley*' or 'thou art the man'.[7] The meaning of such propositions cannot be stated without the notion of identity, although they are not simply statements that Scott is identical with another term, the author of *Waverley*, or that thou art identical with another term, the man. The shortest statement of 'Scott is the author of *Waverley*' seems to be 'Scott wrote *Waverley*; and it is always true of *y* that if *y* wrote *Waverley*, *y* is identical with Scott'. It is in this way that identity enters into 'Scott is the author of *Waverley*'; and it is owing to such uses that identity is worth affirming. (*Logic and Knowledge*, p. 55.)

---

[7] How many modern readers of 'On Denoting' pick up the allusion to Nathan's rebuke of David (see 2 Samuel 12: 7)?

§ 5. 'Descriptions' or 'definite descriptions', as Russell calls these complex expressions like 'the author of *Waverley*', are given a special symbolic expression in *Principia Mathematica*. Using φx as an abbreviation of '*x* wrote *Waverley*', 'the author of *Waverley*' is symbolized by $(\imath x)(\varphi x)$, which can be read 'the *x* such that *x* wrote *Waverley*'. The meaning of symbols of the form $(\imath x)(\varphi x)$ is given by contextual definition, by giving a paraphrase of complete sentences in which they occur. One such definition, which formalizes the general rule given in 'On Denoting', although it does not suffice for defining all occurrences of $(\imath x)(\varphi x)$, is

(R) $\psi((\imath x)(\varphi x)) =_{df} \exists x \{\varphi x \ \& \ [\forall y \ (\varphi y \rightarrow x = y) \ \& \ \psi x]\}$.

With φx abbreviating '*x* wrote *Waverley*' and ψx abbreviating '*x* was Scotch' the *definiens* of the definition just given is the analysis Russell gives of 'The author of *Waverley* was Scotch'. To get his analysis of 'The author of *Waverley* is Scott' (which is no different from 'Scott is the author of *Waverley*') in the formal version, all we need to do is to use *a* to symbolize 'Scott', so that we can substitute $x = a$ ('*x* is the same as *a*') for ψx in the *definiens*, to obtain

(α) $\exists x \{\varphi x \ \& \ [\forall y \ (\varphi y \rightarrow x = y) \ \& \ x = a]\}$.

This is obtained simply by following the rules by which Russell introduces his definite description symbol. $(\imath x)(\varphi x) = a$, the symbolic version of 'The author of *Waverley* is Scott', is simply regarded as a definitional abbreviation of (α).

§ 6. But (α) can be shortened, abbreviated, by the application of rules of inference valid in the logic of identity. Any proposition of the form $\exists x \ (\varphi x \ \& \ x = a)$ entails and is entailed by the corresponding proposition of the form φa. That is to say,

(β) $\exists x \ (\varphi x \ \& \ a = x) \longleftrightarrow \varphi a$

is logically true. Any proposition of the form $\exists x \ (\varphi x \ \& \ x = a)$ can therefore be abbreviated to the corresponding proposition of the form φa. But (α) is of the form $\exists x \ (\varphi x \ \& \ x = a)$: it is obtainable by substituting $\varphi x \ \& \ \forall y \ (\varphi y \rightarrow x = y)$ for φx in $\exists x \ (\varphi x \ \& \ x = a)$. ($\alpha$) can therefore be abbreviated to

(γ) $\varphi a \ \& \ \forall y \ (\varphi y \rightarrow a = y)$.

This is the formal version of Russell's 'Scott wrote *Waverley*; and it is always true of *y* that if *y* wrote *Waverley*, *y* is identical with

Scott', which Russell says is 'the shortest statement of "Scott is the author of *Waverley*"'.

Wittgenstein will use the principle of the logical equivalence of φa and $\exists x \, (\varphi x \,\&\, x = a)$ to obtain another 'shortening' of the Russellian analysis of propositions of the form $a = (\imath x)(\varphi x)$. We shall see how this works in the next chapter. But he will use it to call in question Russell's remark 'The meaning of such propositions cannot be stated without the notion of identity'. He could not have moved in this direction, however, without cashing in on Russell's clear perception of how 'the usefulness of *identity*' can be explained by his Theory of Descriptions.

§ **7.** Before pressing on, however, to examine Wittgenstein's advance on Russell, it is worth returning to take stock of the paradox of identity as set out at the beginning of the chapter. Russell allows that, where 'Scott' and 'Sir Walter' are both being used as proper names, 'Scott is the same as Sir Walter' is a futile tautology. The paradox is allowed its full force where that is concerned. But in 'The author of *Waverley* is the same as the author of *Marmion*' Russell sees a quite different structure. His analysis of this can be stated for this purpose without benefit of logical symbolism. The proposition is designed to assert that being sole author of *Waverley* and being sole author of *Marmion* are both properties of a single person. Someone both wrote *Waverley* and wrote *Marmion* (taking it for granted that no two people wrote either). The structure of the proposition is thus given by identifying the pattern 'Someone both --- and ......' and seeing it as realized by filling the two blanks with the verb-phrases 'wrote *Waverley*' and 'wrote *Marmion*'. The paradox arose from assuming that identity propositions had the job of stating a relationship between objects (an object and itself). On this view the structure of the proposition was that of the pattern '--- is the same as ......' with the blanks being filled in with names. Frege's name for incomplete expressions needing names to complete them to form propositions was 'first-level predicate'; but for reasons stated by P. T. Geach[8] it is preferable to use the word 'predicable'. The

---

[8] Expressions of this kind are called predicates by Geach only when they are attached to names in propositions so that they are being actually predicated of the bearers of the names. They may, however, be called 'predicables' whenever they occur. See P. T. Geach, *Reference and Generality*, 3rd edn., Ithaca and London: Cornell University Press, 1980, § 18.

incomplete expressions '--- is the same as ......', '--- wrote *Waverley*' and '--- wrote *Marmion*' would all be regarded by him as first-level predicables of this type. But 'Someone both --- and ......' is an incomplete expression which yields a proposition when first-level predicables like '--- wrote *Waverley*' and '--- wrote *Marmion*', i.e., verbs or verb-phrases, not names, are used to fill its blanks. Frege called incomplete expressions of *this* sort 'second-level predicables'. So Russell's solution of the paradox can be stated in Fregean terminology by saying that he regards genuine, informative, useful identity propositions as involving, not the first-level predicable '--- is the same as ......', but the second-level predicable 'Somebody both --- and ......'. The mistake, as Russell locates it, is exactly the same as that which gave rise to the paradox of existence. That paradox is engendered by allowing the assumption that existence is a property of objects. Frege would have said that existence was a property of concepts, not of objects—another way of saying that '--- exists' is a second-level, not a first-level, predicable. Frege did not say, but if he had accepted Russell's solution of the paradox of identity he could have said, that identity was a relation between concepts, not objects.[9] Alternatively he could have said that the clear way to express identity was to use the two-place predicable of second level 'Somebody both --- and ......', rather than the illusory two-place predicable of first-level '--- is the same as ......'. With the paradox of identity, as with the paradox of existence, the trouble lies, on this view, in confusing second-level with first-level predicables, in mistaking properties of concepts for properties of objects. Frege did not say this about identity, though he made exactly this point about existence. Russell did not express himself with the help of Fregean terminology as I have just done. And Russell's analysis has to be taken further—through Wittgenstein and beyond. But Russell's analysis thus stated is a good beginning, and it allows us to see the two paradoxes, of existence and identity, as analogous, not only in the pattern of puzzlement they generate, but in the therapeutic treatment needed to allay it.

---

[9] The mistake to which I drew attention at the end of § 3 can now be characterized thus: it is the mistake of thinking that the alternative to seeing identity as a relation between objects is seeing it as metalinguistic, ignoring the possibility of a relation between concepts. Frege would have denied emphatically that a relation between concepts was a relation between names.

WITTGENSTEIN:
IDENTITY NOT A RELATION

§ **1.** Wittgenstein's development of Russell's views on identity begins with a double simplification. As we have seen, according to Russell, any informative identity proposition will have a definite description as at least one of its terms. That is to say, working identity propositions as opposed to idle ones will be either of the form $a = (\imath x)(\varphi x)$ or of the form $(\imath x)(\varphi x) = (\imath y)(\psi y)$. Let us take the simpler of these forms first. But before applying to it the analysis provided by the Theory of Descriptions, it will be convenient to make some general remarks about that theory.

Russell's analysis of propositions containing definite descriptions can be expressed in a number of different ways, and Russell himself rings the changes on these different versions of his theory.[1] In 'On Denoting' he gives the following analysis of 'The father of Charles II was executed'

It is not always false of x that x begat Charles II and that x was executed and that 'if y begat Charles II, y is identical with x' is always true of y. (*Logic and knowledge*, p. 44.)

This is of the logical form

(A) $\exists x \ [(\varphi x \ \& \ \psi x) \ \& \ \forall y \ (\varphi y \rightarrow x = y)]$.

In *Introduction to Mathematical Philosophy*, on the other hand, he gives as an analysis of 'The author of *Waverley* was Scotch' the conjunction of the three propositions:

(B1) 'x wrote *Waverley*' is not always false;
(B2) 'if x and y wrote *Waverley*, x and y are identical' is always true;
(B3) 'if x wrote *Waverley*, x was Scotch' is always true.
(*Introduction to Mathematical Philosophy*, London: George Allen and Unwin, 1919, p. 177).

---

[1] Readers who are willing to take this exposition of Russell's Theory of Descriptions on trust can skip this paragraph and take up again where (D) is introduced.

The logical form of this conjunction is

   (B) $\exists x \, (\varphi y) \, \& \, \{\forall y \, \forall z [(\varphi y \, \& \, \varphi z) \to y = z] \, \& \, \forall w \, (\varphi w \to \psi w)\}$.

In *Principia Mathematica*,[2] however, the analysis, or definition in
use, which he gives of $\psi((\imath x)(\varphi x))$ is of the form

   (C) $\exists x \, \forall y \, [(\varphi y \leftrightarrow x = y) \, \& \, \psi x]$.

The difference between (A), (B), and (C) lies in their length and
in their perspicuity, or that of their ordinary language equivalents.
Brevity is important in the context of *Principia Mathematica*,
perspicuity in that of *Introduction to Mathematical Philosophy*.
(A), (B), and (C) are, of course, logically equivalent, and which of
them Russell selects is of importance only for ease of exposition in
the particular context in which it occurs. In *Introduction to
Mathematical Philosophy*, where his concern is primarily to make
himself readily understood, he selects (B), the conjunctive
analysis. Its three conjuncts can be expressed in simple ordinary-
language terms: (B1) is equivalent to 'At least one person wrote
Waverley', (B2) to 'At most one person wrote *Waverley*', and (B3)
to 'Whoever wrote *Waverley* was Scotch'. In *Principia Mathematica*
his concern is primarily with formal simplicity and elegance: (C) is
the shortest formula available to him.

   Another formula, which is logically equivalent to (A), (B), and
(C) is

   (D) $\exists x \, (\varphi x \, \& \, \psi x) \, \& \, \neg \, \exists y \, \exists z \, [(\varphi y \, \& \, \varphi z) \, \& \, y \neq z]$.

This gives the form of the proposition 'Someone wrote *Waverley*
and was Scotch and no two people wrote *Waverley*'. Any
proposition of the form $\psi((\imath x)(\varphi x))$ is equivalent to one of this
form. In particular, the pattern provided by (D) will provide the
analysis of a proposition of the form $a = (\imath x)(\varphi x)$ by the simple
technique of substituting $a = x$ for ψx. We thus obtain

   (E) $\exists x \, (\varphi x \, \& \, a = x) \, \& \, \neg \, \exists y \, \exists z \, [(\varphi y \, \& \, \varphi z) \, \& \, y \neq z]$.

The first conjunct of this, $\exists x \, (\varphi x \, \& \, a = x)$, is easily seen to be a
mere periphrasis for φa, since (β), i.e., $\exists x \, (\varphi x \, \& \, a = x) \leftrightarrow \varphi a$, is
logically true: 'Someone identical with Scott wrote *Waverley*' is just
another way of saying 'Scott wrote *Waverley*'. That (β) is a logical
truth is, as we have seen (above, Chapter I, § 6), something of which
Russell was aware, and which he made use of in abbreviating (α)

---

[2] A. N. Whitehead and B. Russell, *Principia Mathematica to *56*, Cambridge
University Press, 1962, *14.

to (γ). Russell derives the equivalence of these formulae, i.e. $\exists x \{[\varphi x \;\&\; \forall y \,(\varphi y \rightarrow x = y)] \;\&\; x = a\} \leftrightarrow [\varphi a \;\&\; \forall y \,(\varphi y \rightarrow a = y)]$, from (β) by substituting $\varphi x \;\&\; \forall y \,(\varphi y \;\&\; x = y)$ for φx in (β). Wittgenstein's abbreviation uses (β) itself to abbreviate the first conjunct of (E). This gives, as a shorter formula logically equivalent to (E),

(F) $\varphi a \;\&\; \neg\, \exists x \,\exists y \,[(\varphi x \;\&\; \varphi y) \;\&\; x \neq y]$.

That is to say, the Theory of Descriptions gives 'Scott wrote *Waverley* and no two people wrote *Waverley*' as the analysis of 'Scott was the author of *Waverley*'. That is the first simplification, the simplification of the simpler of the two forms of identity proposition allowed by Russell.

The second simplification takes care of identity propositions which contain two definite descriptions, identity propositions of the form $(\imath x)(\varphi x) = (\imath y)(\psi y)$. Once again we take (D) as the model for analysing such propositions. First we reletter the variables to avoid confusion with variables already used in (D), replacing $(\imath x)(\varphi x) = (\imath y)(\psi y)$ with $(\imath v)(\psi v) = (\imath w)(\varphi w)$. Then, substituting $(\imath v)(\psi v) = x$ for ψx in (D), we obtain

(G) $\exists x \,(\varphi x \;\&\; (\imath v)(\psi v) = x) \;\&\; \neg\, \exists y \,\exists z \,[(\varphi y \;\&\; \varphi z) \;\&\; y \neq z]$.

Once again the first conjunct of (G), $\exists x \,(\varphi x \;\&\; (\imath v)(\psi v) = x)$, can be abbreviated to $\varphi(\,(\imath v)(\psi v)\,)$: 'Someone identical with the author of *Marmion* wrote *Waverley*' is just another way of saying 'The author of *Marmion* wrote Waverley'. So (G) may be abbreviated to

(H) $\varphi(\,(\imath v)(\psi v)\,) \;\&\; \neg\, \exists y \,\exists z \,[(\varphi y \;\&\; \varphi z) \;\&\; y \neq z]$.

Now it is a simple matter to replace $\varphi(\,(\imath v)(\psi v)\,)$ as it occurs in (H) by its *definiens* according to the Theory of Descriptions, namely $\exists x \,(\psi x \;\&\; \varphi x) \;\&\; \neg\, \exists w \,\exists v \,[(\psi w \;\&\; \psi v) \;\&\; w \neq v]$, which is (D) with w and v substituted for y and z and φ swapped with ψ. We thus obtain

(I) $\exists x \,(\psi x \;\&\; \varphi x) \;\&\; \{\neg\, \exists w \,\exists v \,[(\psi w \;\&\; \psi v) \;\&\; w \neq v]$
       $\&\; \neg\, \exists y \,\exists z \,[(\varphi y \;\&\; \varphi z) \;\&\; y \neq z]\}$.

Merely to restore the normal order of variables, we then exchange the second and third conjuncts and the subordinate conjuncts of the matrix of the first conjunct of (I), to obtain

(J) $\exists x \,(\varphi x \;\&\; \psi x) \;\&\; \{\neg\, \exists y \,\exists z \,[(\varphi y \;\&\; \varphi z) \;\&\; y \neq z]$
       $\&\; \neg\, \exists w \,\exists v \,[(\psi w \;\&\; \psi v) \;\&\; w \neq v]\}$.

That is to say, the Theory of Descriptions gives 'Someone wrote both *Waverley* and *Marmion*, and no two people wrote *Waverley*, and no two people wrote *Marmion*' as the analysis of 'The author of *Waverley* was the author of *Marmion*'. This is the second simplification, the simplification of the second form of identity proposition allowed by Russell, namely, that which contains two definite descriptions.

§ 2. We are now in a position to say that every informative identity proposition can take the form either of (F) or of (J). But note that the identity symbol, '=', occurs in (F) and (J) only in its negated form, '≠'. (F) and (J) never use the relational expression '*x* is the same as *y*' ($x = y$), but only the relational expression '*x* is different from *y*' ($x \neq y$). And whatever method is used, in accordance with the Theory of Descriptions, of eliminating definite descriptions, the relational expression $x = y$, whether or not negated, will only ever occur with bound variables in its argument places. In an informative identity proposition the identity predicable, '=', never occurs attached to a proper name. Any such proposition for which we have a real use can be expressed in a form that does not involve $a = b$, or even $a \neq b$, but only $x \neq y$, where x and y are bound variables.

It must be emphasized that the position reached so far is a direct consequence of Russell's Theory of Descriptions. The moves that have been made are all moves that the theory itself legitimizes, or else moves that are valid within the lower predicate calculus. Russell is himself committed to the equivalence of (F) to $a = (\imath x)(\varphi x)$ and (J) to $(\imath x)(\varphi x) = (\imath y)(\psi y)$.

§ 3. The next move is due to Wittgenstein.[3] Let us revise the rules for interpreting quantification and its variables, so that $\exists x \, \exists y \, (\varphi x \,\&\, \varphi y)$ already means what in Russell's interpretation is expressed by $\exists x \, \exists y \, [(\varphi x \,\&\, \varphi y) \,\&\, x \neq y]$. That is to say, $\exists x \, \exists y \, (\varphi x \,\&\, \varphi y)$ will be true only if two different objects satisfy the open sentence φx. Change of variable will now by itself signify change of

---

[3] The considerations which led Wittgenstein to make this move are not exactly manifest in the terse pronouncements of *Tractatus*, 5.53–5.534. My interpretation of them is borrowed entirely from Roger White, whose paper 'Wittgenstein on Identity', *Proceedings of the Aristotelian Society*, 78 (1977–8) is the most illuminating discussion of the topic so far available.

object. $\exists x \; \exists y \; (\varphi x \; \& \; \varphi y)$ will mean 'Something φ's and so does something else'. Generally speaking, a second existential quantifier binding a new variable will be read 'something else': thus the simplest possible formula involving two non-redundant existential quantifiers, and the general form of all such formulae, $\exists x \; \exists y \; (\varphi xy)$, will express the fact that something stands in the relation signified by φ to something else. $\exists x \; \exists y \; (\varphi xy)$ will no longer be implied by $\exists x \; (\varphi xx)$. Given this interpretation of quantification and its variables, (F) and (J), respectively, can be replaced by

(K) $\varphi a \; \& \; \neg \; \exists x \; \exists y \; (\varphi x \; \& \; \varphi y)$

and

(L) $\exists x \; (\varphi x \; \& \; \psi x) \; \&$
$[\neg \; \exists y \; \exists z \; (\varphi y \; \& \; \varphi z) \; \& \; \neg \; \exists w \; \exists v \; (\psi w \; \& \; \psi v)]$.

What has happened in each case is that the subformulae of the form $x \neq y$ have simply been deleted together with the conjunction sign which governed them.

§ 4. I have already pointed out that '$=$', the symbol for identity, remains in (F) and (J) only in the context of negation. Without departing from Russell's own theory and logical principles, we can see that informative identity propositions have no need of a symbol for *identity*, in so far as that is contrasted with a symbol for *difference*. *Affirmation* of identity, as opposed to *denial* of identity, is expressed in (J), as in (L), by the conjunct $\exists x \; (\varphi x \; \& \; \psi x)$. '*Someone* who wrote *Waverley* is identical with *someone* who wrote *Marmion*' is equivalent to, says no more and no less than, 'Someone wrote both *Waverley* and *Marmion*'. It is only the uniqueness expressed by the definite article in '*The* author of *Waverley* is identical with *the* author of *Marmion*' which requires the second and third conjuncts in (J), and contained in them, the clauses expressing difference in the Russellian way, $y \neq z$ and $w \neq v$. What these conjuncts express might be put thus 'At most one person wrote *Waverley*' or 'No two people wrote *Marmion*', and these propositions do not on the face of it seem to involve any relation or the negation of any relation. The Wittgensteinian formula $\neg \; \exists x \; \exists y \; (\varphi x \; \& \; \varphi y)$ seems admirably suited to express such facts. Indeed it seems much better equipped than the Russellian formula to mirror ordinary-language propositions of the form 'No two things φ'.

Wittgenstein fastens on this point. The Russellian way of expressing the fact that *only* a satisfies the function f (understood as meaning merely that no one but a satisfies f) is $\forall x \, (fx \rightarrow x = a)$. Wittgenstein remarks: 'What this proposition says is simply that only a satisfies the function f, and not that only things that have a certain relation to a satisfy the function f' (*Tractatus*, 5.5301).

The paragraph in the *Tractatus* which ends with these words begins with the remark 'It is self-evident that identity is not a relation between objects'. Naturally enough, Wittgenstein does not spend time arguing for a thesis which seems to him self-evident; but I think we can reconstruct what must have been his reasons for denying that identity is a relation. Already in the *Tractatus* there is a hint of the later doctrine that to have meaning an expression must have a use. Russell had already commended his Theory of Descriptions for its ability to explain the 'usefulness' of (*sic*) identity. If our only examples of true identity propositions had been tautologies of the form '$x = x$', which 'no one outside a logic-book ever wishes to say', identity would not be 'worth affirming'.[4] Russell had thus suggested to Wittgenstein the picture of such sentences as idle. The move from the charge of idleness to the charge of meaninglessness was never a difficult one for Wittgenstein to make. The justification for that move is not something which I wish to examine at this point. I shall devote some space to it in Chapter V of this book.

Russell argued that when a name is actually being used as a proper name, any other name which names the same thing can be substituted for it in a sentence without change of sense. Thus if both 'Scott' and 'Sir Walter' are being used as proper names in the sentence 'Scott is the same man as Sir Walter', the sentence means no more than does 'Scott is the same as Scott'. Any true identity proposition formed by filling the gaps in '--- is the same as ......' with names will therefore be equivalent in sense as well as truth value to one of the form '$x = x$'. For Wittgenstein, on the other hand, in a correct *Begriffsschrift* no object will have more than one name; so he cannot find a use for a true identity proposition of the form '$x = y$'.

What account then can be given of propositions like 'Scott is the same man as Sir Walter' or 'St John Stevas is the same politician as

[4] See *Logic and Knowledge*, p. 55.

'St John of Fawsley'? This question has, I hope, been answered already in Chapter I, § 3. In my view, propositions like this, in which '--- is the same as ......' is flanked by two different proper names are to be understood as saying something about at least one of the names. It will never be the case 'outside philosophy' that both the names in such a sentence are actually being used in this context as proper names. I hold that if a sentence is formed by completing '--- is the same as ......' with two proper names which are there being used as proper names, that sentence is doomed to be idle. I am not thereby committed to denying myself the possibility of using a sentence like 'St John is the same man as Bolingbroke' to convey genuine information. When such a sentence is used, the expression '--- is the same as ......' is not being used as a two-place predicate of first level.

This, perhaps, is the occasion for pointing out that, for Wittgenstein, the claim that identity is not a relation and the claim that in an adequate *Begriffsschrift* there would be no need for a sign of identity amount to the same thing. *Relation* is a 'formal concept'. So talk about relations is just misleading talk about the category of certain expressions. To say that in a canonical language there is no two-place predicable of first level which does the work which '--- is the same as ......' appears to do in English is not a *reason* for denying that identity is a relation: it *is* that denial.

Wittgenstein's aphoristic statement of his main thesis about identity is well known: 'Identity of object I express by identity of sign and not by using a sign for identity. Difference of objects I express by difference of signs'. The first of these sentences might have been accepted by Russell, if he had been made to see that his own theory allowed every informative identity proposition to be expressed by sentences either of the form (F) or of the form (J). (J), containing as it does the subformula $\exists x\,(\varphi x\,\&\,\psi x)$, expresses *identity* (as opposed to *difference*) quite adequately by a repeated variable bound by a single quantifier. Wittgenstein is not innovating in his decision to express identity of object by identity of sign. Only in his decision to regard difference of signs, and in particular difference of bound variables, as the expression of difference of objects does he go beyond Russell.

§ 5. I have pointed out already that the formulae (F) and (J), which on Russell's view are all that is necessary for the expression of informative identity propositions, contain the sign for identity only in a position where its argument places are occupied by bound variables. We have $x = y$, but never $a = b$, where a and b symbolize proper names. I owe my appreciation of the importance of this fact to Roger White, and I can do no better than quote his commentary on it:

. . . in the analysis the identity sign only occurs within the scope of quantifiers flanked by variables. [White is thinking of an expression of the form $x = y$.] It is here that a contrast emerges between the identity sign and relational expressions—or, if you prefer at this stage of the argument, more tentatively, other relational expressions. Whereas if we wish to explain the use of a relational expression within the scope of quantifiers, we appeal to its use outside the scope of quantifiers (by saying informally something like 'For "$(\exists x)$ $(\exists y)$ $(x$ loves $y)$" to be true is for some proposition of the form "John loves Mary" to be true'), we have arrived at the point where we explain the use of the identity sign outside the scope of a quantifier by means of an analysis in which it occurs within the scope of a quantifier: we cannot then go on, as we would if identity were a relation, to explain that use by appeal to its use outside the scope of a quantifier without vicious circularity. Here the asymmetry sets the identity sign apart from relational expressions in that we have now to treat the occurrence of the sign within the scope of the quantifier as the basic one. All other uses of the identity sign are to be explained in terms of this basic use, and not vice versa. ('Wittgenstein on Identity', p. 167.)

White makes the point that Frege, at the beginning of 'On Sense and Meaning', asks the question 'Is identity a relation?', and immediately goes on to ask whether, if so, it is a relation between objects, or between names or signs of objects. Frege says that in the *Begriffsschrift* he assumed it was a relation between signs. But this assumption, although it is explicitly made in the introductory 'Explanation of the Symbols', is not taken account of in the formal development of the *Begriffsschrift* itself. Indeed it is actually incompatible with certain of the axioms and theorems of the system. The schema $(x = y) \rightarrow (\varphi x \leftrightarrow \varphi y)$ requires for its validity, and indeed for its intelligibility, that substitutions for x and y have the same meaning in the consequent as they have in the antecedent. They will not have this if Frege's remarks about identity being a relation between signs are taken to apply to this schema: substitutions for x and y will be names which in the antecedent are their own meanings, but in the consequent have their customary meanings, the things they normally name. None of Frege's worries about identity, and neither of his attempts to find solutions for those worries, play any part in the worked out systems of the *Begriffsschrift* or the *Grundgesetze*. They are, as White puts it, idle.

White contrasts Frege's questioning whether identity is a relation with his questioning whether existence is a property. The difficulties of accepting existence as a property are met by the introduction of a symbolic device, corresponding to the quantifiers of contemporary logic, which makes the status of the existential quantifier as a second-level predicate abundantly clear. The whole notational apparatus is designed to show the difference between the logical form of propositions like 'Unfriendly Italians exist' and 'Unfriendly Italians eat snails'. But the formal expression of a proposition like 'Augustus was the same as Octavian' would be in no way distinguished by Frege from that of a proposition like 'Augustus was the brother of Octavia'. Like 'ξ is a brother of ζ', 'ξ is the same as ζ' is treated as signifying a function of two variables taking a truth-value as its value for any pair of objects as arguments (where a 'pair' can be the same object taken twice). The doubts about identity have no consequences for Frege's actual system.

Wittgenstein's proposal, on the other hand, involves fundamental revision of the syntactical rules for the variables of quantification. White shows how this revision follows naturally from the recognition that the basic use of the identity sign is its use within the scope of quantifiers.

Now what are we to say about a sign whose only primitive use—the use to which all other uses may be reduced—is within the scope of quantifiers flanked by two variables: here it naturally suggests itself that we should treat it as belonging with the apparatus of quantification, and that an appropriate representation of it within the *Begriffsschrift* would be one in which it was made part of the quantificational apparatus. ('Wittgenstein on Identity', p. 168.)

The analogy with Frege's treatment of existence is now clear. Just as affirmations of existence took the form $\exists x\ (\varphi x)$, and denials the form $\neg\ \exists x\ (\varphi x)$, so the statement that something which φs is the same as something which ψs takes the form $\exists x\ (\varphi x\ \&\ \psi x)$, and the statement that two different things both φ, the form

$\exists x \; \exists y \; (\varphi x \; \& \; \varphi y)$. Repetition of variable is what shows identity, change of variable what shows difference. 'Someone shaves himself' is of the form $\exists x \; (\varphi xx)$, 'Someone shaves someone else' of the form $\exists x \; \exists y \; (\varphi xy)$. The apparatus of quantification can take care of all these types of proposition.

§ **6.** Note, however, that affirmations of difference are not equivalent to denials of identity. In this there is, in a way, a wider divergence from the surface grammar of ordinary language than there is in the case of affirmations and denials of existence. Whatever their internal structure in Frege and Russell's logical syntax, 'Unfriendly Italians exist' and 'Unfriendly Italians don't exist' remain contradictories.

(i) The φ-er is different from the ψ-er,

however, is not the contradictory of

(ii) The φ-er is the same as the ψ-er,

whether this latter is construed in Russell's fashion after the pattern of (J) or in Wittgenstein's fashion after the pattern of (L). The contradictories of (J) and (L) state that either nothing both φ's and ψ's or more than one thing φ's or more than one thing ψ's, just as, in Russell's view, the contradictory of 'The author of *Waverley* was Scotch' states that either nothing wrote *Waverley*, or that more than one thing did, or that something which was not Scotch wrote *Waverley*. The fact that (i) is not the contradictory of (ii) is a simple consequence of the Theory of Descriptions. Both (i) and (ii) are false if it is not true both that just one thing φs and that just one thing ψs. For Russell, of course, there *are* pairs of propositions of the form $a = b$ and $a \neq b$ which are genuine contradictories; but all true propositions of the form $a = b$ are equivalent to propositions of the form $a = a$, and therefore necessarily true, and all false propositions of the form $a \neq b$ are equivalent to propositions of the form $a \neq a$ and therefore self-contradictory. Wittgenstein leaves us with no resources for forming propositions of this form. Identity is not a separate source of necessary truth.

§ **7.** This last observation is something which is of the greatest importance for Wittgenstein's general theory of necessary truth. The theory is that all necessary truth can in principle be resolved into truth-functional tautologies. The mechanism for this is the reduction of universally quantified propositions to indefinitely extended conjunctions, and existentially quantified propositions to indefinitely extended disjunctions, of atomic propositions: $\forall x\,(\varphi x)$ is reduced to $(\varphi a_1\,\&\,(\varphi a_2\,\&\,(\varphi a_3\ldots\,\&\,\varphi a_n)))$, $\exists x\,(\varphi x)$ to $(\varphi a_1\,\vee\,(\varphi a_2\,\vee\,(\varphi a_3\ldots\,\vee\,\varphi a_n)))$. But Russell's account of identity leaves room for atomic propositions which are logically necessary, though not tautologies in Wittgenstein's sense, namely, propositions of the form $a = a$; and molecular propositions like $\forall x\,(x = x)$ and $\exists x\,(x = a)$, even if reduced in Wittgenstein's manner to conjunctions and disjunctions, would still owe their truth to the atomic propositions of this form out of which they would have to be constituted. $\forall x\,(x = x)$ would be reduced to $(a_1 = a_1\,\&\,(a_2 = a_2 \ldots\,\&\,a_n = a_n))$ and $\exists x\,(x = a_1)$ to $(a_1 = a_1\,\vee\,(a_2 = a_1\ldots\,\vee\,a_n = a_1))$. Identity, as an independent source of necessary truth, would not be eliminable, if $\xi = \zeta$ were retained as an atomic two-place predicable. It is, of course, integral to Wittgenstein's theory of meaning that truth-functional tautology be the only source of logical necessity. He has, therefore, the strongest motivation of an intra-theoretical kind for eliminating this extraneous source of necessity. This, however, should not allow us to overlook the strong extra-theoretical reasons Wittgenstein has, from a consideration of the actual way in which identity propositions work, and as a natural development from the ideas which Frege and Russell hold about identity, for adopting the position I have described with respect to the correct expression for facts involving identity. And these ideas were themselves generated by the Paradox of Identity.

§ 8. The question might well arise: Can the rules for the use of variables which Wittgenstein proposes work in any fully developed predicate calculus? Wittgenstein himself makes no attempt to state the rules, beyond his aphoristic 'Difference of objects I express by difference of sign'. What he does is to give examples: 'Thus I do not write "$f\,(a,b)\,.\,a = b$", but "$f\,(a,a)$" (or "$f\,(b,b)$"); and not "$f\,(a,b).\sim a = b$", but "$f\,(a,b)$" ' (*Tractatus*, 5.531). His examples continue until 5.5321. However, in 1956 Jaakko Hintikka published an article, 'Identity, Variables and Impredicative Definitions',[5] in which he describes in detail two versions of what he calls 'the exclusive interpretation of variables'. The normal interpretation, which Hintikka calls 'inclusive', uses variables in such a way that no coincidences of the values of different variables are excluded. Furthermore, the value of a variable in this normal system may be an individual specified in some other way in the proposition or formula. Thus if John hates himself, '$\exists x \, \exists y \, (x$ hates $y)$' and '$\exists x$ (John hates $x)$' will both be true, even if John hates no one else and no one else hates anyone. It is this kind of coincidence of values of variables which the exclusive interpretations prohibit. However, there are different ways of formulating the rule which determines precisely the coincidences that are to be prohibited. The weaker rule states that a variable bound by a quantifier may not take the same value as that taken by another variable which occurs freely within the range of that quantifier; the stronger rule states that it may not take the same value as that taken by any variable within whose range it occurs. The range of a quantifier is simply the scope of that quantifier, and the range of a variable bound by a quantifier is the scope of that quantifier. The range of a free variable is the whole formula in which it occurs freely.

Using (Ex) and (Ux) as weakly exclusive quantifiers, i.e., in such a way that variables bound to (Ex) and (Ux) obey the weakly exclusive interpretation, (ex) and (ux) as strongly exclusive quantifiers, $(\exists x)$ and (x) as inclusive quantifiers and K as an open sentence, Hintikka gives these rules for translating from exclusive to inclusive quantification:

$(Ex)K$ may be replaced by

(4) $(\exists x)(x \neq y_1 \, \& \, x \neq y_2 \, \& \ldots\ldots x \neq y_k \, \& \, K)$

and vice versa, provided that $y_1, y_2, \ldots y_k$ are all the free variables of $(Ex)K$. Similarly, $(Ux)K$ may be replaced by

(5) $(x)(x = y_1 \lor x = y_2 \lor \ldots\ldots x = y_k \lor K)$

and (5) by $(Ux)K$, provided that all the ys in (5) are the same as in (4). These translation rules are supposed to be applicable even when $(Ex)K$ occurs as a subformula (consecutive part) of a larger formula. For $(ex)K$ and $(ux)K$, we have similar translation rules: $(ex)K$ may be replaced by (4) and vice versa, provided that $y_1, y_2, \ldots y_k$ are all the variables (bound or free) within the range of which $(ex)K$ occurs in the formula in which the replacement is to be made. Under an analogous assumption for $(ux)K$, $(ux)K$ may be replaced by (5) and vice versa. (Ibid., pp. 230 ff.)

Hintikka goes on to provide translations for all inclusively quantified formulae into both sorts of exclusively quantified formulae, and to argue that everything that can be expressed in any of these interpretations can be expressed in each of the others. He also gives three systems of transformation rules, one for each interpretation of the variables, which permit proofs to be constructed and define provability for each variant of the predicate calculus. It seems that he has established both exclusive interpretations as alternatives to the standard interpretation of the predicate calculus as a whole.

§ 9. Hintikka does more than this. He points out that there are sentences in everyday use employing ordinary-language analogues of quantifiers and variables which are naturally understood in a way similar to the exclusive interpretation. Thus 'A man's brother is any man who has the same parents as he' and 'Someone gave ten times more to the collection than anyone at the meeting' are not normally thought of as implying that a man is his own brother or that the man who gave so much to the collection was not at the meeting himself. In geometrical discourse writers sometimes say such things as 'Any two points of a straight line completely determine that line' and sometimes 'Any two distinct points . . .' without meaning something different the second time from the first. It seems that ordinary language uses its equivalents of quantifiers and variables sometimes in an exclusive and sometimes in an inclusive sense. Linguistic intuitions do not establish either the inclusive or the exclusive interpretation as correct.

§ 10. The possibility of giving an exclusive interpretation to informal sentences allows Hintikka to make a startling application of his theory. The great source of difficulty in the theory of sets, and therewith, as many philosophers see it, in providing secure foundations for the whole of mathematics, is the so-called 'abstraction principle'. This states that for every property there is a set whose members are just those objects which possess the property. Using inclusive quantification, the most natural formulation of this principle is the schema

(M) $(\exists x)(y)(y \; \varepsilon \; x \equiv \varphi y)$.

If this schema is valid,

(N) $(\exists x)(y)(y \; \varepsilon \; x \equiv \sim y \; \varepsilon \; y)$

will be a true substitution instance of it, and

(O) $(\exists x)(x \; \varepsilon \; x \equiv \sim x \; \varepsilon \; x)$

will be obtainable from (N) by Universal Instantiation. This, of course, is Russell's paradox. If, however, we use exclusive quantifiers to formulate the abstraction principle, we obtain in place of (M)

(P) $(ex)(uy)(y \; \varepsilon \; x \equiv \varphi y).$[6]

By analogy with (N) we have the true substitution instance of (P)

(Q) $(ex)(uy)(y \; \varepsilon \; x \equiv \sim y \; \varepsilon \; y).$

It will not be possible, however, to derive from (Q) an analogue of (O), namely,

(R) $(ex)(x \; \varepsilon \; x \equiv \sim x \; \varepsilon \; x),$

since the exclusive interpretation of variables will prohibit the variable bound by the universal quantifier in (Q) from taking the same value as one taken by the existentially quantified variable within the scope of which it occurs. The paradox is not derivable under the exclusive interpretation of the abstraction principle.

Hintikka is able to put it more strongly. In his view, (P) has

(S) $(\exists x)(y)(y = x \; \vee \; y \; \varepsilon \; x \equiv \varphi y)$

as its equivalent in terms of inclusive quantification.[7] Corresponding to the steps which led us from (M) to (O) we shall now have the derivation of

(T) $(\exists x)(x = x \; \vee \; x \; \varepsilon \; x \equiv \sim x \; \varepsilon \; x)$

from (S); and, where (O) was self-contradictory, Hintikka claims that (T) is logically true. But this depends on recognizing $(\exists x)(x = x)$

---

[6] The difference between the weakly and the strongly exclusive interpretations emerges in the allowable substitutions for φy in this schema. There was already a limitation on permitted substitutions for φy in (M), but I shall leave the reader to consult Hintikka's paper for the detail of all these restrictions.

[7] Hintikka points out that substituting (S), which is equivalent to $(\exists x)(y)(y \neq x \rightarrow . \; y \; \varepsilon \; x \equiv \varphi y)$, for (M) is tantamount to Frege's attempted way out of Russell's paradox. If (S) is interpreted in such a way as to be equivalent with (P) with weakly, instead of strongly, exclusive quantifiers, this substitution fails in the same way as Frege's attempt. Again, the difference between (S) and Frege's substitute for his original principle of abstraction lies in the substitutions permitted for φy.

as a logical truth, and we shall see in the next section that Hintikka's view about this is not consistent with that of Wittgenstein.

However, in a later paper,[8] Hintikka shows that another paradox *can* be generated from (S), on the assumption that the Universe contains at least two objects. To avert this paradox he proposes yet another formulation of the abstraction principle, namely

(U) $(\exists x)(y)(y \neq x \ \& \ y \neq z_1 \ \& \ y \neq z_2,..., y \neq z_k \ . \rightarrow$
    $(y \ \varepsilon \ x \equiv \varphi y))$,

where the same restrictions on φy obtain as in the interpretation of (S) which made it equivalent to (P) and where z_1, z_2,..., z_k are all the free variables in (U). This amounts to an even more strongly exclusive interpretation of the variables.

Hintikka makes very sweeping claims for this strongly exclusive interpretation of variables as a means of avoiding, not only Russell's paradox, but all the well known paradoxes of set theory. There is no room here to reproduce all these claims or the arguments Hintikka employs to support them. In the second of these articles Hintikka admits that the most strongly exclusive interpretation of the abstraction principle, which makes it equivalent to (U) above, has consequences for axiomatic set theory which may be seen as creating difficulties for those who wish to use set theory as the foundation of mathematics. The usual definitions of a unit set, a couple, a triple, etc., would not be available on this interpretation. He does, however, suggest approximations to the usual definitions, and further axioms may still be found which will make good the deficiency for those who wish to derive arithmetic from set-theoretic axioms. As the reader will discover (see below, Chapter VII), it is not my view that numbers should be identified with sets, ordered pairs, or the like. The interest of set theory will be as a branch of mathematics, not as a basis for mathematics as a whole. It is nevertheless an attractive feature of the exclusive interpretation of the variables of quantification that it can prevent the set theoretical paradoxes, which are the source of intellectual discomfort in their own right, from arising. If a logician is challenged to show that no *inconvénients* follow from an interpretation of quantifiers and variables which, like Wittgenstein's, has no room

---

[8] 'Vicious Circle Principle and the Paradoxes', *Journal of Symbolic Logic*, 22 (1957), pp. 245–9.

for a sign of identity, he can do more than merely respond to the challenge: he can go over to the attack. The power of the exclusive interpretation of variables to prevent the paradoxes of set theory being derived from the principle of abstraction constitutes a positive argument in its favour. Wittgenstein claims that the inclusive interpretation, relying as it does on the possibility of supplementing the quantificational apparatus by a sign of identity construed as a two-place predicable, is just wrong. This claim will be examined later. But this claim is undoubtedly supported by Hintikka's discovery that it is only certain interpretations of variables which make $\exists x \, \forall y \, (y \, \varepsilon \, x \leftrightarrow \varphi y)$ generate paradoxes, and a way to avoid them is to move to more exclusive interpretations. At the very least, exclusive interpretations are made more acceptable as a possible, and in certain contexts, preferable reading of quantifiers and variables by the considerations which Hintikka advances.

§ 11. At one point Hintikka seems to diverge from Wittgenstein, not only on the philosophical merits of the exclusive as opposed to the inclusive interpretation, which he does not wish to press, but on the technical results of adopting one system rather than the other. Hintikka claims that every formula of the system which results from an exclusive reading of the variables admits of the translation into 'the old predicate calculus (with identity), and vice versa' (p. 228). Moreover he claims to have produced a proof of this intertranslatability thesis. It is the 'vice versa' clause which Wittgenstein would dispute. At *Tractatus*, 5.534 we have

And now we see that in a correct conceptual notation (*Begriffsschrift*) pseudo-propositions like '$a = a$', '$a = b \, . \, b = c. \to a = c$', '$(x). \, x = x$', '$(\exists x). \, x = a$', etc. cannot even be written down.

Of the examples Wittgenstein gives here the first two are perhaps irrelevant to Hintikka's claim, because they do not involve quantification or variables at all. To be sure, they would normally be thought to be well-formed formulae of the predicate calculus with identity; but they do not involve the inclusive, or indeed any, interpretation of variables. The last two examples, however, do involve quantifiers and variables, and the exclusive interpretations of these just do not have the resources for expressing what these formulae purport to express. The exclusive interpretation is able to produce translations of formulae whose matrices are truth-functionally compounded out of atomic sentences some, but not all, of which, are of the form $x = y$. It is, however, powerless to reproduce quantified formulae whose only first-level predicable is the supposed two-place predicable '--- is the same as ......'.

What then of the purported proof that every closed formula, L, of the predicate calculus with identity, where the quantifiers are given the inclusive interpretation, can be provided with a translation, $\varphi(L)$, in the exclusively quantified system? One of the formulae whose significance was called into question by Wittgenstein is a closed formula of the predicate calculus with identity, namely, $(x)(x = x)$. The rule for producing $\varphi((x)K)$, the equivalent in an exclusively quantificational system of a formula, $(x)K$, is stated at the top of page 233 of Hintikka's first article. This is the rule which is appropriate for generating an exclusively quantified equivalent of $(x)(x = x)$. The trouble is that the schematic letters K, K_0, K_1, etc., which appear in it essentially, have a sense which has been stipulated at the top of the preceding page. This provides that their substitution instances shall not contain subformulae of the form $x = x$. Does this allow us to regard $x = x$ as a legitimate substitution for K in $(x)K$? The stipulation only forbids us to use as substitution instances for K, etc., formulae which have *subformulae* of the form $x = x$. Can it be supposed that Hintikka wishes 'subformula' to be understood in such a way as to include the limiting case where a formula is a subformula of itself? If so, we could rule out the possibility of a substitution instance for K being of the form $x = x$. This seems prima facie implausible; but only by interpreting it in this way can we make sense of Hintikka's comments, on p. 234, that 'all the identities of L disappear in the transition from L to $\varphi(L)$', and again, on p. 235, that 'if L is closed, $\varphi(L)$ does not contain any identities'. And this interpretation is given further support by his remark, a little later on p. 235, that 'the result we have just proved shows that everything expressible in terms of the inclusive quantifiers and identity may also be expressed by means of the weakly exclusive quantifiers *without using a special symbol for identity*' (his italics). He even adds, in a footnote, 'Wittgenstein was, hence, right in saying that the identity sign is not an essential constituent of the logical notation (*Tractatus* 5.533)'. It seems that he is not prepared to admit expressions such as '$(Ux)(x = x)$' to count as well-formed formulae in an exclusively interpreted predicate calculus.

This calls into question his claim to have proved that anything expressible in the normal predicate calculus with identity is expressible in a language which uses exclusive, in place of inclusive, quantification. Inclusive quantification cannot proceed without 'a special symbol for identity', and the symbol is always treated by Hintikka as a two-place first-level predicable. How can he prevent formulae of the form $(x)(x = x)$ being regarded as well formed in an inclusively interpreted predicate calculus? However, his rule for producing $\varphi(L)$, if my account of it is correct, makes no provision for the case where L is of this form. The rule is the only procedure for producing formulae of the form $\varphi(L)$ where L is introduced by an inclusive universal quantifier, and his proof of intertranslatability depends on an exclusive counterpart being available for every inclusively quantified formula. So his claim seems to require revision.

Would such revision require Hintikka to take back the following remarks?

Also I hope to show that it is not correct to say (as Russell has done) that Wittgenstein tried to dispense with the notion of identity. What a systematic use of an exclusive reading of variables amounts to is a new way of coping with the notion of identity in a formalized system of logic. Under the most natural formalization of the new interpretations, the resulting system is equivalent to the old predicate calculus (with identity): every formula of the latter admits of a translation into the former, and vice versa. ('Identity, Variables and Impredicative Definitions', p. 228.)

As I have been arguing, the words 'vice versa' are not justified. But does he need to justify them in order to rebut Russell's charge?[9] Of course, Wittgenstein had no intention of dispensing with the *notion* of identity. He positively claims that he has a way of *expressing* the identity of objects. All he excludes is *sign* for identity. He would say that all genuine propositions involving identity can be expressed without the help of such a sign. Giving it up is positive gain, if we want to be able to state all the facts we need to state in the least misleading way. The exclusive interpretation of quantification allows us to improve our facility to express the concept of identity, not to suppress it. Hintikka says again:

I do not quite see the superiority ascribed by Wittgenstein to an exclusive interpretation of variables. An exclusive interpretation of variables can be

[9] Russell makes this charge in *The Philosophy of Bertrand Russell*, ed. P. A. Schilpp, Evanston, Ill.: Open Court, 1948, p. 688.

carried out so that it gives us a new way of saying exactly the same things we could say before. (Ibid.)

Hintikka seems here not to be aware that things like '$(x)(x = x)$', which we thought that we could say before, can no longer be said, by reason of the very rules that he constructs for translating from the inclusive to the exclusive system. If he had been fully aware of this divergence between the two systems, Wittgenstein's conviction of the superiority of the exclusive one might have been easier for him to understand.

§ 12. The divergence between the exclusive and the inclusive interpretation is well recognized by White, who indeed emphasizes its significance. Speaking of the formulae listed in *Tractatus*, 5.534, he says

. . . they are also important in that they really do establish beyond question a sense in which, if Wittgenstein has established a *possible* notation for identity, he has given a real sense to the claim that identity is not a relation. For if the identity sign were a relational expression, each of these propositions or phrases would have to make sense, even if they merely expressed obvious logical truths or logical falsehoods. If Wittgenstein's notation is a possible one, then there is a possible notation in which we may do all the work we require with the identity sign, but in which certain propositions, which would have to make sense if the identity sign were a relational expression, have no expression whatever, and are thus in Wittgenstein's terms exposed, not merely as senseless, but as nonsense. In this way we may definitely say that Wittgenstein, by justifying the possibility of his notation, has not merely exhibited a contrast between the identity sign and other relational expressions, or designed a notation which is possible in virtue of the logical properties of identity, and that disguises the relational character of identity, but has produced a notation the possibility of which is incompatible with the idea that identity is a relation—in the most straight-forward sense of a relation we know, that which is described by Frege and employed in his logical writings. In this way, he has done justice to the feeling we alluded to at the outset, that identity is not a relation, and possibly done so in such a way as to show what lay directly behind that feeling. What we have thus shown is that Wittgenstein has argued, from Frege's idea that it is essential for there to be informative identity propositions that proper names should have a sense and not merely a reference, to the possibility of a *Begriffsschrift* which is incompatible with construing the identity sign as a relational expression. That is, he has done what Frege failed even to attempt to do, as a result of which we argued that his worries over the question whether identity was a relation were not articulated to a point where they ceased to be merely idling. We now have what we sought in vain there, genuine repercussions for the *Begriffsschrift* from the nature of identity, which give it a different mode of expression from a relation. ('Wittgenstein on Identity', pp. 169 ff.)

If every formula in the system which results from the exclusive interpretation of the variables had been translatable into the traditional predicate calculus with identity, and vice versa, we should have to meet an objection along these lines: 'So what? You have shown that there is an alternative way of expressing what we normally express with the help of the two-place predicable "--- is the same as ......", but since there is nothing to choose between these two ways of expressing ourselves, you have not shown that identity is *not* a relation.' The traditional way of doing things remains viable, and in this system identity *is* a relation, no matter what possibilities of translation are available. It is as it is with certain Ockhamistic arguments, e.g., that we can dispense with abstract entities like differences of age, because 'There is a difference of age between Sally and June' means neither more nor less than 'Sally is either older or younger than June'. The fact that we do not *have* to appeal to entities like differences of age in order to say what we mean does not show that we cannot understand perfectly well what is going on when we do appeal to such entities, nor that when we say '*There is* a difference of age between Sally and June' what we say is not true.

So it might be objected. But suppose that Wittgenstein is right, suppose that everything we need to say can be said without a sign for identity in a language in which the variables of quantification are given an exclusive interpretation, but that some things which cannot be said in such a language do not need saying anyway, and are in fact nonsense: in that case the possibility and impossibility of translation do real philosophical work. The claim that identity is not a relation is not a mere expression of preference for one out of a number of alternative conventions for using parts of our language: it is a refusal to admit as meaningful certain strings of words and symbols which philosophers have thought would enable them to say things which were both intelligible and important, e.g., the definition of the null class as the class of all objects not identical with themselves. Wittgenstein can be seen as a bull in the china-shop of logic.

§ **13.** Before leaving this attempt to expound Wittgenstein's reasoning for the thesis that identity is not a relation and the significance of his claim, I should like to contrast its consequences with what Saul Kripke says about identity propositions. Russell merely announces the thesis which constitutes one half of the paradox of identity, the thesis, namely, that all true identity propositions are necessarily true. Kripke, following other philosophers such as Ruth Barcan Marcus,[10] deploys an argument to prove the thesis. This starts with the schema expressing the indiscernibility of identicals, which we have already had occasion to notice in connection with Frege (see above, p. 22), namely, $x = y \rightarrow (\varphi x \leftrightarrow \varphi y)$, or, equivalently, $x = y \rightarrow (\varphi x \rightarrow \varphi y)$. Substituting $\square (x = x)$ for φx in this we obtain $x = y \rightarrow (\square (x = x) \rightarrow \square (x = y))$. But since $\square (x = x)$ is a valid schema, we may discharge it from our formula to obtain $x = y \rightarrow \square (x = y)$, which states that if x and y are identical they are necessarily so. The apparent instances of the derived schema which are most strongly counter-intuitive occur where definite descriptions are substituted for x and y in the schema, e.g., 'The author of *Waverley*' and 'The author of *Marmion*', (or just one of them for one of x and y). These Kripke is happy to deal with in the Russellian way by refusing to allow that propositions containing them constitute genuine substitution instances of the schema $x = y$. Where the definite descriptions substituted for both x and y are such that the object which uniquely satisfies the description does so necessarily, e.g., 'The sum of six and thirty' and 'The square of six', there is no problem, since with definite descriptions of this sort substituted for x and y, $\square (x = y)$ is in any case true if $x = y$ is. Kripke calls such definite descriptions, which he describes as designating the same object in every possible world in which they designate any object at all, 'rigid designators'. And he accepts the validity of the schema $x = y \rightarrow \square (x = y)$ where substitutes for x and y are genuine, i.e. non-complex, proper names, since he classifies proper names too

---

[10] Ruth Marcus's arguments are to be found in her paper 'Modalities and Intensional Languages', *Synthese*, 13 (1961); and Kripke's are in 'Identity and Necessity' in Milton K. Munitz (ed.), *Identity and Individuation*, New York University Press, 1971, pp. 135–64.

as rigid designators. Kripke therefore agrees with Russell in regarding 'Scott is the same as Sir Walter' as a necessary truth, where 'Scott' and 'Sir Walter' are both being used as proper names simply to pick out the man so named.

But though agreeing with Russell about the status of such propositions as necessarily true, Kripke is here in conflict with Wittgenstein, and, at a deeper level, with Russell. Russell and Wittgenstein would regard it as a huge mistake to have a single classification—in this case 'rigid designator'—to cover both names and definite descriptions, e.g., both 'Scott' and 'the square of six'. And Wittgenstein, so far from regarding sentences like 'Scott is the same as Sir Walter', or, for that matter, 'Scott is the same as Scott', as necessarily true propositions, regards them as pseudo-propositions, strings of words to which it is strictly impossible to assign a sense. This contrast between the views of Wittgenstein and Kripke will be important at a later stage of my argument (see Chapter VIII).

THE NEED FOR A SIGN OF IDENTITY

§ **1.** I begin with another paradox. Before it can get off the ground, however, I must set out a derivation which involves little more than an ability to apply Russell and Wittgenstein's theories of identity. Consider this proposition

  (1) Boscovich was born in Ragusa and Dubrovnik is a present-day Croatian holiday resort.

Since 'Ragusa' and 'Dubrovnik' are different names for the same town, we can substitute 'Dubrovnik' for 'Ragusa' in (1) without altering the truth-value of (1). For Russell, this substitution can be legitimized by the schema $x = y \rightarrow (\varphi x \leftrightarrow \varphi y)$, which we were considering at the end of the last chapter, since we are here substituting names, not definite descriptions, for x and y in the schema. Wittgenstein, of course, cannot make use of such a schema, since he regards sentences of the form $x = y$ as pseudo-propositions. But we shall see in Chapter VI that the principle which licenses this substitution can be expressed in terms which Wittgenstein would countenance. So both Russell and Wittgenstein would allow the move from (1) to

  (2) Boscovich was born in Dubrovnik and Dubrovnik is a present-day Croatian holiday resort.

In any version of the predicate calculus it has to be possible to derive

  (3) For some town x, both Boscovich was born in x and x is a present-day Croatian holiday resort

from (2). This is existential generalization (EG). Again, both Russell and Wittgenstein would regard (3) as equivalent to

  (4) Some town where Boscovich was born is the same town as a present-day Croatian holiday resort.

(4) in Russell's view is of the form $\exists x \, \exists y \, [(\varphi x \, \& \, \psi y) \, \& \, x = y]$, and

this is equivalent to $\exists x$ (φx & ψx), which is the form of (3). For Wittgenstein $\exists x \, \exists y$ (φxy & $x = y$) is simply an improper way of writing $\exists x$ (φxx) (*Tractatus*, 5.532). Since φx & ψy is a substitution instance of φxy, Wittgenstein will regard $\exists x$ (φx & ψy), which is on anybody's view the logical form of (3), as the proper way of exhibiting the logical form of (4). Russell's version of the logical form of (4), $\exists x \, \exists y$ [(φx & ψy) & $x = y$], 'cannot even be written down' in Wittgenstein's *Begriffsschrift*. So for Russell (3) and (4) are logically equivalent, and for Wittgenstein they are different expressions of the same proposition. On either view it is possible to derive (4) from (3).

Let us now suppose that

(1A) Paul thinks that Boscovich was born in Ragusa and that Dubrovnik is a present-day Croatian holiday resort.

Just as we were entitled to move from (1) to (2), so we may substitute 'Dubrovnik' for 'Ragusa' in (1A) to obtain

(2A) Paul thinks that Boscovich was born in Dubrovnik and that Dubrovnik is a present-day Croatian holiday resort.

However, this claim to have derived (2A) from (1A) will meet with instant protest. The schema $x = y \rightarrow$ ($\varphi x \leftrightarrow \varphi y$) may justify deriving (2) from (1), but is not 'Paul thinks that ---' a referentially opaque context, and is not what we mean by 'referentially opaque context' one in which it is not legitimate to substitute identicals for identicals? Now the term of art 'referential opacity' was devised by Quine (with a little prompting from Russell), and in Quine's paper 'Reference and Modality', where it first gained publicity, it is asserted without qualification that belief-contexts like 'Paul thinks that ---' are referentially opaque.[1] In later works,[2] however, Quine concedes that belief-contexts are sometimes transparent. This can hardly be gainsaid. Suppose we are walking down the street with a black friend newly arrived from Africa. Some hooligans shout racialist abuse at our friend, and we say 'Those ruffians think Elizabeth is a West Indian'. We say this without for a moment supposing that the ruffians in question know Elizabeth's name, and it may be only too obvious, and indeed unfortunate, that the

---

[1] W. V. Quine, *From a Logical Point of View*, 2nd edn., New York and Evanston, Ill.: Harper and Row, 1962.

[2] See, for instance, *Word and Object*, Cambridge, Mass.: MIT Press, 1960, p. 145.

word they use to refer to her is not her name. We are clearly using 'think that ---' as a transparent context, in such a way that we would readily accept 'Those ruffians think that our friend is a West Indian' as an equally good vehicle for expressing our thought. Quine's recognition that some at least of the contexts expressing 'propositional attitudes' are referentially transparent is simply an acknowledgement of the linguistic facts. To agree that (2A) is derivable from (1A) is to indicate that one is understanding these occurrences of 'Paul thinks that ---' transparently. No one could plausibly maintain that understanding them in this way is ruled out by the meaning of psychological verbs.[3]

Given (2A), it seems that we are entitled to infer

(3A) Paul thinks that, for some town x, both Boscovich was born in x and x is a present-day Croatian holiday resort.

(3A) is simply 'Paul thinks that (3)', and (2A) is tantamount to 'Paul thinks that (2)'. (3), as we saw, is an existential generalization of (2), and as such logically entailed by (2). Now it cannot, of course, be maintained in general that any proposition of the form 'x believes that p' is entailed by a corresponding proposition of the form 'x believes that q' merely on the grounds that p is entailed by q. Everyone is unaware of many, if not most, of the logical consequences of what he believes. But no one can be unaware of all the logical consequences of what he believes. Some entailments are so obvious that failure to appreciate them is failure to understand the meaning of the words in which the entailed and entailing propositions are couched. If the entailment of p by q is as obvious as this, the fact that x does not believe that p is a sure sign

---

[3] All I need for my present argument is that 'thinks that ---' in (1A) and (2A) *can* be understood in such a way that (2A) is derivable from (1A). I believe in fact that they *must* be so understood. Those who regard sentences like these as capable of being understood in different ways operate with variously labelled distinctions, 'transparent–opaque', 'direct–indirect', '*de re–de dicto*', which they normally suppose applicable to sentences containing either definite descriptions or proper names (these being confusedly lumped together as 'singular terms'). My own view is that the only sentences which need be disambiguated in anything like this way are those containing definite descriptions and that the distinction which needs to be made in this case is the distinction between what Russell called 'primary' and 'secondary occurrence' of these definite descriptions—a distinction of scope. With proper names no such distinction is possible, and in the case of propositions containing proper names the schema $(x = y) \rightarrow (\varphi x \rightarrow \varphi y)$ is valid without restriction. This view, which I inherit from Prior, is defended in ch. IX of my book *What is Existence?* (Oxford University Press, 1981). I return to the topic in ch. VI of the present work.

that x does not believe that q. Indeed, in these cases, believing that p is a logical criterion for believing that q. Belief is impossible without some degree of understanding, and that degree of understanding includes some at least of the more obvious logical relationships which the proposition expressing the belief bears to other propositions. What I am claiming now is that the relationship of existential generalization is a relationship of this kind. Where p is an existential generalization of q, x's believing that p is a logical criterion for ascribing to x the belief that q. How could Philip believe that Rachel is coming to dinner if he did not believe that someone is coming to dinner? Does Ambrose really think that Martha is Simon's wife if he doesn't even think that Simon is married?

That is my main justification for saying that (3A) is derivable from (2A). A minor point needs clearing up: I said that (2A) was 'tantamount' to 'Paul believes that (2)'. The hedging was due to an awareness that mechanically attaching (2) to the words 'Paul believes that' would produce, not (2A), but (2A) minus the second occurrence of 'that'. My intuitions as a native English speaker lead me to judge that 'x thinks that p and q' is ill-formed, unless it is intended to be understood as '(x thinks that p) and q', as opposed to 'x thinks that (p and q)'. Perhaps to show that the second conjunct is within the scope of the verb of propositional attitude, English idiom requires 'that', if used at all, to be repeated before the second conjunct. The repetition is not intended to suggest any failure on the part of the person whose attitude is being reported to connect the two conjuncts: 'Mary has just heard that Peter has got typhoid and that Peter is on holiday with her daughter; so Mary is in a state of panic.' If Mary had not connected the two things she had heard, she would have no reason to panic. The second occurrence of 'that' has no logical significance, apart from ruling out the possibility of the first type of bracketing: '(Mary has just heard that Peter has got typhoid) and Peter is on holiday with her daughter.' Indeed it is idiomatic, if somewhat slovenly, to omit both occurrences of 'that': 'Paul thinks Boscovich was born in Dubrovnik and Dubrovnik is a present-day Croatian holiday resort' is, not just tantamount to, but exactly what is meant by, 'Paul thinks that (2)'. The minor point could be dealt with by omitting all occurrences of 'that' in this slovenly, though intelligible, way. It need not detain us further.

From (3A) we can derive

(4A) Paul thinks that a town where Boscovich was born is the same as a present-day Croatian holiday resort.

If, with Russell, we hold that (4) is of the form $\exists x \, \exists y \, [(\varphi x \, \& \, \psi y) \, \& \, x = y]$, and that propositions of this form are entailed by corresponding propositions of the form $\exists x \, (\varphi x \, \& \, \psi x)$, we may well consider the entailment so obvious that believing that (4) is a logical criterion for believing that (3). We should then have the same justification for deriving (4A) from (3A) as we had for deriving (3A) from (2A).

If, on the other hand, we accept Wittgenstein's contention that $\exists x \, \exists y \, [(\varphi x \, \& \, \psi y) \, \& \, x = y]$ is ill-formed, and that those who seem to be saying something of this form are really saying something of the form $\exists x \, (\varphi x \, \& \, \psi x)$, we shall be unable to distinguish in respect of logical form between (3) and (4). (3) and (4) are certainly not distinguished in virtue of their content. (3) is got from $\exists x \, (\varphi x \, \& \, \psi x)$ by substituting 'Boscovich was born in x' for φx and 'x is a Croatian holiday resort' for ψx, and (4) is got from $\exists x \, \exists y \, [(\varphi x \, \& \, \psi y) \, \& \, x = y]$ or $\exists x \, (\varphi x \, \& \, \psi x)$, depending on one's acceptance either of Russell's or of Wittgenstein's analysis of such propositions, by making exactly the same substitutions. (3) and (4), therefore, do not differ from each other in respect of their content, and on Wittgenstein's view they do not differ in respect of their logical form. It is difficult to see them as anything other than the same proposition. Propositional identity is a contentious topic, to which we shall have to turn our attention later in this book. Prior, at one time, espoused a version of the identity of indiscernibles as applied to propositions, a view that might be expressed by $(p = q) \leftrightarrow \forall \delta \, (\delta p \leftrightarrow \delta q)$, where δ represents operators forming propositions out of propositions.[4] Whether or not this is acceptable as a definition of propositional identity, as Prior envisaged it, the weakened version $(p = q) \rightarrow \forall \delta \, (\delta p \leftrightarrow \delta q)$, which might be regarded as stating the indiscernibility of identical propositions, seems to be involved in anything that might be accepted as propositional identity. Substituting 'Paul thinks that ---' for δ, this schema licenses the derivation of (4A) from (3A), and, for those who want, vice versa, given that (4) is the same proposition as (3).

[4] A. N. Prior, 'Is the Concept of Referential Opacity Really Necessary?', *Acta Philosophica Fennica*, 16 (1963), p. 192.

On Wittgenstein's view about identity it is difficult to see what any one who thinks that (4) could be thinking, if not that (3). If (4A) asserts that Paul has a genuine belief at all, it must, if Wittgenstein is right, assert what (3A) asserts. It is undoubtedly a consequence of Wittgenstein's account of identity that (4A) is derivable from (3A).

§ **2.** Our derivation, therefore, takes us from (1A) to (4A). Notoriously, however, a proposition like (1A) could be true while the corresponding proposition like (4A) is false. Paul could perfectly well think that Boscovich was born in Ragusa and that Dubrovnik is a Croatian holiday resort and be entirely unaware that a town where Boscovich was born is the same town as a present-day Croatian holiday resort. He might think Boscovich's birthplace was in Bulgaria or Poland. He might hotly deny that Ragusa is or was in Croatia, without prejudice to the truth of (1A). Somewhere along the line a fallacious inference has occurred in the derivation of (4A) from (1A). Which of the three steps is to be questioned?

The last step, from (3A) to (4A), was defended by an *ad hominem* argument. My purpose is to show that Wittgenstein's view, that identity is not a relation, does not, as he thought, have the consequence that we have no need for a sign of identity. I wish therefore to go along with Wittgenstein's view as long as I can; and I do not in any case wish to challenge his thesis that propositions like (3) and propositions like (4) have the same logical form. The fallacious inference must be sought either in the step from (1A) to (2A) or in the step from (2A) to (3A).

The choice between these two will, I believe, in the last resort be unnecessary. The inference from (1A) to (2A) will be amiss, if it is, for the same reason as that from (2A) to (3A). But the fault in question can be diagnosed more easily by first examining the inference from (2A) to (3A).

§ **3.** An initial glance at the two propositions might have led someone to wonder whether a confusion had arisen between (3A) and

(5A) For some town x, Paul thinks that Boscovich was born in x and x is a present-day Croatian holiday resort.

Ex hypothesi the verb 'thinks' in these propositions is being given the transparent interpretation; and just as this interpretation licenses us to infer (2A) from (1A), so it allows us to quantify into the positions occupied by 'Dubrovnik' in (2A) from outside the belief context, thus producing (5A). Just so, when 'believes that' is understood transparently, from 'Philip believes that Cicero denounced Catiline' we can infer that there is someone of whom Philip believes that he denounced Catiline; but when 'believes that' is understood opaquely this inference is invalid. When 'believes that' is understood opaquely, on the other hand, from the fact that Philip believes that Cicero denounced Catiline we do seem to be able to infer that Philip believes that someone denounced Catiline. (This is analogous to the move from (2A) to (3A).) The transparent interpretation allows the quantifier wider scope, the opaque interpretation allows it narrower scope. But these are not exclusive alternatives. The transparent interpretation allows the quantifier wider scope *as well as narrower*. The opaque interpretation, as it were, drives the quantifier inwards, but it does not follow that the transparent interpretation drives the quantifier outwards. Indeed, with 'believes that' interpreted transparently, 'There is someone whom Philip believes to have denounced Catiline' seems actually to entail 'Philip believes that someone denounced Catiline': how could he believe of someone that he did it without believing that someone did it? So (5A) seems to have been a red herring. If (2A), (3A), and (5A) behave like the Catilinian examples, (5A) will entail (3A); and so far from our having to choose between (5A) and (3A) as the proposition entailed by (2A), we cannot have (5A) without (3A). We could in any case get to (3A) from (2A) via (5A); so we cannot be prevented from getting to (3A) direct by fear that we are confusing it with (5A).

§ **4.** But do (2A), (3A), and (5A) behave like the Catilinian examples? Someone who believes (transparently interpreted) that Cicero denounced Catiline believes of Cicero that he denounced Catiline. Does someone who believes (2) believe of Dubrovnik, or of any town, that it was the birthplace of Boscovich and is a present-day Croatian holiday resort? Is asserting (2A), with 'think' understood transparently, tantamount to saying that, in Paul's view, the predicable

(6B) ...... was the birthplace of Boscovich and is a present-day Croatian holiday resort[5]

is truly applicable to Dubrovnik? If that is what (2A) asserts, it looks as though the same must be asserted in (1A), since the transparent interpretation of (1A) and (2A) make each entail the other, given that 'Ragusa' and 'Dubrovnik' are names for the same town. But surely it would be intolerable to attribute to Paul, simply on the strength of the truth of (1A), the view that (6B) is truly applicable to anything at all.

We must distinguish here between (2A) and

(6A) Paul thinks that Dubrovnik was the birthplace of Boscovich and is a present-day Croatian holiday resort.

There need be no hesitation in inferring (3A) from (6A). That case is on all fours with the Catilinian example. What then is the difference between (2A) and (6A)? It is not to be sought in the fact that (2A) contains two occurrences of 'that' to (6A)'s one. That idea has already been scotched. Rather, we need to focus on the difference between the sentences which express the content of Paul's thoughts as stated in (2A) and (6A), respectively, namely, the difference between (2) and

(6) Dubrovnik was the birthplace of Boscovich and is a present-day Croatian holiday resort.

It might be thought that no significance at all attached to the fact that the first half of (2) has 'Boscovich was born in Dubrovnik' whereas the first half of (6) has 'Dubrovnik was the birthplace of Boscovich'. Are not these merely stylistic variations which have no interest at all to the logician? That would indeed be the case if these strings of words were standing by themselves as complete propositions. In that case they could be substituted for each other in any context without change of meaning. As it is, of course, substituting 'Boscovich was born in Dubrovnik' for 'Dubrovnik was the birthplace of Boscovich' in (6) gives the second half of the subordinate clause of (6) the wrong subject. We should be saying that Boscovich was born in Dubrovnik and that Boscovich is a present-day Croatian holiday resort. And if we made the same

---

[5] Expressions with 'B' in their labels are all predicables.

substitution in (6A) we should be attributing to Paul the same stupid confusion between the name of a great scientist and the name of a town. It is important in the context of (6) and (6A), though not in the context of (2) and (2A), that 'Dubrovnik' appears as grammatical subject twice over. To see why this is so, we need to look closely at the construction of (6).

§ 5. Propositions like (6) are not conjunctive propositions with a truth-function as their principal operator. They are formed by attaching a proper name to a conjunctive predicable. The mistake of supposing that 'Boscovich was born in Dubrovnik' could be substituted for 'Dubrovnik was the birthplace of Boscovich' in (6) *salva significatione* was the mistake of treating the latter string of words as a complete proposition wherever it occurs. It is no more a complete proposition in (6) or (6A) than it is in 'Some city less beautiful than Dubrovnik was the birthplace of Boscovich'. To understand (6) we must see it, not as a conjunctive proposition with 'Dubrovnik was the birthplace of Boscovich' as one of its conjuncts, but as the result of attaching the name 'Dubrovnik' to the predicable (6B). What then is the structure of (6B)?

Two strategies have been employed by logicians for explaining the way in which conjunctive predicables of this kind are formed. Let us simplify matters by looking at as brief an example as possible. Take the predicable '--- is old and wise'. Those who favour the notion of satisfaction as the key to explaining the structure of such propositions would explicate this predicable by saying this: an object satisfies the predicable '--- is old and wise' iff it satisfies the predicable '--- is old' and it, the same object, satisfies the predicable '--- is wise'. Those, on the other hand, who use the notion of truth for this purpose would explicate it in this way: a proposition formed by attaching '--- is old and wise' to a proper name, say, 'Catherine', is true iff the proposition 'Catherine is old and Catherine is wise' is true. There is an important difference between these explanations. The satisfaction-type explanation uses in the statement of the truth-conditions the phrase 'it, the same object', whose role we shall be looking into later in the argument. (It would make no difference if the words 'the same object' were omitted from this phrase, or even if the whole phrase were omitted. These are all ways of expressing the concept of identity.) The truth conditions provided by the truth-type explanation, on the other hand, contain no expression involving the concept of identity. Suppose we explain what it is for someone to believe that a given proposition is true by saying that he believes it if he believes that the truth conditions for the proposition are satisfied. On the satisfaction-type explanation, then, someone believes that Catherine is old and wise if he believes that Catherine satisfies the predicable '--- is old' and that she, the same person, satisfies the predicable '--- is wise'. No unfortunate consequences follow from this. On the truth-type explanation, however, someone believes that Catherine is old and wise if he believes that Catherine is old and that Catherine is wise. This is a recipe for trouble, as we shall see if we apply the same procedures to (6A). On the satisfaction-type interpretation, (6A) is true if Paul thinks that Dubrovnik satisfies the predicable '--- is the birthplace of Boscovich' and that it, the same town, satisfies the predicable '--- is a present-day Croatian holiday resort'. Nothing amiss so far. But on the truth-type interpretation (6A) is true if (2A) is true. And given the undoubted entailment of (3A) by (6A), our paradoxical derivation of (4A) from (1A) is back with all its horrors.

We have already appealed to the principle of the indiscernibility of identical propositions: $p = q \rightarrow \forall \delta\, (\delta p \leftrightarrow \delta q)$. We may now use its contrapositive: $\neg\, \forall \delta\, (\delta p \leftrightarrow \delta q) \rightarrow p \neq q$, or its equivalent: $\exists \delta\, \neg\, (\delta p \leftrightarrow \delta q) \rightarrow p \neq q$. If (6A) and (2A) are not to be equivalent, we must recognize a proposition of the form $\delta(6)$ which is not equivalent to the corresponding proposition of the form $\delta(2)$. (6) therefore cannot be the same proposition as (2). Nor can (6) have the same logical structure as (2). (6) contains no proper name that (2) does not contain: they are both propositions about Dubrovnik. If they are distinct propositions their difference must lie, not in what they are about, but in what they say about it. We shall have, therefore, to return again to examining the structure of the predicable (6B), and we shall no longer expect success from a truth-type explanation of its structure, which focuses on the logical equivalence of (6) and (2).

§ 6. A proper appreciation of the structure of (6B) is, I believe, achieved by ignoring (2) and following a direct route from (1) to (6B). This need not surprise us. If both (1) and (2) are transparent contexts for the proper names which occur in them, (2) does not take us any further on our journey than (1). This is because the first step on the journey is to omit the proper names 'Ragusa' and 'Dubrovnik' from (1), and the same result would be obtained by omitting 'Dubrovnik', at each of its occurrences, from (2). What we need first is to form the two-place predicable

(1B) Boscovich was born in --- and ...... is a present-day Croatian holiday resort.

From this we can form a one-place predicable, which is manifestly equivalent to (6B), by inserting the words 'the same town' in the second gap in (1B). This yields

(6B$_1$) Boscovich was born in --- and the same town is a present-day Croatian holiday resort.

It would be a mistake to regard the one-place predicable (6B$_1$) as formed by making 'the same town' one of the arguments of the function expressed by the two-place predicable (1B), as 'Dubrovnik' is argument to this function in (1) and (2). Rather, we should see 'the same town' as simultaneously filling up both argument places in (1B) to form the one-place predicable (6B$_1$). This would stand out more clearly if we had started, not with (1), but with

(1*) Ragusa was the birthplace of Boscovich and Dubrovnik is a present-day Croatian holiday resort,

and proceeded via

(1B*) --- was the birthplace of Boscovich and ...... is a present-day Croatian holiday resort,

which is the two-place predicable formed by omitting the proper names from (1*), to

(6B*) --- was the birthplace of Boscovich and the same town is a present-day Croatian holiday resort.

(6B*) is a mere stylistic variant of (6B$_1$). They are related to each other in the same way as '--- was struck by Peter' is related to 'Peter struck ---'. And each is equivalent in meaning to (6B). (6B), however, does not even have the appearance of being obtained from (1B*) by filling up one of its argument places. It seems to be formed from (1B*) by closing up one of its argument places and thus, almost physically, reducing it to a one-place predicable. (6B) could be got out of (1B*) in this way, though not out of (1B), because each of the names whose omission produced (1B*) was the grammatical subject of a conjunct of (1*), whereas one of the names omitted from (1) to get (1B) was in non-subject position.

§ 7. Indeed, the device of physically closing the gap signifying one of the argument places of a two-place predicable, the device which got (6B) out of (1B*), is available only in a minority of the cases which need to be classified together in this way. Where the two-place predicable is not a complex but an atomic predicable, as are, for example, most transitive verbs, the gap-closing device is clearly not available. Here, however, many languages have a special device, the reflexive pronoun, which does the same work as 'the same town' did to produce (6B$_1$) out of (1B) and as closing the second gap did to produce (6B) out of (1B*). Thus '--- admires himself' is produced out of '--- admires ......' in the same way as (6B$_1$) and (6B) are produced out of (1B) and (1B*).

The recognition that what we have here is not the supplying of one argument to a two-place predicable, leaving the other place empty, but the simultaneous filling up of both places to produce a new one-place predicable, is due to Peter Geach.[6] Geach's doctrine is expressed in two ways, diagrammatically and by the invention of some new symbolism. He writes:

In passing from '--- admires ......' to '--- admires himself' we are not just filling up the second blank with 'himself'; the real logical structure is better brought out by this sort of diagram:

where the place between the parentheses is to be filled with the antecedent of 'himself'. (*Reference and Generality*, § 83)

Again, in § 84, Geach introduces his new symbolism in these words:

What we might well have is a more perspicuous symbolism than '$F(x,x)$' for 'x bears the relation F to itself'—a symbolism showing clearly how a one-place predicable is here formed from a two-place one. Let us use the symbol '$(—;u,v)$' for this purpose; this symbol, which may be read (say) as '--- being both u and v' will form a one-place predicable '$(—;u,v) F(u,v)$' from a two-place predicable, 'u' and 'v' being of course bound variables.

Geach's notation makes it clear that '$(—;u,v) F(u,v)$' is produced from '$F(---,---)$' by making '$F(---,---)$' argument to '$(—;u,v) — (u,v)$' rather than vice versa. We may compare the way in which

---

[6] See *Reference and Generality*, 3rd edn., Ithaca and London: Cornell University Press, 1980, §§ 82–4.

$\exists x \ (\varphi(—)x)$ is produced by making φ argument to $\exists x \ (—(—)x)$ rather than vice versa. In '--- admires himself' '--- admires ......' is to 'himself' as it is to 'someone' in '--- admires someone', not as it is to 'Albert' in '--- admires Albert'.

§ 8. Geach intends his symbolism to be used only in places where the reflexive pronouns of natural languages can be used. It does not correspond to every use of a repeated bound variable in classical logical symbolism. $\forall x \ (\varphi xx)$ gives the logical form of both 'Everyone admires himself' and 'Everyone is both a liar and a thief', since $(\varphi x \ \& \ \psi x)$ is a substitution instance of (φxx), as I pointed out in the first paragraph of this chapter. But the reflexive pronoun is not used to express propositions of the form $\forall x \ (\varphi x \ \& \ \psi x)$. Geach goes out of his way to emphasize this difference:

the repetition of bound variables in 'For any x, $F \ (x,x)$' is essentially different from that in 'For any x, Hx and Gx' or again in 'For any x, for some y, $F(y,x)$ or $G(x,y)$' . . . the latter sort of repetitions can be avoided altogether by joining predicables in a truth-functional way and using the symbol for converse relations: 'For any x, $(H \ \& \ G)x$'; 'For any x, for some y, x (Cnv'$F \cup G$)y'. These devices will not get rid of the repetition in 'For any x, $F \ (x,x)$'. (*Reference and Generality*, § 84)

He is, I think, mistaken at this point. Suspicion is aroused by his contrasting the forms $\forall x \ (\varphi xx)$ and $\forall x \ (\varphi x \ \& \ \psi x)$, as though these were co-ordinate forms of proposition. In fact, as has already been insisted, the latter is simply a more specific form of the former. In *Reference and Generality* Geach explains the 'essential difference' between 'For any x, $F(x,x)$' and 'For any x, Hx and Gx' by noting that in the latter repetition of variables can be avoided by 'joining predicables in a truth-functional way'. Thus 'Hx and Gx' can be written as '$(H \ \& \ G)x$'. But what is involved in this rewriting? How are we to interpret the sign for conjunction when it is inserted between predicate letters, given that its original use is for insertion between propositions? How does Geach explain the construction of conjunctive predicables?

His answers to these questions can be discovered by looking at a theory put forward in his paper 'A Program for Syntax'.[7] Here he

---

[7] This was Geach's contribution to D. Davidson and G. Harman (eds.), *Semantics of Natural Language*, 2nd edn., Dordrecht and Boston, Mass.: Reidel, 1972, pp. 483–97, originally published in *Synthese*, 22 (1970), where 'A Program for Syntax' occupies pp. 3–17.

introduces a recursive rule which secures that, where an operator, e.g., negation, forms a proposition out of a single proposition, the same operator will also form a one-place predicable out of a single one-place predicable. Thus 'It is not the case that ---' will not only form 'It is not the case that it is snowing' out of 'It is snowing', but will form 'It is not the case that --- is stupid' (or '--- is not stupid') out of '--- is stupid'. Turning to operators of more than one argument, he adapts his rule in such a way as to prescribe that where an operator, e.g., conjunction, forms a proposition out of n propositions, the same operator will also form a one-place predicable out of n one-place predicables. Thus, just as 'and' forms 'Catherine is old and Catherine is wise' out of 'Catherine is old' and 'Catherine is wise', so it will form '--- is old and (is) wise' from '--- is old' and '--- is wise'. We are to understand the use of '&' in the formula '$(H \& G)x$' no differently from that of 'and' in 'Hx and Gx'. Geach's rule provides that all that happens when we modify the input into the operation symbolized by 'and' or '&' is that the output is modified in the same way. Thus, if we remove the name or name-variable from the open sentences 'Hx' and 'Gx' to produce the one-place predicables 'H' and 'G', and join the resulting expressions together by '&', we shall get the one-place predicable, '$(H \& G)$'.

It seems to me, however, that he has not made the correct extension of his rule for operators which take more than one argument. What was needed was a rule which resulted, not in the production of a one-place predicable from an n-place operator and n one-place predicables, but in the production of an n-place predicable from an n-place operator and n one-place predicables. Attaching '--- is old' and '--- is wise' to '--- and ......' produces, not '--- is old and (is) wise', but '--- is old and ...... is wise', a two-place predicable which occurs in 'Catherine is old and Lucy is wise' just as much as in 'Catherine is old and Catherine is wise'. If conjunction is the operation which forms '--- is old and (is) wise' out of '--- is old' and '--- is wise', what is the operation which links together these predicables to form the two-place predicable which occurs in 'Catherine is old and Lucy is wise'?

Indeed, I think, it is a mistake to begin with an account of truth-functions which interprets their use with complete propositions as arguments, and supplement this with a rule which extends their use to provide for their taking predicables as arguments. Since propositions can themselves be regarded as no-place predicables,[8] truth-functions can from the start be regarded as operators which form predicables out of predicables. A truth-function of two arguments, like 'and' and 'or', will have an $(n + m)$-place predicable as its value for one n-place and one m-place predicable as its arguments. Thus attaching 'Catherine is old' and 'Lucy is wise', which are no-place predicables (i.e., propositions), to '--- and ......' will yield the no-place predicable (i.e., proposition) 'Catherine is old and Lucy is wise', since $0 + 0 = 0$; and attaching '--- is old' and '--- is wise', which are one-place predicables, to '--- and ......' will yield '--- is old and ...... is wise', which is a two-place predicable.

To obtain the one-place predicable '--- is old and (is) wise', we need, not only conjunction, but also an operator which will convert the two-place predicable '--- is old and ...... is wise' into the one-place predicable '--- is old and (is) wise'. In the same way conjunction by itself is able to produce (1B*), but not (6B), out of the predicables '--- was the birthplace of Boscovich' and '--- is a present-day Croatian holiday resort'. Geach argues, quite correctly, that a proposition formed by filling the gap in, say, (6B) with a given expression will not necessarily be equivalent to a proposition formed by filling the gaps in, say, (1B*) by two occurrences of the same expression: 'Some town was the birthplace of Boscovich and is a present-day Croatian holiday resort' is not equivalent to 'Some town was the birthplace of Boscovich and some town is a present-day Croatian holiday resort'. (6B) has to be recognized as a predicable in its own right, whose occurrence in a proposition does not always produce the same result as joining two propositions by 'and'. But this does not show that conjunction by itself is able to produce (6B) out of two one-place predicables. As the equivalence of (6B) and (6B*) shows, a conjunctive predicable needs for its formation not only the operation of conjunction but an operation expressible by something like 'the same town', or Geach's own functor '$(—;u,v)—(u,v)$'.

§ 9. It seems, then, that Geach has no good reason for resisting a generalization of the account he gives of the work of the reflexive pronoun. Such a generalization will enable it to cover the

[8] See, for example, A. N. Prior, *Objects of Thought*, ed. P. T. Geach and A. J. P. Kenny, Oxford: Clarendon Press, 1971, p. 33.

formation of one-place predicables from two-place predicables of
any variety, molecular as well as atomic. To mark my difference
from him, and for reasons which I will shortly explain, I shall use
the symbolism

$$\Xi u \; [\varphi uu] \; (—)$$

to do the work for which Geach appoints '$(—;u,v)F(u,v)$'. I use
the capital Greek Xi (Ξ) because, its job being to be a sign for
identity, it is not entirely dissimilar from the symbol ($\equiv$) Frege
used for this purpose in *Begriffsschrift*. It is analogous to $\forall$ and $\exists$
in that it is written immediately before a variable, which is then
repeated later in the formula, being on these occasions classified as
a 'bound' variable. (Geach's u and v are bound variables, as he
points out.) The bound occurrences of the variable occur in the
argument places of a many-placed predicable, yielding an open
sentence, which I place within square brackets to emphasize that
this is, as a whole, the operand in the formula. Corresponding to
the open sentence 'x admires x' we have

$$\Xi u \; [\varphi uu] \; x,$$

where the formula in square brackets corresponds to the open
sentence 'x admires y'. $\Xi u \; [---] \; x$ can be thought of as an operator
which converts an open sentence with n free variables (for $n > 1$)
into one with m free variables (for $m < n$). The open sentence
to be so converted has occurrences of the bound variable u
substituted for two or more of its free variables (taking care that
one of the free variables to be thus replaced is x), and is then
placed within the square brackets. If the open sentence which is to
be subjected to this operation has more than two variables, those
that remain after substitution of bound variables still retain their
positions within the square brackets; and the resulting open
sentence can be regarded as having these, together with the final x,
as its free variables. Thus $\Xi u \; [\varphi uu] \; x$, like '$x$ is a self-admirer' has
one free variable; but if we start with an open sentence with five
free variables of the form $\varphi vwxyz$, and substitute bound occurrences of u for v, x, and z, we shall finish with

$$\Xi u \; [\varphi uwuyu] \; x,$$

which is an open sentence with three free variables.

Geach's use of two bound variables, u and v, seems superfluous.
'$(—;u,v)F(u,v)$' cannot be different from '$(—;v,u)F(u,v)$' or

'(—;*u*,*v*)*F*(*v*,*u*)'. So '(—;*u*,*u*)*F*(*u*,*u*)' would be as good as '(—;*u*,*v*)*F*(*u*,*v*)' for this purpose. Two occurrences of the variable in the 'bound' positions are necessary as I shall explain in the next chapter. The distinction between *u* and *v* in the operator '(—:*u*,*v*)' is due largely, I think, to this being read as '(--- being both *u* and *v*)', which, unfortunately in my view, reimports the idea of identity as a relation at the point where we want to replace it. Ξ*u* is, there-fore, capable without repetition of *u* of doing the work done by '(—;*u*,*v*)'. The blank written before the semi-colon I reposition at the extreme right of the formula. This is to accord with the practice, initiated by Łukasiewicz, of writing functors to the left of arguments. Geach's whole complex symbol '(—;*u*,*v*)*F*(*u*,*v*)' is a functor whose argument would have to be written at its extreme left. In this it follows ordinary English, where, to take the case of Geach's memorable example 'Satan pities himself', 'Satan' is written to the left of 'pities himself', and permits the easy reading '(Satan being both *u* and *v*) pities (*u*,*v*)'. Nevertheless, the benefits by way of settling painlessly endless questions about scope which follow from adopting Łukasiewicz's practice outweigh all other considerations, and convince me that Ξ*u* [φ*uu*] *a* is the best way to represent 'Satan pities himself' with φ*xy* standing for '*x* pities *y*' and *a* for 'Satan'.

At the beginning of this section I remarked that I had chosen Xi as the operator to perform the task I have been describing because its job was to be a sign of identity. So far I have done little more than explain its syntactical category. If I am to justify my claim that it is a sign of *identity*, I shall need to say more about its 'semantics'. Enquiries about the semantics of an expression usually expect to be satisfied by statements of the truth-conditions of propositions in which it occurs. In the case of the Xi operator this is not difficult. For given interpretations of φ and *y*, any proposition of the form Ξ*u* [φ*uu*] *x* is true iff the corresponding proposition of the form φ*uu*, where the interpretation given to *x* is assigned to each occurrence of *u*, is true. As far as truth-conditions are concerned, Wittgenstein's identity of sign (the fact of the repetition of the name constituting the interpretation of *u*) is just as good as my sign of identity. But, as is well known, in contexts involving propositional attitudes, expressions which in isolation have the same truth-conditions are not substitutable *salva veritate*. To be given the semantics of Ξ*u* [φ*uu*] *x* is not to be given enough.

But how can an expression which is not relational in form be a sign of *identity*? It is reasonably clear how the Xi operator can be regarded as a regimented version of the reflexive pronouns of natural languages, but it seems extravagant to describe it as the canonical expression of the concept of identity itself. And yet this is exactly what I mean to do.

In so far as the word 'same', in English, is the principal expression of the concept of identity, we may note that in phrases like (6B$_1$) the work done by the phrase containing the word 'same' is exactly the same as that done by the reflexive pronoun. (6B$_1$), like '--- admires himself', is a possible interpretation of '$\Xi u \, [\varphi uu] \, (—)$', and here the work done by 'it, the same town' is that symbolized by the Xi operator. It is tunnel vision on the part of philosophers who consider the concept of identity to look only at examples where the word 'same' occurs as part of the apparently relational expression '--- is the same as ......'.

Even in the case of propositions containing this expression, it is possible to defend my contention that the concept of identity, as it occurs in them, is more appropriately represented by the Xi operator. The substance of this claim can, I think, be appreciated best by analogy with Quine's claim that existence is what the existential quantifier expresses.[9] Quine would hold that propositions to the effect that so-and-so's exist should be seen as having the logical form represented by an existential quantifier followed by a sentence containing a variable bound by that quantifier. His view is the one previously put forward by Frege and Russell, namely, that existential propositions are not in the business of predicating anything of objects, but have the role of predicating something of concepts (Frege) or of propositional functions (Russell). This, in their eyes, is the only form that a genuine existential proposition can take. Attempts to predicate existence of objects produce only nonsense. In the same way, I wish to maintain that the propositions we principally have in mind when we talk of identity propositions—propositions like 'The author of *Waverley* was the same as the author of *Marmion*'—are propositions whose true logical form can be represented by the Xi operator. It is this operation which is doing the real work in genuine identity propositions, just as it is existential quantification which is doing

---

[9] See W. V. Quine, *Ontological Relativity and Other Essays*, New York and London: Columbia University Press, 1966, p. 97.

the real work in genuine existential propositions. These are the crucial elements in affirmations of identity and existence, respectively.

Frege and Russell found it necessary to reject as abortive attempts to form propositions by attaching 'exist' or 'is' to a proper name used as a proper name. 'Lloyd George exists' would, in Russell's eyes have had no more sense than 'Lloyd George is numerous'. My position would come out most clearly if I were similarly to regard as abortive attempts to form propositions by filling both the places of the purported two-place first-level predicable '--- is the same as ......' with proper names used as proper names. In propositions like 'St John is the same as Bolingbroke', as I argued in Chapter I, § 3, at least one of the names is not being used as a proper name. But I intend to postpone until Chapter V my main consideration of the question whether such strings of words are significant propositions—whether, that is, there *is* an identity relation. However this may be, the propositions which we normally refer to as identity propositions, which are capable of conveying information, which are actually of use to people 'outside logic-books', as Russell says, or, in the Wittgensteinian phrase, 'outside philosophy', do not involve a two-place first-level predicable of this sort. What they do involve is an operator having the characteristics of my Xi operator. It is for this reason that I find it natural to use Wittgenstein's phrase 'sign of identity' to describe this operator.

§ 10. Armed with this symbolism (6B), $(6B_1)$, and $(6B^*)$ can be rewritten as

$(6B_2)$ Ξu [Boscovich was born in u and u is a present-day Croatian holiday resort] (—),

This is a one-place predicable formed out of (1B) by means of what I call 'the identity operator', Ξu [(—)uu] (—). (In this representation of the operator the first blank is the place to be filled by the two-place predicable and the second blank the place that will remain unfilled until the one-place predicable is converted into a proposition.) We are now in a position to explain the difference between (6) and (2). (6) is formed by attaching (6B) to the proper name 'Dubrovnik'. (6B) is formed by closing the second gap in $(1B^*)$; and this produces the same result as filling the second gap in

(1B) by 'the same town', as in (6B*). This operation is more perspicuously exhibited if we operate on (1B) by means of Geach's operator '(—;*u*,*v*)' or the identity operator, which is my adaptation of it. So where (2) and (1) are formed by attaching two occurrences of a proper name, or one occurrence of each of a pair of proper names, as arguments to the predicable (1B), (6) is formed by first attaching (1B) as argument to the identity operator, and then attaching a proper name to the one-place predicable obtained in this way. The structure of (2) and (1) is given by the two-place predicable (1B) and occurrences of proper names. The structure of (6) is given by (1B), together with the identity operator, which has the role of forming a one-place predicable out of a two-place predicable, and the single occurrence of a proper name. The conceptual content of (6) is thus greater than that of (2), although it contains fewer words. They are thus distinct propositions, although logically equivalent (as are 'John has six children' and 'The number of John's children is the double of the half of six'). The equivalence of (1A) and (2A) is explained by the fact that the only difference between them is the substitution of one name for another name of the same object. Leibniz's Law applies here, since we are giving the transparent interpretation to 'thinks that'. The non-equivalence of (2A) and (6A) is explained by the fact that the substitution of (6) for (2), which is what differentiates them, is the substitution of a logically equivalent, but not identical, proposition. Leibniz's Law does not apply.[10]

The fallacious reasoning which took us from (1A) to (4A) can now be exposed with (6A)'s help. It was the move from (2A) to (6A) which tempted us; but we have seen now that it should not be made, and why it should not be made. To nail down the mistake more firmly, the symbolism of the identity operator can be used to display the move from (2A) to (6A) as a case of the operator-shift fallacy. (2A) is equivalent to

(2A$_2$) $\varXi u$ [Paul thinks that Boscovich was born in u and that u is
        a present-day Croatian holiday resort] Dubrovnik.

This equivalence is guaranteed by the fact that propositions of the form $\varphi x x$ and those of the form $\varXi u[\varphi u u]x$, as we have already

---

[10] See Prior, 'Is the Concept of Referential Opacity Really Necessary?', *Acta Philosophica Fennica*, 16 (1963), for the distinction between such cases in respect of Leibniz's Law.

noted, share the same truth-conditions. That is to say, $(\varphi xx) \leftrightarrow (\Xi u[\varphi uu]x)$, is a logically valid schema. 'Paul thinks that Boscovich was born in x and that x is a present-day Croatian holiday resort' is a legitimate substitution instance for φxx in this schema. But from this we cannot infer

(6A$_2$) Paul thinks that (Ξu [Boscovich was born in u and u is a present-day Croatian holiday resort] Dubrovnik),

which is the same proposition as (6A). 'Boscovich was born in x and x is a present-day Croatian holiday resort' is another legitimate substitution instance for φxx in the schema $(\varphi xx) \leftrightarrow (\Xi u [\varphi uu] x)$, so that (2) is logically equivalent to (6). But it is not the same proposition, and with δ read as 'Paul thinks that' the schema $[\Box (p \leftrightarrow q)] \rightarrow [\delta p \leftrightarrow \delta q]$, as opposed to $[p = q] \rightarrow (\delta p \leftrightarrow \delta q)$, is not valid. The transition from (2A), which is tantamount to (2A$_2$), to (6A), which is the same as (6A$_2$), involves failure to notice a scope distinction. In (2A$_2$) the identity operator has wider scope than the operator 'Paul thinks that ---'. In (6A$_2$) it is 'Paul thinks that ---' which has wider scope.

§ **11.** The paradox which I introduced at the beginning of this chapter can thus be solved if we are prepared to recognize the identity operator. Wittgenstein would not have been prepared to recognize it, since he held that identity could always be expressed by identity of sign, without recourse to a sign for identity. The investigation of intentional contexts shows, I believe, that Wittgenstein was mistaken in this. That was the purpose of the attempt to show where fallacy occurred in the attempt to derive (4A) from (1A). But I do not regard Wittgenstein as having been mistaken in denying that identity is a relation. The symbol '=' is understood as expressing a two-place first-level predicable, and it is difficult not to see '--- is the same as ......' in the same light. 'Ξu' is obviously not of this category. It is an operator whose function is to convert a two-place predicable into a one-place predicable. What Frege had (idle) doubts about was whether identity was a relation, and Wittgenstein pronounced emphatically that identity was *not* this. Both of them were expressing views about the syntactical category of the concept of identity. But these were negative views. In the case of existence Frege went on to propound an affirmative view about its syntactical category. He not only refuted the view that

'---exist' is a first-level predicable, but also established its role as a second-level predicable. The syntactical revolution he thereby brought about has to be repeated for the concept of identity. Just as Kant saw that 'existence is not a predicate', so Wittgenstein saw that 'identity is not a relation'. What existence and identity *are* remained in both cases to be discovered.

SAME AND SELF

§ 1. Geach's symbolism for the identity operator is not the only device already current for giving apt expression, in a correct *Begriffsschrift*, to the concept of identity. There is a paper of Quine's, entitled 'Variables Explained Away', first published in 1960[1] and reprinted in his *Selected Logic Papers*,[2] which provides alternative machinery. Neither Geach nor Quine sets out explicitly to clarify the concept of identity or discuss the meaning of the word 'same'. Geach, as we have seen, is concerned to give an account of the logic of reflexive pronouns in natural languages. Quine's aim is to throw light on the role of variables on Logic and Mathematics by developing an alternative apparatus which will do the same work. Nevertheless, I hope to show that Quine's ideas too are able to assist us in our attempt to understand identity.

Indeed, the reason for explaining in laborious, though necessary, detail the mechanics of Quine's variable-free notation, is to show how a particular language devised by a formal logician can reproduce in a generalized fashion devices available only piecemeal in certain areas in certain languages. None of the variety of morphemes corresponding in different natural languages to 'self' and 'same' in English and to the middle voice in Greek provides a unified means of expression available for what I believe to be a single concept of identity. A proper understanding of the operation of 'reflection' as explained by Quine will, I hope, serve to justify this view that behind all this diversity of verbal expression a single concept is at work. The exercise requires a certain extension of Quine's vocabulary. As is well known, Quine proposes to eliminate 'singular terms' from his canonical language. The work done by names in natural language can, in his view, be performed better by quantifiers, variables, and predicables. His

[1] *Proceedings of the American Philosophical Society* (1960).
[2] New York: Random House, 1966, pp. 227–35.

symbol for 'reflection' is needed, therefore, only for the elimination
of repeated individual variables. I propose to extend its use to the
elimination of repeated individual constants, i.e., names, and
repeated expressions, variable and constant, of other categories,
e.g., predicables and propositions. I believe that the concept
expressible by 'Ref' has an ability to transcend categories and a
topic-neutrality equal to that of the quantifiers.

§ 2. It is best, however, to begin where Quine begins, with
an account of how the system of variables as used in first-order
predicate calculus can be replaced. The main work that variables
do can be illustrated by looking again at one of the forms discussed by Geach, 'For any x, for some y, $F(y,x)$ or $G(x,y)$'
($\forall x \exists y \ [\varphi yx \lor \psi xy]$). A proposition which has this form is
'Everyone has someone who hates him or whom he fears'. The
variables here perform three functions. The first is that of
indicating, with the help of the quantifiers to which they are bound,
which of the two quantifiers, the universal or the existential, has
wider scope. Ordinary language does not always avoid ambiguity
in this regard. Instead of 'Everyone has someone who hates him or
whom he fears' we might have written 'Someone either hates or
is feared by everyone'. This, however, might be interpreted as
being, not of the form $\forall x \ \exists y \ (\varphi yx \lor \psi xy)$, but of the form
$\exists y \ \forall x \ (\varphi yx \lor \psi xy)$—or, equivalently, reléttering the variables,
$\exists x \ \forall y \ (\varphi xy \lor \psi yx)$. English word order does not require that the
vernacular quantifier (e.g., 'some') which occurs first in the
sentence have wider scope than the one (e.g., 'every') which
occurs second. 'Some number is the successor of every number' is
not doomed to falsehood. Formal quantifier notation, on the other
hand, gives wider scope to a quantifier the further to the left it
occurs in the formula.

The second function performed by variables is not peculiar to
formal languages. English, though not every natural language, has
a word order which rigidly determines the sense of the words in the
matter of the direction of relations. 'Some boy is loved by every
girl' is about boys being loved by girls, not about girls being loved
by boys, even if the scope of the quantifiers is ambiguous.
(Inflected languages accomplish this disambiguation by case-
endings, not by word order.) So long as we stick to the two-place
predicable '--- is loved by ......' the order in which the phrases

'some boy' and 'every girl' occur is determined entirely by this fact—the fact that we are talking about boys being loved by girls. It is not available to mark the distinction between the interpretation which understands it as being of the form $\forall x \; \exists y \; (\varphi xy)$, where φxy means 'x loves y', and that which understands it as being equivalent to $\exists y \; \forall x \; (\varphi xy)$ (or $\exists x \; \forall y \; (\varphi yx)$). But left–right ordering serves in English, as in formal languages, to express the direction of a relation, and this, their second function, can also be represented by the use of variables.

§ 3. The logical notation of quantifiers and variables, therefore, uses left–right ordering to express both distinctions of scope and direction of relations. This is why in $\forall x \; \exists y \; (\varphi yx)$, to change the example, each of the variables occurs twice, once immediately after a quantifier and once in the open sentence φyx (y loves x). Where x ranges over boys and y over girls the fact that y precedes x in the matrix informs us that the proposition is about girls loving boys, but the fact that $\forall x$ occurs to the left of $\exists y$ shows us that what is intended is that every boy has some girl who loves him, rather than that there is some one girl who loves every single boy. Cross reference is achieved by each variable being repeated, occurring once with the prenex quantifiers and once in the matrix of the formula. Its position in the matrix shows the direction of the relation—shows that we are talking about the love which girls have for boys. But the fact that the variable which is on the left here is tied to the quantifier which occurs to the right in the prenex position, and vice versa, shows that 'every boy' is intended to have wider scope than 'some girl'.

§ 4. Already, in choosing idiomatic English sentences to express these distinctions, I have rung the changes between 'x is loved by y' and 'y loves x'. The availability in many (all?) natural languages of the passive voice allows us to reverse the direction of the relation without reversing the left–right ordering of the names of the *relata*. The symbolism of *Principia Mathematica* included a similar device for reversing the direction of a relation or two-place predicable. Instead of changing the direction of xRy by substituting yRx, we can write, in Russell's symbolism, x Cnv' Ry. Geach, as we have already seen, made use of this by rewriting 'For any x, for some y, $F(y,x)$ or $G(x,y)$' as 'For any x, for some $y(\text{Cnv'}F \cup G)y$'.

Geach's purpose was to turn a disjunction of open sentences into a single open sentence employing a disjunctive predicable. I can turn 'x is older than y or x is poorer than y' into 'x is older or poorer than y' without more ado. That is because x and y occurred in the same order in each disjunct. But if I want to replace the disjunction of open sentences 'y is older than x or x is poorer than y' by a single open sentence employing a disjunctive predicable, I must first transform this into 'x is younger than y or x is poorer than y', before proceeding to 'x is younger or poorer than y'. Given unlimited use of an inversion operator such as 'Cnv' ', I can always transform formulae containing two-place predicables so that the order of variables in the prenex quantifiers is the same as their order in the matrix of the formula. Instead of distinguishing $\forall x \; \exists y \; (\varphi yx)$ from $\forall x \; \exists y \; (\varphi xy)$ by reversing the order of the variables at their second occurrence, I can write $\forall x \; \exists y \; (\text{Cnv' } \varphi xy)$ and $\forall x \; \exists y \; (\varphi xy)$. But now the order of the variables is invariant: always alphabetical, and therefore idle. The variables no longer contribute anything to our understanding of these formulae. Similarly, if the order of 'someone' and 'everyone' always has to indicate which has the wider scope, so that 'Someone loves everyone' has to be taken as being of the form $\exists x \; \forall y \; (\varphi xy)$, to get a proposition having the form $\forall y \; \exists x \; (\varphi xy)$ we will have to write 'Everyone is loved by someone'. The four possibilities, $\exists x \; \forall y \; (\varphi xy)$, $\forall x \; \exists y \; (\varphi xy)$, $\exists x \; \forall y \; (\varphi yx)$ and $\forall x \; \exists y \; (\varphi yx)$ are thus represented by 'Someone loves everyone', 'Everyone loves someone', 'Someone is loved by everyone', and 'Everyone is loved by someone', or, in variable-free symbolism, by $\exists \forall \varphi$, $\forall \exists \varphi$, $\exists \forall$ Cnv' φ, and $\forall \exists$ Cnv' φ. The twin functions performed by the variable, scope indication and indication of the direction of relations, can be performed by variable-free quantifiers with the help of the inversion operator.

§ 5. The third function performed by variables can be explained by taking a further look at Geach's example 'For any x, for some y, $F(y,x)$ or $G(x,y)$'. Each variable occurs three times in this formula. The reason for its occurrence both in the matrix and with the prenex quantifiers has been explained already. But x and y are each repeated in the matrix itself. Geach himself has a way of eliminating this repetition: '$F(y,x)$ or $G(x,y)$' is changed into '$x(\text{Cnv'}F \cup G)u$'. Given the conventions we have just described the whole formula could be rendered variable free as $\forall \exists$ Cnv'$F \cup G$. Similarly, Geach's 'For any x, Gx and Hx' can be changed into $\forall$ G & H. But, as Geach emphasizes, nothing we have so far said has indicated a way in which we might cut down on the number of variables in 'For any x, $F(x,x)$'. Geach's own rendering of this, 'For any x, $(x;u,v)F(u,v)$' does not reduce the number of variables, whatever else it does; nor does my own version $\forall x$ (Ξu [φuu] x).

Someone may well ask, 'Why complicate the identity operator with variables at all? Why not write $\forall x$ (Ξu [φuu] x) as $\forall x$ ($\Xi \varphi x$), or indeed as $\forall \Xi \varphi$?' Quine indeed does something very like this. He does not have a primitive operator corresponding to the universal quantifier, but he does represent the existential quantifier by 'Der' and negation by 'Neg'. Since $\forall x = \neg \exists x \neg$, the universal quantifier can be represented by 'Neg Der Neg'. Quine's equivalent for Ξ is 'Ref', and his equivalent for $\forall \Xi \varphi$ is therefore 'Neg Der Neg Ref φ', which represents $\forall x$ (φxx) of the traditional predicate calculus. No bound variables are required.

If two-place predicables were all we had to concern ourselves with, there would be no answer to the questions asked in the last paragraph. But, as Geach makes clear, we have to deal with n-place predicables for $n > 2$. Blackmail can involve one person threatening a second with exposure to a third. But we can envisage the possibility of A threatening B with exposure to A (where B doesn't know the identity of the blackmailer), or of A threatening B with exposure to B (where the blackmailer doesn't know the identity of the person he is blackmailing). We therefore need to distinguish between a situation which has the form Ξu [φuyu] x from one which has the form Ξu [φyuu] x. Ξu [φuuy]x is also possible, though hard to envisage in the case of blackmail.

§ 6. Suppose, however, that we could transform any three-place predicable in such a way that a repeated variable always occurred in second and third position—suppose, that is, that of the three bracketed formulae in the last sentence [φyuu] was the only one we required. In that case, the open sentence $\forall x$ (φyxx) ('y threatens everyone with exposure to himself') could safely be written $\forall \Xi \varphi y$. No bound variable would be needed. In English we can do something similar to this: 'A threatens B with exposure to B' is already of the desired form, but 'A threatens B with exposure to A' can be transformed with the help of the passive voice into 'B

is threatened by A with exposure to A', which is also of the desired
form. Symbolically, writing φxyz for 'x threatens y with exposure
to z', we could render 'x is threatened by y with exposure to z'
by Cnv' φxyz, making 'Cnv'' the symbolic analogue of the passive
voice. 'A threatens B with exposure to A' will then be expressible
by a sentence of the form Cnv' φyuu. One of the required
distinctions will then be got by the contrast between φyuu and
Cnv' φyuu.

This, then, will enable us to turn φuyu into the desired form
φyuu. But how can φuuy be got into this form? To achieve this,
Quine, as it were, splits the inversion operator. Instead of 'Cnv'',
which was perfectly adequate so long as we were concerned only
with two-place predicables, Quine has a major inversion operator
'Inv' and a minor inversion operator 'inv'. Just as, according to the
convention we adopted in the last paragraph, 'Cnv'' had the effect
of transposing the occupants of the first two argument places of a
many-place predicable, so 'inv' has the effect of transposing the
occupants of the last two argument places. Thus invφxyz is
equivalent to φxzy. Major inversion is a more momentous business, as might be expected; it produces a formula equivalent to
one obtained by transposing the occupant of the last argument
place of the operand to the first argument place, and shifting
everything else one place to the right. Thus Inv φxyz is equivalent
to φzxy, Inv $\varphi xyzw$ to $\varphi wxyz$, and so on. Major inversion can
usefully be iterated, whereas it would obviously be futile to iterate
'inv' or 'Cnv''. Thus Inv Inv $\varphi xyzw$ is equivalent to Inv $\varphi wxyz$, and
so to $\varphi zwxy$. For our purposes 'Inv' is all we need to get every
three-place predicable which is to be attached to the identity
operator into the φyuu form. Of the three possibilities φyuu is
already in this form, φuyu becomes Inv φyuu, and φuuy, which we
lacked the resources to alter in the way desired, becomes Inv Inv
φyuu. The three possibilities are thus φyuu, Inv φyuu, and Inv Inv
φyuu. The occurrences of u are now all clearly redundant.
Deleting them, and the occurrence of u with the Xi-operator which
bound them, we obtain the three open sentences $\Xi\ [\varphi y]\ x$,
$\Xi\,[\text{Inv } \varphi y]\ x$, and $\Xi\,[\text{Inv Inv } \varphi y]\ x$. Since we have already adopted
Quine's 'Inv' as the major inversion operator, we may as well use
his 'Ref' instead of my recently invented Xi-operator. The square
brackets I introduced also now seem superfluous; so let me rewrite
our three possibilities as Ref φyx, Ref Inv φyx and Ref Inv Inv φyx.

These correspond to '*y* threatens to expose *x* to *x*', '*x* threatens to expose *y* to himself (i.e., to *x*)' and '*x* threatens to expose himself to *y*'. Thus, together with inversion operators, 'Ref' can perform the third of the functions performed by variables, the function they perform in virtue of allowing themselves to be repeated in the matrices of formulae.

The operation symbolized by 'Ref' is called by Quine 'reflection'. Reflection can be iterated, as inversion can. Imagine a four-place predicable occurring in the proposition 'A threatens B to expose C to D'. If we changed this to 'A threatens B to expose C to C', we could recognize this as being of the form Ref φxyz. A further change to 'A threatens B to expose B to B' will have the form Ref φxyy, and this can obviously be expressed by Ref Ref φxy. 'A threatens B to expose A to A' will be of the form Ref Inv Ref φxy.

§ 7. So far I have considered only those propositions which could be expressed in English by the use of the reflexive pronoun, and which Geach's operator was supposed to illuminate. My Xi-operator and Quine's reflection operator are supposed to be more general than this. They are supposed to cover all cases expressible in the traditional predicate calculus by the repetition of a variable or variables in the matrices of quantified formulae. To revert to Geach's original examples, they must cover propositions of the forms 'For any *x*, *Gx* and *Hx*' and 'For any *x*, for some *y*, *F(y,x)* or *G(x,y)*' as well as the simpler 'For any *x*, *F(x,x)*'. The difference between the last example and the others is that the open sentence in it is an atomic open sentence, formed by attaching variables to a single, non-complex predicable. The open sentences in the other examples are formed by truth-functional combinations of other open sentences. The molecular open sentences thus formed can be analysed, not only as being constructed by truth-functions out of existing open sentences, but also as being produced by attaching variables to a predicable with as many places as there are variables or different occurrences of a variable in the resulting open sentence. Thus, corresponding to the open sentence '*F(y,x)* or *G(x,y)*' there is a four-place predicable '*F*(---,......) or *G*(---,......)'. This itself can be regarded as the result of omitting all the names from the dummy proposition '*F*(Matthew, Mark) or *G*(Luke, John)', or each occurrence of each name from '*F*(Mark, Matthew) or *G*(Matthew, Mark)'. Predicables are simply what we get by punching out names, or occurrences of names, from propositions. It does not matter in the least whether those propositions are atomic or molecular, they are still propositions and predicables can be formed from them. '*F*(Matthew, Mark) or *G*(Luke, John)' is analysable as the result of attaching the names 'Matthew', 'Mark', 'Luke' and 'John' to the four-place predicable '*F*(---, ..., ---, ...)'. The whole proposition is thus of the form $\varphi xyzw$. (The same would have to be said if we considered not the dummy, but the real proposition, 'Matthew hates Mark or Luke is feared by John'.)

In order that Quine's operations of inversion and reflection can get to grips with molecular open sentences of this sort it is essential that all the variables be written at the end of the sentence. φxy v ψzw is indeed of the form $\varphi xyzw$, but to obtain the result Quine needs we will write it as Disj $\varphi\psi xyzw$.[3] (This could, of course, represent open sentences of the form φx v ψyzw or φxyz v ψw, but in the case of any given constant substituted for φ or ψ we should know, in virtue of our knowledge of its meaning, whether it was a one-place, two-place, or three-place predicable.) Given that all our open sentences can be written in this form, we can change Geach's '*F*(*y*,*x*) or *G*(*x*,*y*)' to Disj $\varphi\psi yxxy$ and this to Inv Disj $\varphi\psi xxyy$, and this to Ref Inv Disj $\varphi\psi xxy$, and this to Inv Ref Inv Disj $\varphi\psi xyx$, and this to Inv Inv Ref Inv Disj $\varphi\psi yxx$, and this to Ref Inv Inv Ref Inv Disj $\varphi\psi yx$. In this way what was expressed by repetition of variables in Geach's molecular open sentence, can be expressed without such repetition, but with repeated operations of inversion and reflection.

§ 8. We can now use this Quinean symbolism to mark the distinctions we drew at the end of the last chapter. First, let us abbreviate. Let φx represent 'Boscovich was born in *x*', ψy '*y* is a present-day Croatian holiday resort', δ 'Paul thinks that' and *a* 'Dubrovnik'. Then (2A₂) of Ch. III becomes

(2A₃) Ref δ Conj $\varphi\psi a$

---

[3] Quine in fact introduces only Cartesian multiplication to represent conjunction, writing $(F \times G)xy$ for *Fx* and *Gy*. Geach, in 'A Program for Syntax', see above, ch. II, n. 7. uses Imp *FGxy* to represent *Fx* → *Gy*, and I will follow his Polish style of writing a truth function to the left of its arguments—an arrangement I need for one of the theses I advance in ch. VII, below. I therefore represent, not only φx v ψy by Disj $\varphi\psi xy$, but φx & ψy by Conj $\varphi\psi xy$.

and (6A$_2$) becomes

(6A$_3$) δ Ref Conj $\varphi\psi a$.

What about (3A)? To translate this into Quine's symbolism we need to recall an item of the variable-free language which we encountered briefly in § 5 above. This is 'Der', which stands for 'derelativization'. The aim of the Quinean enterprise, it may be remembered, is to get rid of variables without losing the power to say the things we say by their means. Most of the translations we have so far effected produce open sentences, e.g. Ref φx, which still have free variables at their extreme right. Reflection is one way of reducing the number of these variables, as when the two variables of φxx are reduced to the single variable of Ref φx. If this variable is bound by an initial quantifier, and the binding of a variable made the occasion for its deletion, we can continue the process of reducing the number of variables, in this case to nought. 'Der' corresponds to the existential quantifier. So instead of $\exists x\,(\varphi xx)$ we can write Der Ref φ, and for Geach's 'For any x, $F(x,x)$' Neg Der Neg Ref φ. Variables are thus completely 'explained away'.

So what of (3A)? Using the abbreviations already used to obtain (2A$_3$) and (6A$_3$), we turn (3A) into

(3A$_3$) δ Der Ref Conj $\varphi\psi$

Similarly (6) becomes

(6$_3$) Ref Conj $\varphi\psi a$

and (3) and (4) are both representable by

(3/4$_3$) Der Ref Conj $\varphi\psi$.

In using a to stand for 'Dubrovnik' (and let b now stand for 'Ragusa'), I have departed from Quine's programme, in so far as he makes provision only for individual variables, not individual constants. His free variables are eliminated, beginning from the right, in one of two ways: either they are subjected to reflection, or they are first bound to the existential quantifier, and then both quantifier and variable are deleted in exchange for 'Der', written on the extreme left of the open sentence which is its range. I propose to legitimize the introduction of individual constants (in defiance of Quine's view about 'singular terms'), and allow them to occupy the positions occupiable by variables in open sentences and to be subject to the same treatment. Repetition of

names can then be eliminated in the same way as repetition of
variables. (2) of § 1 of the last chapter becomes

   (2_3) Conj $\varphi\psi aa$,

and by using reflection, which is a truth-preserving logical
operation, we can turn this into (6_3). Derelativization can then
turn (6_3) into ($3/4_3$), and emerges as prima facie the same
transformation as existential generalization (EG). It too is
truth-preserving, so that (6_3) logically entails ($3/4_3$). We get
from (2_3) to ($3/4_3$) by successive application of reflection and
derelativization.

§ **9.** And here is an answer to a question which may well have
bothered an attentive reader. 'Why has there been this mammoth
diversion via (6), (6A), ($6A_3$), etc.? Is not (3) itself the existential
generalization of (2), and has it not been agreed that δp entails δq
where q is the existential generalization of p?

Arguments were indeed advanced in favour of the view that we
were logically bound to ascribe to Paul belief in the existential
generalizations of his beliefs. Armed with the apparatus of
reflection and derelativization we can now, I think, separate out
what is true from what is false in this view. In so far as existential
generalization coincides with derelativization it remains plausible
that propositions of the form $\delta\varphi a$ entail corresponding propositions
of the form $\delta \exists x (\varphi x)$. 'Paul thinks Susan is coming to dinner' and
'Paul thinks someone is coming to dinner' are of these forms,
respectively, and the entailment relation clearly holds here. But
(2A) and (3A) are also, in the ordinary understanding of quantification, clearly of these forms. It would be normal to see (2), despite
the repeated occurrence in it of 'Dubrovnik', as being of the form
ϕa. It is possible to regard 'Brutus killed Brutus' as saying of
Brutus what 'Cato killed Cato' says of Cato, and Frege would see
in both an occurrence of the one-place predicable 'ξ killed ξ'. Each
of these propositions, and for that matter (2), is regarded as
obtained by attaching a proper name to this one-place predicable,
and propositions which are thus formed are precisely those which
are said to be of the form φa. Exactly the same reasoning would
force us to regard (3) as being of the form $\exists x (\varphi x)$. Existential
generalization cannot be conceived in any other way.

We can obtain 'Someone is coming to dinner' from 'Susan is
coming to dinner' by derelativization. We can obtain 'Someone

killed Brutus' from 'Brutus killed Brutus' by the same transformation. These are of course also existential generalizations. But there
is another existential generalization of 'Brutus killed Brutus',
namely '$\exists x$ (x killed x)' which is not obtainable by derelativization
alone—any more than the mere substitution of the word 'someone'
for one or both of the occurrences of the proper names in 'Brutus
killed Brutus' can produce a proposition having the meaning of
$\exists x$ (x killed x). This is because, where a quantifier can bind an
indefinite number of occurrences of a variable which replaces
repeated occurrences of a proper name, placing 'Der' in front of a
proposition allows us (*salva veritate et congruitate*) only to delete
one occurrence of a proper name. The quantifier $\exists x$ can by itself
take us from φaaa to $\exists x$ (φxxx); but a single 'Der' can only take us
from φaaa to Der φaa. To get to an equivalent of $\exists x$ (φxxx) we
should need two applications of reflection as well as one of
derelativization: the equivalent of $\exists x$ (φxxx) is Der Ref Ref φ.

Certainly, if Paul thinks that Susan is coming to dinner he thinks
that someone is coming to dinner, but this is because 'Someone is
coming to dinner' is the derelativization, not because it is the
existential generalization, of 'Susan is coming to dinner'. You
cannot get to something equivalent to $\exists x$ (φxx) by derelativizing
φaa, but you can get to it by derelativizing Ref φa. Similarly, (3)
can be seen as the derelativization of (6), which is of the form Ref
φa, as its variant (6_3) makes clear, whereas it cannot be seen as the
derelativization of (2), which is of the form φaa. The truth behind
the claim that we must attribute to a person a belief in the
existential generalization of what he believes, is that this holds
only when the existential generalization coincides with the
derelativization. The thesis that can be maintained is that a
proposition of the form 'x thinks that p' is entailed by a corresponding proposition of the form 'x thinks that q' where p is the
derelativization of q.

Traditional predicate calculus allows us to see in the move from
(2) to (3) only existential generalization. Quine's analysis shows
the fine detail of the logical steps taken in this case. There is not
one move here but two: reflection followed by derelativization.
The first corresponds to the move from (2) to (6), the second to
that from (6) to (3). The revised principle, which requires us to
attribute to a man belief only in the derelativizations of what he
believes, countenances the move from (6A) to (3A), but not that

from (2A) to (6A). If it is proper to speak of the legitimacy of substituting logical consequences of p for p in propositions of the form 'Paul thinks that p' as a sort of transparency of the context, we may say that 'Paul thinks that' is a context which is transparent with respect to derelativization, but opaque with respect to reflection. Contexts which are transparent with respect to the substitutivity of identicals may be opaque with respect to reflection. Thus I may believe of John Paul II that in the conclave that elected him he voted for Wojtyla, and may therefore be properly said to believe of Wojtyla that he voted for Wojtyla. It does not follow that I believe that Wojtyla voted for himself. In 'Variables Explained Away', Quine has nothing to say about propositions containing proper names; but, having adapted his symbolism to take account of them, we may say that where a and b name the same object it is permissible to move from $\delta\varphi ab$ to $\delta\varphi aa$, but not from either to δ Ref φa.

§ 10. Referential opacity can thus be said to force us to single out reflection as a distinct logical operation. We might call this the 'transcendental deduction' of the concept of identity. It was the same argument which, in the last chapter, forced us to single out an operator expressible by Geach's '$(—;u,v)$' or my 'Ξu [ ] x'. All these are, in my view, adequate expressions of the concept of identity, that is to say, of the concept expressed in English by the word 'same'. It is notable that when philosophers have concerned themselves with the meaning of the word 'same' they have almost always treated it as a fragment of the supposed two-place predicable '--- is the same as ......'. They have not paid attention to its use in phrases like 'the same town', as in $(6B_1)$ and $(6B^*)$ of the last chapter. I drew attention there to the similarity between the way in which a phrase like 'the same town' works and that in which a reflexive pronoun converts a two-place into a one-place predicable by filling up simultaneously both argument places. 'Himself', 'itself', and 'the same A' (where A is proxy for a sortal or count-noun) are natural language's equivalent of 'Ref' or 'Ξu [ ] x'. I already drew attention to the way in which English can produce the effect of converting a proposition of the form φaa to one of the form Ref φa simply by closing up, without filling, the second gap in the two-place predicable represented by φ. This is how (6B) is produced from $(1B^*)$. This method is not always available (it could not be used on (1B)), any more than the reflexive pronoun is always available for doing the work of 'Ref'. But where it is, we have the pleasing phenomenon of a logical operation being achieved by deletion rather than addition of a word or words. (2) is changed to (6) by the omission of the word 'Dubrovnik', but the change has the same effect as that of expanding φaa into $\Xi u [\varphi uu]\, a$ —a much less economical procedure.

A further way in which ordinary English can express the move from a proposition of the form φaa to one of the form $\Xi u [\varphi uu]\, a$ is by inserting the tiny word 'it' instead of the phrase 'the same town' in the gap indicating the second place of the two-place predicable.[4] The pronouns 'it', 'he', 'she', etc., used in this way, were compared by Quine as well as Geach with the bound variables of quantification, and it is entirely in keeping with this doctrine, and a development of it, to use an operator whose explicit function is to form predicables from predicables, to do part of the work done by the pronouns of ordinary language. Geach argued that the reflexive pronouns were not playing a 'referential' role in pro-positions like 'Satan admires himself'. Although in this English sentence 'himself' occupies a position which could also be occupied by 'Beelzebub' or by a repeated occurrence of 'Satan', whose job *would* be to refer to the objects whose names they are, the job of 'himself' is shown by Geach to be quite different. The same argument will show that the job of 'it' in 'Some man who owns a donkey beats it' is not to refer to a particular donkey ('let alone an 'arbitrary' donkey), but to help produce a predicable ripe for derelativization. Geach's arguments have been challenged in two heavyweight articles by Gareth Evans,[5] against which Geach has defended himself. I cannot go over this ground here. Suffice it to say that the claim I am making about the use of the word 'same' has to expect opposition from two sides. The opposition I have kept my sights on during the greater part of my argument is from those who see the essential use of 'same' as being in the larger phrase 'is the same as', which they construe as a two-place

---

[4] Indeed, it is idiomatic to combine the two methods by writing, e.g., 'Dubrovnik was the birthplace of Boscovich and it, the same town, is a present-day Croatian holiday resort'. Note that instead of writing 'and it, the same town' we might simply have written 'which'.

[5] G. Evans, 'Pronouns, Quantifiers, and Relative Clauses (I) and (II)', in *Canadian Journal of Philosophy*, 7 (1977), pp. 467–536, 777–97. Geach's reply is in vol. 8 (1978), pp. 375–9.

predicable. The other opposition may be expected from those who explain identity in terms of co-reference. Such philosophers are willing, perhaps, to grant that the fundamental use of the word 'same' is to be seen rather in phrases like 'the same town' in (6B₁) or 'the same woman' in 'Henry VIII married a woman and later had the same woman beheaded'. This phrase 'the same woman', although it helps to construct a predicable uniquely satisfied by Catherine Howard,[6] should not be construed as 'referring to' that woman, as these philosophers would wish. Members of this school insist on giving an account of the meaning of phrases like 'the same town', 'the same woman', along with the pronouns 'he', 'she', 'it', 'herself', etc., in terms of reference, treating them as quasi-names, referring to the same objects as their antecedents. But co-referentialists and relationists are equally in the wrong. The use of 'same', in whatever phrase it is embedded, is to be interpreted, not as part of a name, nor as part of a predicable, but in terms of an operator which forms predicables out of predicables. That is how $\varXi u$ [ ] x is intended, and it is what 'Ref' is manifestly about. The concept of identity is understood by understanding the concept of reflection.

§ 11. I have already indicated that the identity operator is a generalized replacement for the reflexive pronoun. In other words, the concept of *same* is no other than the concept of *self*. The way in which 'self' can occur prefixed to a noun or participle, e.g. 'self-deceiver', 'self-refuting', shows how closely the way 'Ref' works resembles natural language uses of 'self'. 'Richard is a self-admirer' might be rewritten 'Ref admires (Richard)'. The French *'se'* behaves in exactly this way: 'Richard se déteste' could be translated 'Ref hates (Richard)'. There are indeed languages with special inflexions of verbs expressing reflexivity, e.g., the Greek 'middle' voice, the Hebrew hithpa'el, where surface grammar indicates most clearly what is going on at a deeper level. The verb

---

[6] Anne Boleyn was not a woman whom Henry married and later beheaded, since his attempt to marry her was null and void, whether his previous marriage to Catherine of Aragon was valid or not. If it was, he committed bigamy in attempting to marry Anne Boleyn. If it had not been, the same reason (previous sexual involvement of the partner with a sibling) which made his marriage to Catherine of Aragon invalid would have made Anne Boleyn's marriage to him invalid, since Anne's sister had previously been his mistress. On any view Elizabeth I must be regarded as illegitimate.

in the middle voice does not present the least appearance of a two-place predicable. The modification of the radical, active-voice, form of the verb shows that a predicable is being formed out of a predicable. 'Ref' might be described as a morpheme which, when prefixed to a verb, converts it from the active to the middle voice.[7]

§ 12. This observation can be taken a stage further. Quine showed how the elimination of variables was to be accomplished by a team of operators including the reflection and the inversion operators. Both reflection and inversion operators form predicables out of predicables. Where $n > 1$, reflection forms an $(n-1)$-place predicable out of an n-place predicable, inversion an n-place predicable out of an n-place predicable. What 'Ref' does, the middle voice does in languages that have a middle voice. What 'Inv' or 'Cnv'' does, the passive voice does in, I suppose, every language. The passive voice is not so widely applicable as 'Inv': 'Man bites dog' will go into 'Dog is bitten by man' as well as into 'Inv bites (dog, man)'; but 'Peter is on the left of Paul' has no natural-language passive form to parallel 'Inv is on the left of (Paul, Peter)'—all that is available in ordinary language is the *ad hoc* inverted form 'Paul is on the right of Peter'. Nevertheless, we have in the English passive construction a limited analogue of inversion, and a native expression of an operation which forms predicables out of predicables. Those whose education introduced them to the passive and the middle voices should find no difficulty in grasping the ideas of inversion and reflection.

§ 13. English and German philosophers who write reams on 'the Self' or '*Das Selbst*' have sometimes wryly reflected (if I may be excused the word) on the difficulty of translating their profundities into French. Flew[8] once made a great fuss of the fact that in English other than philosophers' English, '-self' occurs only as a suffix to pronouns, 'myself', 'herself', 'themselves', etc. When the French turn their minds to the Transcendental Unity of Apperception they tend to discourse about '*le moi*' and '*le soi*', not about '*le*

[7] Cf. Stephen E. Toulmin, 'Self-knowledge and knowledge of the "Self"', in Theodore Mischel (ed.), *The Self: Psychological and Philosophical Studies*, Oxford: Basil Blackwell, 1977. I am grateful to Dr Steven Collins for drawing my attention to this paper.

[8] See A. G. N. Flew, 'Selves', *Mind*, 58 (1949).

même', which is what they would have to do if they wished, like us, to peel off the suffix which makes reflexive pronouns reflexive. But a thought is thereby suggested. French has a single word, or morpheme, '*même*', to do what English does with two, 'self' and 'same'. Greek too uses modifications of the same word '*autos*' to express 'the same' (*ho autos*) and 'himself' (*heauton*). German uses not only '*selbst*' in '*sich selbst*' for 'itself', but '*derselbe*', which is obviously the same word, for 'the same'. What is more, a look at the *Oxford English Dictionary* under 'self' will reveal that 'self' was anciently used in just the way 'same' is now used. Instead of 'the same man who was here last week' our ancestors would have said 'the self man who was here last week'.[9] 'Selfsame' is thus self-explanatory. Drapers' English retains a trace of this: if I want the facings or the cuffs or the collar of a garment to be of the same colour as the main part, I ask for it to be 'self-coloured'.

§ **14.** The evidence begins to look overwhelming. The concept of *same* just *is* the concept of *self*—the self-same concept. There is a special twist to the word 'self', which Locke's discussion of personal identity may have done more to stimulate than anything else, and which explains why the French translation is often '*le moi*'. But more of this later. We are still moving in the regions of topic neutrality, and nothing so committed as the Ego must be allowed to disturb the purity of the discussion at this stage.

§ **15.** Let the doctrine be stated with maximum implausibility: 'My mother-in-law is the same as my physiotherapist', 'Someone is deceiving himself', and 'There is a number which is its own square' are all of the same logical form, a form which we may symbolize by $\exists x \; \varXi u \, [\varphi uu] \, x$ or Der Ref φ. In traditional form the first comes out as '$\exists x \; (x$ bore my wife & x alone gives me physiotherapy)', the second as '$\exists x \; (x$ is deceiving $x)$' and the third as '$\exists x \; ($the square of x is $x)$'. What we need in order to recognize the common form here is above all to see that removing names from a complex, e.g., conjunctive, proposition, as well as from an atomic one, can

---

[9] Dr Collins has drawn to my attention the following lines from Shakespeare: 'It is the stars, the stars above us, govern our conditions; Else one self mate and mate could not beget such different issues' (*King Lear*, IV. iii. 34 ff.), and Mr Stephen Elphick has found similar occurrences in *Antony and Cleopatra*, V. i. 21 and *The Comedy of Errors*, V. i. 10.

produce a two-place predicable. In each case there is the repetition of a variable bound by a quantifier. The considerations of referential opacity force us to isolate and give expression to the concept whose implicit presence was shown by the repetition of the variable. We do need a sign for identity in addition to being able to repeat an identical sign.

Where disagreement comes with Wittgenstein, however, is not only over this sign for identity, but in a failure of parallelism between the concept of identity and the concept of difference. I have already pointed out that neither on Russell's view of identity (except where it is idling) nor on Wittgenstein's, is difference the contradictory of identity. The concept of difference and the concept of identity do not enjoy that intimate union which comes when one is the mere negation of the other—a union so close that we can say *eadem scientia oppositorum* (to know what oddness is is to know what evenness is). But if difference is not the negation of identity, Wittgenstein could still allow himself the balanced dictum: identity I show by identity of sign, difference by difference of signs. That balance is one which I cannot allow myself to endorse. For where difference is concerned, my view is no different from Wittgenstein's. The exclusive interpretation of variables (which means that difference of variable is to express difference of object), in my view as in his, is the best way to express difference. The resources of the traditional predicate calculus thus interpreted are adequate, and indeed precisely what we need, to state such facts. Enough to say '$\exists x\ \exists y$ (x bore my wife & y alone gives me physiotherapy)' to assert the distinction between physiotherapist and mother-in-law. This is not of the form Neg Der Ref φ, let alone of the form Der Neg Ref φ: it is not that no one is related to me in both these ways, nor that someone at least is not so related to me, but that someone is related to me in one of these ways and someone *else* in the other. If the concept *same* is the concept *self*, the concept *different* is the concept *else*. I claim to have provided a transcendental deduction of the need for a sign to express the concept of sameness. I make no such claim for elsehood.

EXTENSIONALISTS AND RELATIVISTS: AN EIRENIC INTERLUDE

§ 1. Wittgenstein is very fierce about identity as a relation: 'in a correct *Begriffsschrift* pseudo-propositions like "$a = a$", "$a = b$. $b = c. \rightarrow a = c$", "$(x).x = x$", "$(\exists x).x = a$", etc., cannot even be written down' (*Tractatus*, 5.534). Russell is equally combative on the subject of existence:

'though it is correct to say "men exist", it is incorrect, or rather meaningless, to ascribe existence to a given particular x who happens to be a man (*sic*). Generally, "terms satisfying φx exist" means "φx is sometimes true"; but "a exists" (where a is a term satisfying φx) is a mere noise or shape, devoid of significance.' (*Introduction to Mathematical Philosophy*, London, George Allen and Unwin, 1919, p. 165.)

According to Wittgenstein it is as absurd to construe 'My mother-in-law is the same as my physiotherapist' as being of the same logical form as 'Peter is on the left of Paul' as it would be to suppose that 'My sister and my secretary are identical' is of the same logical form as 'My sister and my secretary are lackadaisical'. Russell frequently compares inferring 'Socrates exists' from 'Men exist and Socrates is a man' with inferring 'Socrates is numerous' from 'Men are numerous and Socrates is a man'. If we follow these authors, any attempt to construe '--- exist' as a one-place, or '--- is the same as ......' as a two-place, first-level predicable, results only in gibberish.

§ 2. But is it not possible quite simply to lay down truth-conditions for propositions having '--- exist' or '--- is the same as ......' as predicates of the forbidden type? Any proposition formed by attaching '--- exists (or has existed)' to a proper name is true. The predicable '--- exist' has as its extension the universal class. Similarly, the extension of the two-place predicable '--- is the same as ......' is the class of all pairs such that the pair consists of just one object taken twice. Pairs such as ⟨Brutus, Brutus⟩, ⟨Caesar, Caesar⟩, ⟨Augustus, Augustus⟩, ⟨Augustus, Octavian⟩, ⟨Karol Wojtyła, John Paul II⟩, and so on, satisfy the predicable '--- is the same as ......'. It is not difficult to specify the set of pairs of this kind or to understand how to continue the series of examples I have begun. 'A semantics' is thus given for '--- exist' and '--- is the same as ......', understood as first-level predicables. What right has Russell or Wittgenstein to deny that they have any meaning?

§ 3. Where '--- exist' is concerned, it is possible to raise the following objection: if there is such a thing as the class of existents, it has to be the same as the class of things which are either square or not square, the class of things which are married if married, and, indeed, the class of things which are self-identical. But this makes it impossible to explain the meaning of '--- exist' simply in terms of its extension. Such a procedure would fail to differentiate it from the indefinite number of tautological predicables with which it would be co-extensive.[1]

Some philosophers, however, might wish to question whether in fact everything that exists is either square or not square. They would be inclined to say that points, lines, and volumes, not to speak of symphonies, recipes, and disembodied spirits, are neither square nor not-square; and that since there is no way of deciding, in the case of snakes, gnats, or rose-trees, whether they are married or unmarried, the molecular predicable 'married if married', whose sense depends on the ability to affirm or deny the atomic predicable it contains of any given subject, cannot meaningfully be ascribed to such objects either. Others would cheerfully ascribe 'not-square' and 'not-married' to everything whatsoever to which 'square' and 'married' cannot truly be ascribed, and so would re-instate the difficulty for believers in universal properties. This dispute can perhaps be left unsettled, because those who are unwilling to call the sound of a trumpet 'not-square', but who are happy nevertheless to treat 'exist' as a predicable that applies truly to

---

[1] Gareth Evans in *The Varieties of Reference* (Oxford: Clarendon Press, 1982, p. 348) seems to be alluding to this difficulty when he suggests that a first-level predicable 'exist' would have *Bedeutung* but no *Sinn*, and that it is therefore 'a formal, or logical, predicate'. The footnote on the same page extends this to 'the identity predicate'.

everything, will have no good reason to deny that all and only those things which exist satisfy the open sentences $x = x$ and $\exists y\, (\, y = x)$. Those who have Wittgensteinian doubts about the significance of strings of words like 'x is identical with itself' or 'x is the same as something' will not be disturbed by the objection that the class of objects which satisfy these purported sentences also satisfy the sentence 'x exists'. They will probably be the same people who question the significance of '--- exist' as a predicate of objects in the first place.

§ 4. These predicables whose extension, it is claimed, coincides with that of '--- exist', are all, be it noticed, complex. Either they are formed out of simpler predicables by one sort or other of truth-functional combination, or they are one-place predicables constructed by reflection or derelativization from two-place predicables. This gives the friends of existence-as-a-property a line of defence. They can say that '--- exist' is the only predicable which is true of absolutely everything and which is also simple or non-complex. To be sure, its meaning differs from that of predicables like '--- is married if married' or '--- is identical with something'; but that is because these other predicables have the meaning they have in virtue of the meaning of the words like 'if', 'identical', 'married', and 'something' out of which they are constructed. The word 'exist', on the other hand, is simple: that is to say, it does not have the meaning it has in virtue of the meaning of any proper part of itself. It is the only such word which applies to any and every object.

How do they know that it is? How do they know that there are not many such words waiting to be introduced into our language? How do they know that '--- is', in certain of its uses, though applying to just the same objects as '--- exist', does not say something completely different about them? How do they know that there are not many properties each of which which all objects possess, and that different people use the word 'existence' to signify different properties from amongst this group, although there is no way of discovering which of these properties any particular user of the word intends to pick out. Perhaps a single individual, without knowing it, may mean one thing by the word on Mondays, Wednesdays, and Fridays and another on Tuesdays, Thursdays, and Saturdays.

§ 5. The difficulties which attend those who claim to use '--- is the same as ......' as a two-place first-level predicable are slightly less acute. Just as the friends of existence-as-a-property had to respond to the challenge to distinguish existence from *being either square or not-square*, and from *being married if married*, so the friends of identity-as-a-relation have to explain what distinguishes it from *being the double of the half of*, or *being ten feet to the right of what it is ten feet to the left of*. Easier for them to insist that there are many pairs of objects which are not spatially related to any objects, or which have no size. *Being* double, or on the left, implies the possession of certain characteristics, even if *not being* square, or *not being* married, does not. So there does not seem to be any complex relation which holds between any object whatsoever and itself with which identity might be confused, as *being self-identical* or *identical with something* could be confused with *existing*. But the sceptical doubts about the uniqueness of the alleged simple property of existence could be paralleled in the case of identity. Given that you and I agree on the pairs of objects we think satisfy '*x* is the same as *y*', how do we know that there is just one such sentence satisfied by those pairs? How do we know that I am picking out the same relation as you are?

§ 6. Perhaps these worries can be quieted. Perhaps it does not matter if there are many properties signified by '--- exist' and many relations by '--- is the same as ......'. This, it might be urged, would only make Russell and Wittgenstein's positions further, if anything, from the truth. Those who are impressed by the teachings of Frege, Russell, and Wittgenstein in these matters can, I think, afford to be more generous than their teachers. They can concede that there is a one-place predicable whose extension is the universal class and a two-place predicable whose extension is the class of pairs consisting of each object taken twice over. They will still wish to say that these predicables do not occur in the propositions which in real life find expression with the help of the words 'exist' and 'same'. The analysis of '--- exist' as a second-level predicate in propositions like 'Unfriendly Italians exist' is too well known to require comment; but the use of the word in propositions like 'The Great Western Railway ceased to exist in 1947' or 'I might never have existed', which have seemed more favourable to the cause of existence-as-a-property, resist this sort of analysis.

Being self-identical is not a feature that the GWR lost in 1947, nor is *being the same as something* a property I might never have possessed. Whether or not the three sentences '*x* exists', $x = x$, and $\exists y \, (y = x)$ pick out the same property, as Quine and others have claimed, they do not pick out a property which will help us to understand the notions of contingent existence, coming to exist, or ceasing to exist. Nor is existence, if construed as a property which all objects possess, going to behave differently from being a woman —a property which all women possess—in fictional contexts. If there is such a property as existence, Anna Karenina will possess it in exactly the same way as she possesses the property of being a woman. Analysis of the concept of existence is going to be no more help to us than analysis of the concept of womanhood in understanding the logical peculiarities, if any, of fiction.[2]

Nor are the interesting questions about identity answered by the alleged relation, whose definition is 'that relation which every object bears to itself'. How can propositions which assert the existence of such a relation ever be informative? How could we ever be ignorant of the fact that such a relation obtained, where it did obtain, or that it did not, where it did not? Why does the substitution of identicals break down where it does break down? Could the study of such a relation help to explain the evident connection in many languages between the word for 'same' and the word for 'self'? How is it that so much of Mathematics consists in establishing equations, if all that an equation does is to affirm this least interesting of all relations? We can include identity, if we like, as Russell did, in our analysis of propositions like 'Scott is the author of *Waverley*', but even Russell quickly saw that its affirmative occurrence is superfluous given the truth of (β); and the way it remains hauntingly in its negative occurrence, restricted to a position within the scope of quantifiers, very soon summoned Wittgenstein to exorcise it. There may perhaps be a relation definable in the way logicians require; but most of us can do very well without it.

§ 7. Kripke, in *Naming and Necessity*,[3] has some fun at the expense of writers who, like me, think that they can do without

---

[2] I have said a good deal on these topics in my *What is Existence?*, Oxford: Clarendon Press, 1981, particularly chs. IV, V, and X, and pp. 286–8.

[3] Saul Kripke, 'Naming and Necessity' in D. Davidson and G. Harman (eds.)

identity as a relation between objects. 'Some philosophers', he says, 'have found the relation so confusing that they change it'. The change he considers is the view maintained by Frege in *Begriffsschrift*[4] that identity is not a relation between objects, but between names of objects. But Kripke's main argument is supposed to work for any analysis of identity propositions other than that which takes them at their face value, as asserting a relation between objects. His ploy is to grant to someone who adopts such a view his account of *identity*, and introduce into our language an 'artificial relation', *schmidentity*, stipulated as holding only between an object and itself. He supposes that the same problems will arise for schmidentity as were originally supposed to arise for identity. In particular the problems which originally arose for the question whether Cicero is identical with Tully will now arise in connection with the question whether Cicero is schmidentical with Tully, and these problems will not be solved by supposing that schmidentity is a relation between names. Kripke therefore concludes that the manoeuvre of introducing a relation between names is useless for solving the original problems about identity propositions. Identity as a relation between objects, whatever word we use to signify it, will not go away, and its problems will remain to be solved.

The step in Kripke's reasoning which I think mistaken is the step where he says 'the question whether Cicero is schmidentical with Tully can arise'. What is intended by this talk of 'a question arising'? If schmidentity is really a relation between objects, the question whether Cicero is schmidentical with Tully is schmidentical with the question whether Cicero is schmidentical with Cicero (if questions are objects). Does *this* question arise? Certainly few people are likely to ask it, and fewer still to be in doubt about the answer. If the question 'Is Cicero schmidentical with Cicero?' is not going to trouble them, neither is the question 'Is Cicero schmidentical with Tully?', because it is the same question. What may well trouble them is whether the words 'Is Cicero schmidentical with Tully?' express the same question as the words 'Is Cicero

---

The Semantics of Natural Language, 2nd edn., Dordrecht and Boston, Mass.: Reidel, 1972, pp. 309 f. My response to Kripke has much similarity to that provided by Thomas V. Morris in *Understanding Identity Statements*, Aberdeen University Press, 1984, pp. 50–3.

[4] See above, ch. I, § 3.

schmidentical with Cicero?'; but *that* question is just the question 'Do the names "Cicero" and "Tully" name the same man?', and is a question, in Kripke's terms, not about schmidentity, but about identity. Whether or not a relation holds between a pair of objects, or an object and itself, is a question completely specified once the relation is specified and the objects (or object) are specified. If a question arises when the objects are specified in one way but not in another, that is a question about which objects are being specified (what the names name), not about whether the relation holds. Kripke's schmidentity, by his own stipulation, gives rise to no such questions, and it is not problematic or paradoxical in the way that identity is. By the same token it is of no interest to philosophers. The hypothesis that there is a relation such as schmidentity is supposed to be ('nothing but the smallest reflexive relation'[5]) is one of which most of us have no need.

§ **8.** There is, however, one school of thought which has need of this hypothesis, namely, those philosophers who hold that identity is relative. In their view it is possible for x to be the same A as y without being the same B as y. For them '--- is the same as ......' is elliptical: by itself it does not determine a relation, but in conjunction with a sortal expression it does determine one. The words '--- is the same ...... as ---' can be thought of as an operator which produces a two-place predicate when its second argument-place is filled with a common noun of the appropriate sort. It seems that if identity is relative, sameness must be a relation.

This becomes clear if we consider a proof that can be given of the anti-relativist thesis 'For every φ, for every ψ, if x is the same φ as y, then if ψx, x is the same ψ as y', when this thesis is translated into the language of the Xi operator or reflection. The relativist thesis requires, in any case, to be distinguished from the thesis that identity is elliptical, or needs to be kind-indexed. The latter is the view that when x is said to be the same as y, it is always legitimate to ask 'The same *what* as y?' When identity propositions are cast in the form represented by (L) in Chapter II, this thesis that identity is elliptical reappears as the thesis that quantification must always be restricted. Instead of saying that the one who is F is the same as the one who is G, the elliptical view insists on saying that the one

---

[5] Kripke, 'Naming and Necessity', n. 50.

who is *F* is the same *A* as the one who is *G*. Analogously the Wittgensteinian who holds the elliptical view will not say that, for some *x*, both *x* alone is *F* and *x* alone is *G*. Rather he will say that there is an *A*, namely *x*, such that both *x* alone is *F* and *x* alone is *G*. The variable *x* will be explicitly restricted to range over members of the class of *A*s, instead of ranging over objects in general. So, if we accept the elliptical view but reject the relativist view, the thesis we have to prove, in Wittgenstein's terms, is 'Whatever *A* and *B* may be, if there is an *A*, namely *x*, such that both *x* alone is *F* and *x* alone is *G*, and *x* is a *B*, then there is a *B*, namely *y*, such that both *y* alone is *F* and *y* alone is *G*'.

Let us attempt a *reductio ad absurdum* proof of this thesis. We begin by supposing that, for some *A*, for some *B*, there is an *A*, namely *x*, such that both *x* alone is *F* and *x* alone is *G*, and *x* is a *B*, and that it is also the case that there are *B*'s, *y* and *z*, such that both *y* alone is *F* and *z* alone is *G*. We may take as an example Locke's fiction of the prince who swaps bodies with the cobbler. We will suppose that the cobbler was called Jan and that he mended Locke's shoes yesterday, whereas the prince was called Stanislas and opened Parliament the day before. According to Locke, it is possible that the one who mended Locke's shoes yesterday was the same person, though not the same man, as the one who opened Parliament the day before. Using restricted quantification with an exclusive interpretation of variables, we should have to say that

(iii) For some person, *x*, *x* alone mended Locke's shoes yesterday and *x* alone opened Parliament the day before,

and that

(iv) For some man, *y*, for some man, *z*, *y* alone mended Locke's shoes yesterday and *z* alone opened Parliament the day before.

(iii) entails that

(v) For every person, *x*, if *x* mended Locke's shoes yesterday, *x* opened Parliament the day before.

(iv) entails that

(vi) For every man, *x*, if *x* mended Locke's shoes yesterday, *x* did not open Parliament the day before.

But the person who mended Locke's shoes yesterday, namely Jan, was a man. Then by (v) Jan opened Parliament the day before yesterday, and by (vi) he did not do this. We have a contradiction. This contradiction can, I think, be generalized. The supposition with which this paragraph began does indeed lead to an absurdity.

It will be objected[6] that 'Jan' is the name *for* and *of* a man and the name *of*, but not *for*, a person. The same is true of 'Stanislas'. Jan, though a person, and the same person as the one who opened Parliament the day before yesterday, is not the same man as the one who opened Parliament the day before yesterday. Jan mended Locke's shoes yesterday, but by (vi) he did not open Parliament the day before. Stanislas opened Parliament the day before yesterday, but by the same token he did not mend Locke's shoes on the following day. Who then was the person who did both these things? We have as yet no name for him. Let us call him Casimir. 'Casimir' is the name *for* and *of* a person, and the name *of*, but not *for*, a man. It is not an alternative to 'Jan', nor yet to 'Stanislas', since they are names for men, not persons. But how does this person, Casimir, come into the story?

The model Geach offers us is that of a name associated with an office which may be held by different people at different times. His examples are drawn from the College of Heralds: 'Bluemantle', 'Rouge Dragon', and the like. But few of us, I fear, have reliable intuitions where the supervision of heraldic matters is concerned. To use an example from more widely shared experience, we may recall that the leader of a pack of Wolf Cubs is called 'Akela'. Cubs will use 'Akela' in the vocative, and without a definite article, as indeed people will say 'Yes, Minister' or 'I'm afraid I disagree, Vice-Chancellor'. But although 'Akela' is similar in these ways to proper names, it is different from them in that it is subject to temporal qualification. Mrs Parsons, let us suppose, is Akela at the moment. But last year it was Miss Summerfield. And we say quite naturally, 'The Akela in 1984 was Miranda Brown', just as we say 'The Prime Minister in 1935 was Stanley Baldwin'. But we do not similarly have a use for 'The Stanley Baldwin in 1935'. As Aristotle noticed, names are used without temporal qualification.[7] We may well begin to doubt whether 'Akela', or for that matter 'Casimir', is a name at all.

[6] See P. T. Geach, *Reference and Generality*, 3rd edn., Ithaca and New York: Cornell University Press, 1980, § 91.

[7] Aristotle, *Categories and De Interpretatione*, tr. J. L. Ackrill, Oxford: Clarendon Press, 1967, 16^{a}19.

'Casimir alone mended Locke's shoes yesterday and Casimir alone opened Parliament the day before' is the proposition of which (iii), above, is the existential generalization. Similarly we might say

(vii) Akela, and no one else, built up a strong pack in 1987, and Akela, and no one else, held a successful barbecue last week.

Would it be compatible with (vii) to deny that some one man or woman both built up a strong pack in 1987 and held a successful barbecue last week? It is essential to the relativist position that (iii), and presumably its existential instantiation, be compatible with (iv), and therefore with the denial that some one man both mended Locke's shoes yesterday and opened Parliament the day before. But how could someone claim that the man or woman who built up the pack in 1987 was different from the man or woman who held a successful barbecue last week, and continue to maintain that (vii) is true? Suppose that we rephrase (vii) as follows:

(viii) In 1987 Akela, and no one else, built up a strong pack, and last week Akela, and no one else, held a successful barbecue.

This would indeed be compatible with denying that the same man or woman built up the pack in 1987 and held the barbecue last week. The sense of (viii) could, I think, be brought out by inserting 'the then' before the first occurrence of 'Akela' and 'our present' before its second occurrence. But this would make it clear that 'Akela' in (viii) was being used, not as a proper name, but as the equivalent of a definite description like 'the woman who held the position of leader of the cub pack at the time'. And whereas repetition of a proper name entitles us to pass from a proposition like (vii) to, say 'Akela, and no one else, built up a strong pack in 1987, and she, and no one else, held a successful barbecue last week', substituting 'she' for the second occurrence of 'Akela' in (viii) alters its sense completely. I suspect that this ability of a word like 'Akela' to pass from being used as a proper name to being used as a 'truncated' definite description goes some way to explain the plausibility of the relativist argument.

Another source of strength for the argument is the surface resemblance between propositions of the form '*x* is the same man as y' and 'x is the same age as y', 'x is the same height as y' or 'x is the same nationality as y'. Of course, x can be the same age as y without being the same nationality. This is because propositions of the form 'x is the same age as y' or 'x is the same nationality as y' can be given the analysis 'For some F, both x is F and y is F', where 'F' takes as its substitution instances expressions like 'thirty years old' in the first case, or like 'Algerian' in the second.[8] And, of course, 'For some F, both x is F and y is F' and 'For some F, both x is F and y is not F' can be true together. This analysis, however, is inappropriate to propositions of the form 'x is the same man as y'. The surface similarity veils a deep difference. As has already been argued at length, '--- is the same man as ......' and the like are often analysable as two-place predicables of second, rather than as first level: they are equivalent to expressions of the form 'For some man x, both x --- and x ......', where the blanks have to be filled with predicables of first level. It is in fact misleading to talk about 'propositions of the form "x is the same man as y"' at all. The use of x and y here suggests that the expressions substitutable for them are names, whereas we should hold that a definite description is required to occupy at least one of these positions. There is no such problem in the case of the description 'propositions of the form "x is the same age as y"'. Expressions like '--- is the same age as ......' are quite straightforward two-place predicables of first level, where the blanks can to be filled with proper names. To assimilate '--- is the same man as ......' to '--- is the same age as ......' is to treat predicables of different level as though they were of the same level. It is to make the same mistake as those who fail to distinguish between the logical forms of 'Tame tigers do not exist' and 'Tame tigers do not growl'.

We can now see that there is something gravely wrong with the sentences the Relative Identity Theorists need to construe as true propositions. 'The one who mended Locke's shoes yesterday is the same age, but not the same height, as the one who opened Parliament the day before', containing as it does two definite descriptions, must be regarded as an existential generalization of a proposition in which two proper names occupy the positions taken up by those definite descriptions. In our example, the names 'Jan' and 'Stanislas' will provide the instantiation needed. 'Jan mended

[8] This sort of analysis, involving repeated predicative variables bound by an existential quantifier, is discussed in ch. VIII, § 1.

Locke's shoes yesterday, and Stanislas opened Parliament the day before, and Jan is the same age, but not the same height, as Stanislas' is perfectly in order. But if we substitute 'person' and 'man' for 'age' and 'height', the third conjunct gives rise to difficulties. 'Jan is the same person, but not the same man, as Stanislas' will be ill-formed if the proper names are here being used as proper names. If they are being mentioned rather than used, as I claimed was the case with the two names in 'St John was the same politician as Bolingbroke', we shall once again have an existential generalization for which it is impossible to find an instantiation. Taking them in this way yields a proposition equivalent to 'The one we call "Jan" is the same person, but not the same man, as the one we call "Stanislas"'; and for an existential instantiation of this, we shall have to go to something like 'We call Casimir "Jan", and we call Casimir "Stanislas", and Casimir is the same person, but not the same man, as Casimir'. This, however, has as its third conjunct a sentence involving the very same problematic use of '--- is the same person, but not the same man, as ......'. *Expellas furco, tamen usque recurret.* The Relative Identity Theorist cannot produce sentences which have the meaning he wishes to attach to them unless he construes '--- is the same person, but not the same man, as ......' as a first-level predicable.

§ 9. Relativists about identity, then, will not be able to maintain their thesis if forced to express the facts about identity and difference in a Wittgensteinian language. For them identity, or relativized identity, must be a relation. They, it seems, have an interesting use for the otherwise boring relation which, in an eirenic spirit, I was prepared to give away to those who wanted it.

However, the relation about which I feel generous may yet prove worthless to the relativity theorists. The admission of its existence was extorted from me by arguments of a severely extensionalist character. It was foisted on me as the relation defined by the set of ordered pairs {⟨Brutus, Brutus⟩, ⟨Caesar, Caesar⟩, ⟨Augustus, Augustus⟩, ⟨Augustus, Octavian⟩, ⟨Karol Wojtyla, John Paul II⟩, . . .}. The prince who swapped bodies with the cobbler, according to our story, was called Stanislas, and the cobbler with whom he swapped, Jan. Since Stanislas, in Locke's view, was the same person as Jan, the ordered pair ⟨Stanislas,

Jan⟩, like the ordered pair ⟨Octavian, Augustus⟩, belongs to the extension of the identity relation. But since Stanislas was not the same man as Jan, the pair ⟨Stanislas, Jan⟩ is a member of the complement of the relation. Again a contradiction. The relativists, perhaps, will wish to distinguish two ordered pairs here, the pair consisting of the person, Stanislas-Jan, taken twice over, and the pair consisting of the two men Stanislas and Jan. But extensionalists cannot stomach such distinctions. Sets and sets of sets are obtained by working from the bottom up. Given that we know the reference of 'Stanislas' and that we know the reference of 'Jan', the reference of the ordered pair ⟨Stanislas, Jan⟩ is uniquely determined. There can be no two pairs obtainable from the references (or reference) of the two names.

Those who believe that persons and men are simply composite entities built up of space–time slices will, of course, have a way of distinguishing the pair of persons ⟨Stanislas^P, Jan^P⟩ from the pair of men ⟨Stanislas^m, Jan^m⟩. Stanislas^m and Jan^m can be supposed to be those collections of space–time slices which, on Locke's view, would make up the *men*, Stanislas and Jan, respectively. 'Stanislas^{P1}' and 'Jan^{P2}', on the other hand, may be regarded as alternative names for the collection of space–time slices, beginning with something with the bodily appearance *and* memories and mental characteristics of the prince, and finishing with something with the same memories and mental characteristics, but with the bodily appearance of the cobbler, which Locke would have counted as a single person. By the same token 'Jan^{P1}' and 'Stanislas^{P2}' will be alternative names for the Lockean person made up of the remaining slices. The ordered pairs ⟨Stanislas^{P1}, Jan^{P2}⟩ and ⟨Jan^{P1}, Stanislas^{P2}⟩ will then be members of the set which is the extension of the identity relation, whereas the ordered pair ⟨Stanlislas^m, Jan^m⟩ will be a member of its complement. But this will give no comfort to the relativists about identity. What we have described is a system of sets built up from four distinct individuals, i.e, collections of space–time slices, (i) Stanislas^m, (ii) Jan^m, (iii) the individual corresponding to the alternative names 'Stanislas^{P1}' and 'Jan^{P2}', and (iv) the individual corresponding to the alternative names 'Jan^{P1}' and 'Stanislas^{P2}'. We do not have a clear instantiation of the formula 'x is the same A, but not the same B, as y' where the substitutions for 'x' and 'y' have unambiguous reference. It is not clear whether such an instantiation should be said to involve one individual or two (that is what '*A*' and '*B*' are supposed to disambiguate), but undoubtedly four individuals are too many. The extensionalist account of identity again seems incompatible with the relativist account.

If this is so, the extensionalist account of identity is of no interest to philosophers. It may succeed in specifying a concept, that is to say, a way in which words could be used. It does not pick out the concept which people actually do use in sentences involving the word 'same' and its synonyms. And it lacks even the interest it might have had if its use had facilitated descriptions of bizarre thought-experiments of the kind made familiar by Locke in his discussion of personal identity. Kripke can have his schmidentity if he likes; but he is wrong in thinking that it will enlighten or entertain us by generating a paradox of schmidentity.

IDENTITY AND INDISCERNIBILITY

§ 1. How much has to go if we follow Wittgenstein's ungenerous line and treat all attempts to use '--- is the same as ......' as a first-level predicable as 'pseudo-propositions'? Wittgenstein himself stigmatizes in this way the traditional axioms expressing the transitivity and reflexivity of identity. No doubt the axiom expressing symmetry $\forall x\, \forall y\, \{(x = y) \to (y = x)\}$ would have to go as well. But what of 'Leibniz's Laws', namely, that of the Identity of Indiscernibles and that of the Indiscernibility of Identicals? These are traditionally regarded as controversial, unlike those which set up identity as an equivalence relation. Nevertheless, a doctrine which treated their formulations as pseudo-propositions, which maintained that they 'could not even be written down in a correct *Begriffsschrift*', would take most philosophers by surprise.

Can the Law of the Identity of Indiscernibles be written down? If we had no Wittgensteinian scruples to worry us, we might use the following formula to express this law:

(LL1) $\forall x\, \forall y\, [\forall \varphi\, (\varphi x \leftrightarrow \varphi y) \to x = y]$.

This is clearly equivalent to

(LL1$_1$) $\neg\, \exists x\, \exists y\, [\forall \varphi\, (\varphi x \leftrightarrow \varphi y)\, \&\, x \neq y]$.

What (LL1$_1$) is supposed to state is that there are no two (distinct) objects, x and y, such that whatever is true of x is true of y, and vice versa. But according to Wittgenstein this is adequately stated by

(LL1$_2$) $\neg\, \exists x\, \exists y\, \forall \varphi\, (\varphi x \leftrightarrow \varphi y)$.

That is to say, the conjunct $x \neq y$ can simply be lopped off the formula (LL$_1$), as similar conjuncts were lopped off the Russellian analyses of identity propositions. Thus, (F) and (J) of Chapter II gave way to (K) and (L). Given the exclusive interpretation of variables, $(LL1_2)$ says what Leibniz wished to say: no two things have all their properties in common. This is precisely how Wittgenstein interprets the issue:

Russell's definition of '=' is inadequate, because according to it we cannot say that two objects have all their properties in common. (Even if this proposition is never correct, it still has sense.) (*Tractatus*, 5.5302.)

By 'Russell's definition', he means the definition which makes $\forall\varphi \ (\varphi x \leftrightarrow \varphi y)$, which is the antecedent of (LL1), the *definiens* of the consequent, $x = y$. By 'this proposition' he means the contradictory of $(LL1_2)$, namely $\exists x \ \exists y \ \forall\varphi \ (\varphi x \leftrightarrow \varphi y)$. Wittgenstein does not express a view as to which of the two is true, $(LL1_2)$ or its contradictory. He merely wishes to say that $(LL1_2)$ is not true by definition, as Leibniz and Russell would have it. He might have had added that it cannot be as a definition that it is true, since it lacks a *definiendum*: the conjunction of (LL1) and its converse cannot be a *definition* of $x = y$, because there is no such relation to be defined. We can thus settle how the Identity of Indiscernibles is to be expressed in a Wittgensteinian language, even if the rules of such a language do not enable us to settle its truth value.

§ 2. The converse of (LL1) is

(LL2) $\forall x \ \forall y \ [x = y \rightarrow \forall\varphi \ (\varphi x \leftrightarrow \varphi y)]$,

which expresses the Indiscernibility of Identicals. This is not easy to translate, as is (LL1), into a notation which uses the exclusive interpretation of variables in place of a sign for difference. We need to go back to the Russellian thesis about true identity propositions, namely, that they escape from triviality only if they are of the form $a = (\imath x)(\varphi x)$ or of the form $(\imath x)(\varphi x) = (\imath y)(\psi y)$. If we ignore this, and make use of propositions of the form $a = b$, we get the following result: in an instantiation of (LL2), e.g., $a = b \rightarrow \forall\varphi \ (\varphi a \leftrightarrow \varphi b)$, the antecedent will be true only if it means the the same as $a = a$. But if so, the consequent will mean the same as $\forall\varphi \ (\varphi a \leftrightarrow \varphi a)$, which is equally trivial.

What then of the two possible non-trivial types of instantiation of (LL2)? These are:

(LL2$_1$) $a = (\imath x)(\varphi x) \rightarrow \forall\psi \ (\psi a \leftrightarrow \psi((\imath x)(\varphi x)))$

and

(LL2$_2$) $(\imath x)(\varphi x) = (\imath y)(\psi y) \rightarrow \forall\chi \ (\chi((\imath x)(\varphi x)) \leftrightarrow \chi((\imath y)(\psi y)))$

The antecedents of these can be replaced directly by their Russellian translations, (F) and (J), and the consequents can be analysed in accordance with the pattern given by (D). (LL2$_1$) is thus equivalent to the formula

(LL2$_{1A}$) (F) → [∀ψ (ψa ↔ (D))],

and (LL2$_2$) is equivalent to the formula whose abbreviation is

(LL2$_{2A}$) (J) → [∀χ ((D$_1$) ↔ (D$_2$))],

where (D$_1$) is obtained from (D) by substituting χ for ψ, and (D$_2$) by substituting χ for ψ and ψ for φ. Wittgensteinian considerations, which allow us to move from (F) and (J) to (K) and (L) in the antecedents of (LL2$_{1A}$) and (LL2$_{2A}$), respectively, also allow us to drop all conjuncts of the form $x \neq y$ from (D), (D$_1$) and (D$_2$). The Wittgensteinian versions of (LL2$_1$) and (LL2$_2$), written out in full will therefore be:

(LL2$_{1B}$) [φa & ¬ ∃x ∃y (φx & φy)] → ∀ψ {ψa ↔
        [∃x (φx & ψx) & ¬ ∃y ∃z (φy & φz)]}

and

(LL2$_{2B}$) {[∃x (φx & ψx) & ¬ ∃y ∃z (φy & φz)]
        & ¬ ∃w ∃v (ψw & ψv)} → ∀χ {[∃x (φx & χx)
        & ¬ ∃y ∃z (φy & φz)] ↔ [∃x (ψx & χx)
        & ¬ ∃y ∃z (ψy & ψz)]}.

What (LL2$_{1B}$) says is that if *a* φ's and no two things φ, then, whatever ψ may be, *a* ψ's iff both something φ's and ψ's and no two things φ; and what (LL2$_{2B}$) says is that if something both φ's and ψ's and no two things φ and no two things ψ, then, whatever χ may be, something φ's and χ's and no two things φ iff something ψ's and χ's and no two things ψ. (LL2$_{1B}$) and (LL2$_{2B}$) are theorems of the predicate calculus with variables exclusively interpreted.

§ 3. How then do we explain the widespread belief that the Indiscernibility of Identicals (Leibniz's Law) has only a limited application—that it does not apply in 'intentional' contexts? Let us adopt a convenient abbreviation of Prior's.[1] Any one of the formulae (A)–(D) may be regarded as an expansion of ıxφxψx, which may be read as 'The x such that φx ψ's'. Then $(LL2_{1B})$ can be abbreviated to

$(LL2_{1C})$ $(K) \rightarrow \forall \psi \, (\psi a \leftrightarrow \imath x \varphi x \psi x)$

and $(LL2_{2B})$ to

$(LL2_{2C})$ $(L) \rightarrow \forall \chi \, (\imath x \varphi x \chi x \leftrightarrow \imath y \psi y \chi y).$[2]

Given that Dubrovnik was the birthplace of Boscovich, and that Paul thinks that Dubrovnik is a Croatian holiday resort, it follows by $(LL2_{1C})$ that Paul thinks that the birthplace of Boscovich is a Croatian holiday resort. All we need do is to substitute 'Dubrovnik' for a, 'Boscovich was born in x' for φx and 'Paul thinks that x is a Croatian holiday resort' for ψx. Again, given that the town where Edna spent her holiday last year was the birthplace of Boscovich and that Paul thinks that the town where Edna spent her holiday last year is a Croatian holiday resort, it follows, this time by $(LL2_{2C})$, that Paul thinks that the birthplace of Boscovich is a Croatian holiday resort. For this, we need to substitute 'Edna spent her holiday last year in x' for φx, 'Boscovich was born in y' for ψy and 'Paul thinks that $x(y)$ is a Croatian holiday resort' for $\chi x(y)$.

But of course there is a sense in which we wish to deny that Paul thinks that the birthplace of Boscovich is a Croatian holiday resort, despite the assumptions we have made about him and Edna. This is precisely the phenomenon that prompts people to say that 'Paul thinks that ---' and other contexts of this sort are 'referentially opaque' or 'intentional'. What has happened is that we have now interpreted 'Paul thinks that the birthplace of Boscovich is a Croatian holiday resort' as being, not of the form $\imath x \varphi x \psi x$ or $\imath y \psi y \chi y$, but as being of the form $\delta \, (\imath x \varphi x \psi x)$ or $\delta \, (\imath y \psi y \chi y)$. Here the substitution made for ψx and χy is not 'Paul thinks that $x(y)$ is a Croatian holiday resort', but simply '$x(y)$ is a Croatian holiday resort', and 'Paul thinks that ---' is what is substituted for δ. The fallacious inferences are thus of the forms $(K) \rightarrow \forall \psi \, [\delta \, (\psi a) \leftrightarrow \delta \, (\imath x \varphi x \psi x)]$ and $(L) \rightarrow \forall \chi \, [\delta \, (\imath x \varphi x \chi x) \leftrightarrow \delta \, (\imath y \psi y \chi y)]$, which are not substitution instances of $(LL2_{1C})$ and $(LL2_{2C})$, and are invalid. The first interpretation of 'Paul thinks that the birthplace of Boscovich is a holiday resort' took it as being of the form $\imath x \varphi x \delta \, (\psi x)$ or $\imath y \psi y \delta \, (\chi y)$, and these forms are legitimate sub-

[2] Using '(K)' and '(L)' to abbreviate the formulae set out with these labels in § 3 of ch. II.

stitutions for $\imath x\varphi x\psi x$ and $\imath y\psi y\chi y$, though $\delta(\imath x\varphi x\psi x)$ and $\delta(\imath y\psi y\chi y)$ are not. The difference between the interpretation which gives a valid, and that which gives an invalid, inference is a difference between two ways of fixing the scope of δ ('Paul thinks that ---'). Where the scope given to δ is narrow, that given to $\imath x\varphi x(\,-\,)$ and $\imath y\psi y(\,-\,)$, the definite description operators, is wide. This corresponds to what Russell called the definite description's having 'primary occurrence', and the inference on this interpretation is valid. The definite description's having 'secondary occurrence' corresponds to $\imath x\varphi x(\,-\,)$ and $\imath y\psi y(\,-\,)$ having narrow, and δ wide, scope. When this interpretation is given, the inference is invalid. Scope distinctions are capable of doing all the work of sorting out the problems for which Quine invented the label 'referential opacity', and which earlier authors discussed under the heading of 'intentionality'.[3]

§ 4. Suppose that Paul thinks, mistakenly, that Ragusa is in Albania. In that case he does not think that the birthplace of Boscovich is in Croatia. But, of course, interpreted in the first of the two ways I suggested, 'Paul thinks that the birthplace of Boscovich is a Croatian holiday resort' is true, given the assumptions we made about him and Edna. It seems then that we want to say that Paul does and that he does not, think that the birthplace of Boscovich is a Croatian holiday resort. We seem to be saying (given the earlier interpretations) that $\imath x\varphi x\,[\delta(\psi x)\ \&\ \delta(\neg\ \psi x)]$, and therefore that $\imath x\varphi x\delta(\psi x\ \&\ \neg\ \psi x)$. Does it follow that Paul believes of one and the same town that it is and is not a Croatian holiday resort'? Has he abandoned the Principle of Non-Contradiction?[4]

---

[3] This way of dealing with these problems, already implicit in Russell's 'On Denoting', was explicitly developed in A. F. Smullyan's paper 'Modality and Description', *Journal of Symbolic Logic*, 13 (1948), pp. 31–7 (repr. in L. Linsky (ed.), *Reference and Modality*, in the 'Oxford Readings in Philosophy' series, Oxford University Press, 1971, pp. 35–43), and was taken up several times by A. N. Prior in 'Is the Concept of Referential Opacity Really Necessary?', pp. 195–6, and in *Objects of Thought*, Oxford: Clarendon Press, 1971 (see above ch. III, § 1, n. 4).

[4] This is precisely the problem to which Quine addresses himself in 'Quantifiers and Propositional Attitudes', *Journal of Philosophy*, 53 (1956), repr. in Quine, *The Ways of Paradox*, New York: Random House, 1966, and in L. Linsky (ed.), *Reference and Modality*, when he finds himself obliged to affirm '(15) Ralph believes $z(z$ is a spy) of Ortcutt' and '(22) Ralph believes $z(z$ is not a spy) of Ortcutt', but draws back from affirming '(23) Ralph believes $z(z$ is a spy z is not a spy) of Ortcutt'. It is also what Saul Kripke refers to as 'A Puzzle about Belief' in

For a start, it is important to make it clear that *we* have not abandoned the Principle of Non-Contradiction. 'Paul does not think that the birthplace of Boscovich is a Croatian holiday resort' is quadruply ambiguous. It can be taken (1) as being of the form $\neg\,\delta(\imath x\varphi x\psi x)$, or (2) as being of the form $\delta\neg\,(\imath x\varphi x\psi x)$, or (3) as being of the form $\imath x\varphi x\neg\,\delta\,(\psi x)$, or (4) as being of the form $\imath x\varphi x\delta\,(\neg\,\psi x)$. This is because we have to choose, not only between taking a definite description to have primary occurrence and taking it to have secondary occurrence, but between interpreting a proposition of the form 'x does not believe that p' as being of the form $\neg\,\delta\,(p)$ and interpreting it as being of the form $\delta(\neg p)$. We are not concerned with propositions ascribing to Paul thoughts about the birthplace of Boscovich in which 'the birthplace of Boscovich' has secondary occurrence; so we can dismiss (1) and (2) above. We seemed to have reason to affirm 'Paul thinks that the birthplace of Boscovich is a Croatian holiday resort', where this proposition is understood as having the form $\imath x\varphi x\,\delta\,(\psi x)$. It would certainly involve us in an offence against the Law of Contradiction if we affirmed 'Paul does not think that the birthplace of Boscovich is a Croatian holiday resort' if this were taken to be of the form $\imath x\varphi x\neg\,\delta\,(\psi x)$ ((3) above). Although not themselves contradictories, $\imath x\varphi x\delta\,(\psi x)$ and $\imath x\varphi x\neg\,\delta\,(\psi x)$ are contraries and together imply a contradiction.[5] So it is just false that Paul does not think that the birthplace of Boscovich is a Croatian holiday resort, where this is understood in sense (3).

What we have to admit is that this proposition is true in sense (4). Since Paul does not believe that a town can be in both Albania and Croatia, and he believes of the birthplace of Boscovich that it is in Albania, he must believe that it is not in Croatia. And if we hold that a man believes of something that is in fact φ that it is ψ, and that he believes of this same thing that it is χ, we can hardly

his paper of that name in A. Margalit (ed.), *Meaning and Use*, Dordrecht: Reidel, 1979. Kripke hesitantly (see his n. 7) assumes that the *de re–de dicto* distinction applies to propositions like 'Ralph believes that Ortcutt is a spy', and restricts his attention to what he regards as the *de dicto* occurrences of proper names in such propositions, whereas Quine takes himself to be considering *de re* occurrences. Since I take the view (see above, ch. III, § 7, n. 4.), 'that proper names are scopeless and that for them the *de dicto–de re* distinction vanishes', which, according to Kripke (ibid.), 'has considerable plausibility', Quine's puzzle and Kripke's seem to me to coincide. I address myself to Kripke's central argument below (§ 9).

[5] Namely, $\forall x[\varphi x \rightarrow \delta\,(\psi x)]$ & $\exists x\,[\varphi x$ & $\neg\,\delta\,(\psi x)]$.

deny that he believes of it that it is ψ and that it is χ: i.e.,
$\imath x \varphi x\, \delta(\psi x) \rightarrow [\imath x \varphi x\, \delta(\chi x) \rightarrow \imath x \varphi x\, \delta(\psi x\ \&\ \chi x)]$. It was a principle
very similar to this which allowed us to move from (2A) to (2A$_2$)
in Chapter III. A man may be taken to believe the conjunction of
the propositions which he believes. Nor can we abandon this
schema and the principle it embodies just in the case where the
substitute for χ is of the form $\neg\ \psi$. Since, therefore, we are
committed to $\imath x \varphi x\, \delta(\psi x)$, on this interpretation of φ, ψ and δ, and
to $\imath x \varphi x\, \delta(\neg\ \psi x)$, we must concede that $\imath x \varphi x\, \delta(\psi x\ \&\ \neg\ \psi x)$ is also
true.

The earlier suggestion, therefore, that the facts as I have described
them make it necessary to affirm $\imath x \varphi x\ [\delta(\psi x)\ \&\ \neg\ \delta(\psi))$,
must now be rejected; but the suggestion that we have to say
that $\imath x \varphi x\ [\delta(\psi x)\ \&\ \delta(\neg\ \psi x)]$ and thus $\imath x \varphi x\, \delta(\psi x\ \&\ \neg\ \psi x)$ still
stands. *We* are not forced to contravene the Law of Contradiction:
do we have to impute such a contravention to Paul?

§ 5. It is here that we need to have recourse again to the Xi-
operator which was introduced in Chapter III. Just as there was a
distinction to be drawn between (2A$_2$) and (6A$_2$), so now we need
to distinguish

(7A) $\imath x \varphi x\ \Xi u\ [\delta(\psi u\ \&\ \neg\ \psi u)]\ x$

from

(8A) $\imath x \varphi x\, \delta\{\Xi u\ [\psi u\ \&\ \neg\ \psi u]\ x\}$.

(7A) ascribes to Paul a belief about what is in fact the same town
(the birthplace of Boscovich), namely, that it is and that it is not a
Croatian holiday resort. He has this belief in virtue of the fact that
Ragusa is the birthplace of Boscovich and is believed by Paul not
to be in Croatia, but is where Edna took her holiday last year and
is believed by Paul (under this description) to be in Croatia. (8A),
on the other hand, ascribes to Paul the belief that some town
which is in Croatia *is the same as* some town which is not in
Croatia. The concept of identity, expressed by the Xi-operator, is
part of the content of Paul's thought according to (8A), whereas
according to (7A) it plays a part in our description of the state of
affairs, but escapes from that clause in our description which says
what Paul actually thinks. Once again, the problems of intentionality
can be solved by making careful scope-distinctions.

Modern philosophy tends to interpret the Principle of Non-Contradiction *propositionally*, as forbidding assertions of the form *p* & ¬*p*. The Aristotelian tradition tended to interpret it *predicatively*, as forbidding the ascription of contradictory predicates to the same thing. A man would only knowingly contravene the Law of Contradiction in this version if what he said or thought was known by him to involve, not only contradictory predicates, but the predication of them *of the same thing*. This is what is attributed to Paul by (8A), but not by (7A). In affirming (7A), therefore, we no more impute violation of the Principle of Non-Contradiction to Paul than we violate it ourselves.

§ 6. In the variable-free notation described in Chapter IV, we can say that (7A) implies

(7A₁) Der Ref δ Conj ψ Neg ψ,

whereas (8A) implies

(8A₁) Der δ Ref Conj ψ Neg ψ.

Contexts like 'Paul thinks that ---' are seen once again to be, in the terminology used earlier,[6] opaque with respect to reflection. When I used this description before, I was concerned to contrast reflection with derelativization. The contrast I wish to make now is with proper names. Using *a* to stand for 'Dubrovnik' and *b* to stand for 'Ragusa' and interpreting the other symbols as before, we may say that

(9A) δ(ψ*a* & ¬ ψ*b*),

and, by the same principle that allowed us to pass from (1A) to (2A), we may say that

(10A) δ(ψ*a* & ¬ψ*a*).

This formula can be interpreted, not only, as has just been suggested, as 'Paul thinks that Dubrovnik is a Croatian holiday resort and that Dubrovnik is not a Croatian holiday resort', but as 'Ralph believes that Ortcutt is a spy and that Ortcutt is not a spy' and as 'Pierre believes that London is pretty and that London is not pretty'.[7] These propositions have been taken by philosophers as obviously false, given a modicum of logical acumen on the part of the believers, and as providing *reductio ad absurdum* arguments

---

[6] See ch. IV, § 9.
[7] See § 4 of this chapter, n. 4. The example about London is Kripke's.

against various principles which allow them to be deduced from plausibly true premises. Most commonly the principle which is supposed to be called in question in this way is the Principle of Substitutivity of Identicals (LL2), which just now allowed us to pass from (9A) to (10A). Quine seems to think that what has to be abandoned is the Agglomeration Principle, which allows us to pass from $\delta(p)$ & $\delta(q)$ to $\delta(p$ & $q)$, whereas Kripke casts suspicion on what he calls the 'Disquotational Principle' and the 'Principle of Translation'. Paul, Ralph, and Pierre are all assumed to be logically conformist, in the sense that they can be relied upon not to believe a proposition that is manifestly self-contradictory. That is to say, as a minimum, that they will not believe anything of the form $(p$ & $\neg p)$. But do these interpretations of (10A) attribute to any of these people a belief of the form $(p$ & $\neg p)$? It is an assumption of Kripke's argument, which he does not call in question, that they do.

A proposition of the form ψa & $\neg\psi a$ is, of course, also of the form $(p$ & $\neg p)$. ψa is a possible substitution instance of p. And in truth-functional contexts we could not suppose that substituting $(\psi a$ & $\neg\psi a)$ for $(p$ & $\neg p)$ made any difference to truth or validity: $(\psi a$ & $\neg\psi a) \rightarrow q$ is as valid a formula as $(p$ & $\neg p) \rightarrow q$. But does the same principle hold in belief-contexts?

§ 7. To answer this last question we need first to return to the alleged paradox involved in admitting the truth of (10A). From (10A) we may infer

(11A) Ref δ Conj ψ Neg ψa

(which could be derelativized to $(7A_1)$). But we may not infer

(12A) δ Ref Conj ψ Neg ψa

(which could be derelativized to $(8Aa_1)$). The reason for this is that (12A), but not (10A) or (11A), changes the conceptual content of the thought ascribed to Paul by (9A). My claim is not just the negative one that (10A) and (11A) do not add anything to the content of the thought ascribed to Paul by (9A). It is indeed true that they do not, and this is something which I have shortly to explain. But (12A) asserts that Paul has a thought which explicitly contains 'Ref', an expression, in my view, of the concept of identity. Paul's thought is richer as described by (12A) than as described by the earlier propositions.

Against this, it will be urged that (10A) and (11A) change, if they do not add to, the description of Paul's thought given in (9A). Does not Paul's thought as described by (10A) contain the name 'Dubrovnik' where (9A) had 'Ragusa'; and does not the description of Paul's thought given by (11A) contain only one occurrence of one name where (9A) had two names? To make good my claim, I have to set out what I believe to be some fundamental facts about proper names.

Controversy has arisen over whether proper names have sense as well as meaning, connotation as well as denotation. Those who urge that they do not have insisted that the job of a proper name is simply to pick out its bearer, to say what it is that the proposition in which it occurs is about. Nothing is needed in order to explain the function of the proper name except the link which attaches it to the thing named. On the other hand, those who hold that a proper name must have sense point to the fact that the person who uses the name must have some way of singling out the object to which it is linked, must have some way of indicating what it is that is being named. Sense, it is maintained, is a cognitive concept, and an account is due of what it is that a person must know in order to be said to know how to use the name. This consideration applies just as much to the person who understands what is being said when he hears or sees a proposition which contains the name as to the person who utters or writes the proposition in the knowledge of what it means.

The point that is sometimes neglected is that what is known by the speaker, enabling him to make meaningful use of a name, need not be the same as what is known by the hearer, enabling him to understand what is meant by its use. That each should know something, that each should have a way available to him of distinguishing the object named from other objects, is no doubt essential. Nevertheless, all that is required for successful communication is that the object which the speaker means to single out be the same as the object which the hearer takes him to mean. It is not necessary that the ways in which speaker and hearer identify the object in question be the same. The method of identification is not part of the content of the thought which the speaker intends to communicate.

This is not an empirical matter to be established by investigating the intentions of speakers. Nor is it a sufficient condition for an expression's being used as a name that the speaker intends, in using it, to do no more than single out an object for a hearer's attention. Thus, suppose that I say 'The doctor's wife has grown some magnificent orchids' intending you merely to get the information that Marjorie, who lives with the doctor but is not in fact married to him, has had this horticultural success: I do not therby use 'the doctor's wife' as a proper name. Despite the fact that Marjorie's being married to the doctor was not something I intended you to believe as a result of hearing my remark, my use of the phrase 'the doctor's wife' to pick out Marjorie depended on the fact that many people, if not necessarily yourself, assume, on the basis of circumstantial evidence, that they are married. My use of 'wife' in these circumstances was not unrelated to the connection between the meaning of the word 'wife' and the institution of marriage. If, on the other hand, I used the phrase 'The Wife of Bath' to refer to a rose-tree in my garden—'The Wife of Bath has done very well this year'—the meaning of the word 'wife' in English would here have nothing, unless, perhaps, by way of historical explanation, to do with my meaning. Someone who had not the faintest idea of what a wife is, but who knew which rose-tree I meant, could understand what I said. In order to communicate with this name there is no need for it to be seen as a complex expression, as having parts which are themselves independently significant. 'The doctor has a wife who grows orchids' would be a legitimate inference from the earlier statement we were considering; but if the hearer were to infer from the other statement that some woman who comes from Bath had done very well this year, it would be a sure sign that he had misunderstood it. 'The Wife of Bath' so used is semantically and syntactically simple. This is necessary if an expression is to be a proper name. A definite description will not meet this condition, even though it can be intended simply to pick out the object which satisfies it; and this is one reason why the speaker's intention is insufficient for establishing that an expression used by him is being used as a proper name.

It may well be that, on a particular occasion, a speaker's intentions have been fulfilled if his hearer has understood who or what it was he was speaking about. This fact, however, does not guarantee that the means he used for this purpose was a proper name. The phrase 'The man drinking a glass of Martini' might be used in that way, but this does not make it a proper name. There is another reason for this. For a word to be a proper name it must be part of the rationale of its existence in the language that it has this sort of use, namely, that a speaker's purpose in using it is achieved if and only if his hearer knows which object he is speaking of. It is because 'Marjorie' has the use it does in the language that no information *about* Marjorie is intended to be conveyed by its use. Not so with 'the doctor's wife'.

§ **8.** Furthermore, for every proper name there must be just one object which any user's purpose at any time is to identify to his hearers. This is not the case with demonstratives or demonstrative phrases, which in other ways resemble proper names. 'That one over there' or 'This puddle' may be used simply to identify an object of discourse, but it is part of their meaning that they are usable on different occasions, in different contexts, to identify different objects. It has been thought[8] that proper names too behave in this way. It could have been the case that only one man had ever been called 'John', but it could not have been the case that only one object was ever indicated by 'this'. There is not just one name 'John' which will serve to indicate now one man, now another, depending on who uses it, where and when. There are as many different proper names written and pronounced 'John' as there are and have been men called John. The word 'John' is equivocal, like the word 'rake'. If I say 'That old rake is here again' meaning that someone has once again left a particular garden tool lying around on the lawn, and you think I am indicating that our dissolute uncle has just arrived, you have misunderstood what I meant. More specifically, you have taken me to be using one word when in fact I was using another. As dictionary entries show, there are two words spelt 'rake'. Proper names do not often get entries in dictionaries; but the Classical Dictionary, for example, has several different entries under 'Cato'. We should regard these as different names. Understanding a particular historian's use of 'Cato' involves knowing whether he is referring to the elder or the younger Cato.

It is, in a sense, an accident if different men have the same name. Within any given context of discourse people do not share

[8] See L. J. Cohen, 'The Individuation of Proper Names', in Z. van Straaten (ed.), *Philosophical Subjects: Essays presented to P. F. Strawson*, Oxford: Clarendon Press, 1980.

names. In a family, for instance, care is taken to give different names to different children. Parents do not give the name 'John' to more than one of their sons;[9] and in religious communities a novice is not given the name 'Sister Agnes' if there is already a Sister Agnes alive in the community. It may not be a historical accident, a gigantic coincidence, that so many men in Christendom have been called 'John'; but our many uses of the word 'John', like those of the word 'rake', constitute a case of what the medievals called *per accidens* equivocation. The meaning of 'John' in respect of its use to name one man is not dependent on or connected with its use to name another.

Whereas 'John', used of St John the Baptist, means something different from 'John', used of St John the Evangelist, 'Ragusa', used to name the town which is in fact the birthplace of Boscovich, means the same as 'Dubrovnik', also so used. This is, as it were, the converse of the doctrine I have just been preaching. What is typographically the same name, used of different people, constitutes semantically more than one name each with its own distinctive meaning; and what are typographically different names, used of the same person or place, are semantically the same name. They stand, at least, in the same relation to each other as 'rouge' stands to 'red', or, to take an example of synonyms within one language, as 'commence' stands to 'begin'. ('Ragusa' and 'Dubrovnik' may perhaps be regarded as belonging to different languages, to Italian and Croatian, respectively; but the case is not importantly different from two names like 'Sion' and 'Jerusalem', which may both be regarded as belonging to English.) The point is that the function in language of 'Ragusa' is exactly the same as that of 'Dubrovnik'—the same, that is, in terms of what Frege called 'sense'. Where Frege's 'tone' is concerned there may, of course, be differences: I may deliberately choose to call the town 'Ragusa' in order to tease my friend, who is a sensitive Croatian nationalist. From the point of view of the thought conveyed, a proposition like (2), which contains 'Dubrovnik', is indistinguishable from a proposition like (1), similar in every respect except for containing 'Ragusa' in a place where the other contains 'Dubrovnik'. That is why (1A) entails (2A), and vice versa.

---

[9] My own ancestors in the Eighteenth Century christened more than one of their sons 'Thomas', but the later Thomases were so christened only after their predecessors had died, usually in infancy.

§ 9. So, if your thought was a thought expressed with the help of the use (as opposed to the mention) of a proper name, it does not matter if I use another name for the same person, place or thing when I report your thought. I do not distort Queen Mary's thought if I report her as thinking that George VI was a more responsible monarch than Edward VIII, although in her inner discourse she no doubt used the names 'Bertie' and 'David'. The thought is totally and adequately identified if we know which objects it is a thought about and what it is that is being thought about those objects. Indeed there is a sense in which the subject of a thought escapes the thought entirely. When I report that Queen Mary thought that Bertie made a good king, I state that a certain relation held between George VI and his mother, the relation of his being thought by her to have made a good king. It is a mistake to think of every proposition which reports a 'propositional attitude' as having the form 'x thinks (or the like) that p'. Rather, expressions like 'thinks that', which we may symbolize by δ', should always be understood as forming n-place predicables out of $(n-1)$-place predicables. Thus, taking φx as 'x has made a good king', a as 'Queen Mary', and b as 'George VI', $\delta'\varphi ba$ says that George VI was thought to have made a good king by Queen Mary; and taking ψxy to mean 'x is a more responsible monarch than y was', and c to mean 'Edward VIII', $\delta'\psi bca$ reports the thought I attributed to Queen Mary in the first place. If Queen Mary, one summer's day, had simply had the thought 'It's hot', our report of the incident would indeed have the form $\delta'pa$, but only because a proposition is the limiting case of a predicable, a no-place predicable.[10] But no thought Queen Mary had which can be reported by a proposition of the form $\delta'\varphi ba$ can also be reported by one of the form $\delta'pa$. And in particular, 'Queen Mary thought that Bertie made a good king' is not of this form.

This has a corollary which some may find surprising. It can be regarded as a fundamental principle of logical analysis that any proposition which admits of analysis into an n-place predicate attached to n names or occurrences of names admits also of analysis into an $(n-1)$-place predicate attached to $n-1$ names or occurrences of names. But this does not apply to words which follow 'Queen Mary thought that ---', 'John thought that ---', or

---

[10] Cf. my remarks in *What is Truth?*, Cambridge University Press, 1976, pp. 9–10, and ch. III n. 8.

the like. The principle I am talking about can be illustrated as follows: 'Peter struck Malchus' can be analysed as being of the form φab ('--- struck ......' attached to 'Peter' and 'Malchus'), or as being of the form ψa or χb ('Peter struck ---' attached to 'Malchus', or '--- struck Malchus' attached to 'Peter'), or as being of the form p ('Peter struck Malchus' attached to nothing). It can be regarded as containing a two-place, a one-place, or a no-place predicable. And 'John thought that Peter struck Malchus' can similarly be supposed to contain the three-place predicable '--- thought that ...... struck ---', or the two-place predicable 'John thought that --- struck ......', . . . and so on, down to the no-place predicable which is itself. But though we can analyse this proposition as being of the form $\delta'\varphi abc$ we cannot analyse it as being of the form $\delta'\psi ac$ or $\delta'\chi bc$ or $\delta'pc$.

One way of putting this point is to say that in the proposition 'John thought that Peter struck Malchus' 'Peter struck Malchus' does not occur as a syntactically coherent string. The suggestion that it does is an illusion, due to the occurrence of these words in sequence. But we should no more regard 'Peter struck Malchus' as a separately significant unit in this context than we should regard 'Plato was bald' as a separately significant unit in the context 'The man who taught Plato was bald'. Neither do the predicables '--- struck Malchus' or 'Peter struck ---' occur in the proposition 'John thought that Peter struck Malchus'. If we think of 'John' as the interpretation for c in the formula $\delta'\varphi abc$, we may be tempted to see the formula as equivalent to $\delta'\psi ac$, with ψ corresponding to φb ('struck Malchus') or to $\delta'\chi bc$, with χ corresponding to φa ('Peter struck ---'), but we are hardly likely to suppose that any equivalent formula can be found with a predicable-letter corresponding to φc: no predicable formed by attaching 'John' to 'struck' occurs in 'John thought that Peter struck Malchus'. But the transparent analysis of the verb 'think' as it occurs in this proposition is intended to result in all three names 'John', 'Peter', and 'Malchus' having the same role in the proposition. Taking ψ to represent the three-place predicable '--- thought that --- struck ---', we can use Quine's major inversion operator 'Inv'[11] to produce Inv ψ, which may be read '--- was thought by --- to have been struck by ---': ψabc ('John thought that Peter struck Malchus') is clearly equivalent to

[11] See ch. IV, § 6.

Inv ψbca ('Malchus was thought by John to have been struck by Peter'). Here there is nothing in the symbolism, or in the natural-language version, to suggest that we have occurrences of the one-place or no-place predicables 'Peter struck ---', '--- struck Malchus' or 'Peter struck Malchus'.

We can construct a further argument against the view that these predicables occur in 'John thought that Peter struck Malchus'. Suppose, not only that Malchus was thought by John to have been struck by Peter, but also that Gaius was thought by John to have been struck by Simon, and that, unbeknown to John, Simon and Peter were identical. Since these contexts are all being interpreted transparently, if Gaius was thought by John to have been struck by Simon, Gaius was thought by John to have been struck by Peter. So it is true of both Malchus and Gaius that they were thought by John to have been struck by Peter. But, given John's ignorance of Simon's identity with Peter, we cannot say that John thought that it was true of both Malchus and Gaius that they were struck by Peter, nor that John thought that Peter had struck two people. Using the symbolism already available, we can say that ($\delta'\varphi abc$ & $\delta'\varphi adc$), and even that $\delta'(\varphi ab$ & $\varphi ad)c$, but not that $\delta'(\chi b$ & $\chi d)c$, nor that δ' Conj $\chi\chi bdc$, nor that δ' Der Der Conj $\chi\chi c$. It does not follow from the fact that both Malchus and Gaius were thought by John to have been struck by Peter that some one predicable was thought by John to hold of both of them. And the explanation of this is that the predicable 'Peter struck ---' does not occur in the proposition 'John thought that Peter struck Malchus'. A similar argument could be found to show that '--- struck Malchus' does not occur in this proposition either.

Nor does the proposition 'Peter struck Malchus' occur in it. If John thinks that Peter struck Malchus but thinks that Simon did not strike him, it is true of Peter both that he is thought by John to have struck Malchus and that he is thought by John not to have struck Malchus. So we have ($\delta'\varphi abc$ & $\delta'\neg\varphi abc$), and indeed $\delta'(\varphi ab$ & $\neg\varphi ab)c$, but it is not fair to hold it against John that he believes something of the form (p & $\neg p$): where p is 'Peter struck Malchus', we do not have $\delta'(p$ & $\neg p)c$, nor even ($\delta'pc$ & $\delta'\neg pc$).

We are thus able to answer the question asked at the end of § 6 of this chapter. In the context of (10A), which we should now rewrite as $\delta'(\psi b$ & $\neg \psi b)a$, (ψb & $\neg \psi b$) does not occur as a separately significant, syntactically coherent, string. So 'Pierre believes that London is pretty and that London is not pretty' is no more of the form 'Pierre believes that p' than 'The man who taught Plato was bald' is of the form 'The man who taught p'. Nor is the simple 'Pierre believes that London is pretty' of the form 'Pierre believes that p'. It is of the form $\delta'\varphi ab$, but there is no more reason on this account for taking it to be of the form $\delta'pb$ than for taking it to be of the form $\delta'pa$.

If we wish to say that Pierre has no (obviously) self-contradictory beliefs we can formulate our assertion in this way, using δ' for 'believes that' and a for 'Pierre':

(PISC$'$) $\neg\, \exists p\, [\delta'(p\ \&\ \neg\, p)a]$.

This would give the propositional form of the Principle of Pierre's Immunity to Self-Contradiction (PISC). If we wished to give the equivalent predicative form of the principle, which says that Pierre never holds one and the same thing to have contradictory predicates, we should need more than

(PISC$''$) $\neg\, \exists x\, \exists \varphi\, \delta'(\varphi x\ \&\ \neg\varphi x)a$.

What we should require is

(PISC$'''$) $\neg\, \exists x\, \exists \varphi\, \delta'(\Xi u\, [\varphi u\ \&\ \neg\, \varphi u])xa$.

If the amended form of (10A), $\delta'(\psi b\ \&\ \neg\, \psi b)a$, is true this does not constitute a counter-example to either (PISC$'$) or (PISC$'''$). It does constitute a counter-example to (PISC$''$), but then we have no reason to suppose that (PISC$''$) is true. Of course people can believe contradictory things of the same object, provided they do not realize that it is the same object about which they hold these things. Kripke's puzzle is solved by rejecting his assumption that to suppose Pierre to believe that London is pretty and that London is not pretty is to attribute to him a self-contradictory (logically incoherent) belief.

He uses this assumption more than once in his argument. As I indicated in § 4 above, it would be more disastrous if the cases we have been considering were to lead us to violate the Law of Non-Contradiction ourselves by asserting propositions of the form $(\delta'\varphi ba\ \&\ \neg\, \delta'\varphi ba)$ than if they were to lead us to assert propositions of the form $(\delta'\varphi ba\ \&\ \delta'\neg\varphi ba)$ or even $\delta'(\varphi b\ \&\ \neg\varphi b)a$. Kripke, supposing that a proposition of this last form is also of the form $\delta'(p\ \&\ \neg\, p)a$, argues that, given that Pierre believes that London is not pretty $(\delta'\neg\varphi ba)$, if he were to believe also that London *is* pretty $(\delta'\varphi ba)$, he would believe both that London is pretty and that London is not pretty ($\delta'(\varphi b\ \&\ \neg\ \varphi b)a$, which would be to ascribe to him a contradictory belief. Given that he is logically conformist, we can argue that if he believes that London is not pretty he does not believe that London is pretty ($\delta'\neg\varphi ba \rightarrow \neg\delta'\varphi ba$). So our grounds for attributing to him both the belief that London is pretty and the belief that London is not pretty are grounds for simultaneously affirming and denying the proposition that Pierre believes that London is pretty ($\delta'\varphi ba\ \&\ \neg\ \delta'\varphi ba$). Not only does Pierre contradict himself, but we ourselves are forced to do so. Once, however, we reject the assumption that ($\delta'\ (\varphi b\ \&\ \neg\varphi b)a$ is of the form $\delta'\ (p\ \&\ \neg p)a$, we prevent this argument from going through.

Why should anyone think that 'Pierre believes that London is pretty and that London is not pretty' ascribes to Pierre a self-contradictory belief? One reason, I think, is that if I were to say 'I believe that London is pretty and that London is not pretty' I would be indicating (though not asserting) that I believe that one and the same town both is and is not pretty. Identity is shown by repeating a proper name, even if so repeating the name is not to say that anything is the same as anything. What I show by announcing 'I believe that London is pretty and that London is not pretty' is my belief that the town believed by me to be pretty is the same as the town believed by me not to be pretty. Similarly, what I show by announcing 'Pierre believes that London is pretty and that London is not pretty' is *my* belief that the town believed by Pierre to be pretty is the same as the town believed by him not to be pretty. But this is not to ascribe to *him* a belief that one and the same town is both pretty and not pretty, although the similar announcement about myself purports to *show*, though not to *say*, that I have this incoherent belief. But the paradox attaching to the announcement 'I believe that London is pretty and that London is not pretty' no more carries over to the announcement 'Pierre believes that London is pretty and that London is not pretty' than the paradox attaching to 'I believe that seven sevens are forty-seven, but they aren't' carries over to the remark 'Pierre believes that seven sevens are forty-seven, but they aren't'. Our belief that Pierre in the circumstances envisaged is being said to hold a logically incoherent belief may stem in part from a failure to distinguish the effects of first-person ascriptions from those of third-person ascriptions of belief.

Thus we must say of δ' that while it can form an $(n+1)$-place predicable out of an n-place predicable, it cannot form an n-place predicable out of an n-place-predicable-and-a-name. It can form predicables only out of what may be called 'pure predicables'. It cannot operate on names at all. Where atomic propositions are concerned, only those whose analyses involve no predicable of polyadicity greater than nought (e.g., 'subjectless' propositions like 'It's hot') can take the place of p in propositions of the form $\delta'pa$. 'Queen Mary thought it was hot' was of this form, but this form does not cover the other propositions we have been considering, propositions formed by more than one name or occurrence of a name. Verbs of propositional attitude on this account are modifiers, not of propositions, but of pure predicables. Proper names escape entirely from the scope of δ', that is to say, they do not serve to specify in any way what is thought. Prior's distinction between the two senses of 'object of thought', *what we think* and *what we think of*,[12] needs to be made even sharper: *what we think of* cannot even form part of *what we think*. The object of thought in the first of Prior's senses is mediated entirely by what Frege would have called *Begriffswörter*. Our thought is related to particulars, but cannot embrace them.

What a thought is about, on this view, is not part of the thought. The thought is entirely encapsulated in the predicable on which δ' operates to form the complex predicable of the form $\delta'\varphi$. Strictly speaking, there are no singular thoughts or judgements. The context of thought is always entirely general, consisting, in the terminology of Aquinas and Russell, wholly of universals, or, in the terminology of Kant, wholly of concepts as opposed to intuitions. This view was widely accepted in the Middle Ages and was advocated by as recent a philosopher as C. S. Peirce.[13] The human intellect does not apprehend particulars.

§ 10. This, then, is the rationale for the mutual entailment of (1A) and (2A). The names 'Ragusa' and 'Dubrovnik' do not enter into the specification of what Paul thinks at all. (1A) asserts a three-term relation as holding between a man named 'Paul', a town

[12] A. N. Prior, *Objects of Thought*, Oxford: Clarendon Press, 1971, p. 3. Prior was wrong, in my view, in identifying *what we think* with propositions.

[13] Peirce's views are reported by Prior, in *Objects of Thought*, pp. 145–8, where he cites passages from Peirce's *Collected Papers*, iii, p. 419.

named 'Ragusa' and a town named 'Dubrovnik'. This relation, expressed by the three-place predicable '--- thinks that Boscovich was born in --- and that --- is a present-day Croatian holiday resort', is said by (2A) to hold between exactly the same things as it is said to hold between by (1A). What (1A) and (2A) say is thus exactly the same.

This view of proper names also enables us to understand, even if we do not accept, Wittgenstein's prohibition on having in his canonical language more than one name for any given object. There was, I fear, an unadmitted distortion of Wittgenstein's doctrine involved in my presenting the derivation of (4A) from (1A) as an *ad hominem* argument designed to force Wittgenstein to admit the need for a sign of identity. Within Wittgenstein's system there is no room for propositions like (1) and (1A) which use two names for one thing. But it is only if (1) and (1A) do use two names for one thing that we are entitled to pass from them to (2) and (2A). And the complete freedom which I am claiming to pass backwards and forwards between (1) and (2) and between (1A) and (2A) does in a way correspond to Wittgenstein's intuition that there is only room for one name for one thing. If the function of a name is simply the communication from one language-user to another of what it is that is being talked about, and the function of a particular name is entirely determined by the identity of the object named, there can be no distinction of function between two names of the same object. From the point of view of the job done by the two names, they might just as well be one. Semantically, as I expressed it earlier, they *are* one.

§ 11.   There is nothing in all this which my argument in Chapter III needed to dispute. It is not part of my thesis that either (1) or (1A) says anything more or less than (2) or (2A). (1) and (2) can be regarded as the same proposition, and the same holds for (1A) and (2A). What (1A) serves to highlight, however, is the fact that something can be thought by someone to stand in a certain relation to itself without his realizing that the relation is in this way reflexive. (1A) is of the form $\delta'\psi bca$, and since b and c in this case name the same thing it is also of the form $\delta'\psi bba$. But since nothing except the predicable, symbolized here by ψ, but instantiated in this case by (1B), is, as it were, absorbed by the 'operator of propositional attitude', δ', the mere repetition of b

does not make any difference to what Paul thinks. It is quite otherwise with (6A), which is of the form δ 'Ref ψba. Here the two-place predicable δ 'Ref ψ(---, ...), which serves to express the relation between Paul and Dubrovnik (Ragusa), contains reflection as part of its structure. Dubrovnik *is thought by* Paul *to be the birthplace of Boscovich and a present-day Croatian holiday resort.* The italicized portion of the last sentence is a two-place predicable which occurs in (6A). This predicable just does not occur in (1A) or (2A). It is formed by δ ' out of the one-place predicable (6B), which, as we have seen, is equivalent to (6B₁), in which the concept of identity, implicit in (6B), is given overt expression. Where (6A) contains this two-place predicable, formed by δ ' out of the one-place predicable (6B), (1A) and (2A) contain only the three-place predicable formed by δ ' out of (1B). They differ only in the names they attach to this predicable, and this difference can do nothing to change the thought thereby attributed to Paul.

§ 12. Where names are being used to name the object, rather than being mentioned (as in ' "Cicero" has six letters'), the substitution of a different name for the same object can never affect the truth value of the proposition in which the substitution is made. This is the other way in which the Indiscernibility of Identicals (LL2) can be expressed. If identity is not a relation, (LL2) cannot be interpreted with proper names substituted for both x and y. As we have seen, where a definite description is substituted for either x or y or both, an interpretation can be given ((LL2₁ᵦ) and (LL2₂ᵦ)) which eliminates '=' as a two-place predicable. Where the substitution legitimated by the Indiscernibility of Identicals is of proper name for proper name, as in (2) and (2A) where 'Dubrovnik' is substituted for 'Ragusa', this legitimation will have to come from a metalinguistic version of (LL2). Such a version might be provided by

(LL2ₘ) If there is something of which both a and b are names, then for every $φ$, $φa$ is materially equivalent to $φb$.

Here again the principle can be stated without using '--- is the same as ......' as a two-place predicable. Moreover, it is impossible for it to admit of exceptions. Apparent exceptions, as when 'Tully' is substituted for 'Cicero' in ' "Cicero" has six letters', will be found to involve the occurrence of a proper name which is not on this

occasion being used as a proper name.[14] This inexorability of
$(LL2_m)$ is a consequence of the logical status of proper names, as I
have tried to state it earlier in this chapter. The sole and total
contribution that proper names make to the meaning, and thus to
the truth value, of a proposition is the specification of the object or
objects they are about. Two names which specify the same object
will thus make the same contribution to the meaning of the
proposition. Substituting one for the other will make no difference
to its meaning, let alone its truth value.

This discussion of proper names, and the version of the Principle
of the Indiscernibility of Identicals, namely $(LL2_m)$ which is a
consequence of their role in language, has, it is hoped, explained
the contrast between the opacity of contexts like 'Paul thinks
that ---' with respect to reflection, or identity, and their transparency with respect to names. It is predicables, not names, which
determine the content of thoughts. The concept of identity is the
concept of an operator which forms predicables from predicables.
It is therefore able directly to affect the content of thoughts in a
way that substitution of names cannot do. In the Kantian sense of
'concept', identity is a concept, not an intuition. And in understanding this contrast between the role of identity and the role of
names, we have been able to understand the metalinguistic sense
in which the identicals can be said to be indiscernible.

§ 13. Let me now attempt a summary of this chapter. The view of
identity which this book is concerned to defend leaves open the
question of the Identity of Indiscernibles. It allows a clear
statement of the thesis that indiscernibles are identical, but cannot
by itself determine whether that thesis is true. Where the
Indiscernibility of Identicals is concerned, our view of identity
distinguishes two versions of the thesis. One, which can be
couched in the object language, is expressible as the conjunction
of two theorems of the predicate calculus (with variables exclusively
interpreted), namely $(LL2_{1B})$ and $(LL2_{2B})$. The other, which has
to be stated in the metalanguage, can take the form $(LL2_m)$. Both
versions of the thesis, however, are true. Apparent exceptions,
which have given rise to talk of 'referential opacity' and 'intentionality', disappear when care is taken to make the necessary

---

[14] I have discussed these cases in *What is Existence?*, pp. 227–30, 236–41.

distinctions of scope and the necessary distinctions between the use and the mention of proper names. Neither the thesis of the Identity of Indiscernibles nor that of the Indiscernibility of Identicals is a 'pseudo-proposition' on our account of identity: the latter is not only a genuine proposition, but a true one.

ARITHMETICAL EQUATIONS

§ 1. Arithmetic begins with adding and subtracting, multiplying and dividing. 'Four and five make nine', 'Twice three is six': this is where we start. But these propositions, when put into symbols, take the forms '$4 + 5 = 9$' and '$2 \times 3 = 6$'; and Frege taught us to regard the '$=$' here as the sign of identity. These equations seem to assert a relation between a number and the sum or product of a pair of numbers. Nor do we seem to be advancing very far beyond the starting point if we move to propositions like '$2 + 10 = 3 \times 4$', where the sum of two numbers is said to be identical with the product of two others. If we are deprived of identity as a relation, how are we to express any of these elementary truths?

§ 2. 'Four and five make nine' does indeed express a relation, but it is a three-term, not a two-term, relation. That is the first point to establish if we are to solve these problems. Using '$Snmk$' to abbreviate 'The sum of n and m is k', I must now indicate how it is to be understood, without falling into the circularity of treating 'is' as the so-called ' "is" of identity'.[1] 'The sum of n and m is k' means 'For any φ, for any ψ, if there are at most n things which φ, then if there are at most m things which ψ there are at most k things which either φ or ψ'. Abbreviating 'There are at most n things which φ' to $nx\varphi x$, my definition of $Snmk$ is as follows:

(D1) $Sn,m,k =_{\mathrm{df}} \forall \varphi \, \forall \psi \, \{ny\varphi y \rightarrow [my\psi y \rightarrow kz(\varphi z \vee \psi z)]\}$.

An instance of this is:

(D2) $S4,5,9 =_{\mathrm{df}} \forall \varphi \, \forall \psi \, \{4x\varphi x \rightarrow [5y\psi y \rightarrow 9z(\varphi z \vee \psi z)]\}$.

---

[1] In much of this chapter I follow the line of thought set out by Dale Gottlieb in his book, *Ontological Economy*, Oxford: Clarendon Press, 1980, particularly in the chapter entitled 'Substitutional Arithmetic'. However, I make various adjustments to his analyses, chiefly by using statements of number of the form 'There are *at most* n objects which φ', and by using the exclusive interpretation of variables.

Propositions like $5y\psi y$ ('There are at most 5 things which ψ'), following Frege,[2] I call statements of number (*Zahlangaben*). 'There are at least 5 things which ψ' and 'There are exactly 5 things which ψ' are also statements of number. They are all answers, of a sort, to the question 'How many things ψ?'. 'There are at most 5 things which ψ' and 'There are at least 6 things which ψ' are contradictories, so if one is a number statement the other has to be. Conjunctions of number statements are number statements, and 'There are exactly 5 things that ψ' is equivalent to the conjunction of 'There are at most 5 things that ψ' and 'There are at least 5 things that ψ'. Using $5\#y\psi y$ for 'There are exactly 5 things which ψ' I can give the following partial definition:

(D3) $5\#x\varphi x =_{df} (5y\varphi y\ \&\ \neg\ 4\varphi y)$.

To make this fully general I should have to use an expression having the sense of 'the successor of n', and for this, at the moment, I do not have the conceptual resources. I shall acquire them later in the chapter.

§ 3. The challenge which has to be met in this chapter is a challenge to provide an account of elementary arithmetical equations which does not require for their expression a sign for identity which is a two-place first-level predicable. This is met by introducing a three-place predicable '$S(—, —, —)$', and there is an immediate need to give an account of this predicable without reintroducing the identity relation in its explanation. Responding to this need I have given a brief outline of a Nominalist interpretation of propositions of the form '$Snmk$', whose merits I hope to demonstrate later. However, it must be emphasized at the start that the Wittgensteinian thesis that we can do without a relation of identity does not compel the philosopher of mathematics to adopt a Nominalist position.[3] It would be possible to introduce the three-place predicable $S(—, —, —)$ by means of the following axioms:

$S0mm$
$Snmk \rightarrow Sn'mk'$,

[2] G. Frege, *The Foundations of Arithmetic*, tr. J. L. Austin, Oxford: Basil Blackwell, 1959, § 47.
[3] I am grateful to the referee of the Oxford University Press for convincing me of the need to emphasize this point.

where 'n' ' stands for 'the successor of n'. To do this is, of course, to define 'S' in terms of the successor function; but that is something which is required anyway, since it will need to be used, and explained, in connection with the third and fourth of Peano's axioms, namely,

$\forall n \; \forall m \; (n' = m' \rightarrow n = m)$
$\forall n \; (\neg \; n' = 0)$

Here again identity can be dispensed with by introducing a new two-place predicable '--- is the successor of ......', which can be abbreviated to '$H(—, —)$'. Peano's axioms can now be expressed thus:

$\neg \; \exists n \; \exists m \; \exists k \; (Hkn \; \& \; Hkm)$
$\neg \; \exists n \; H0n,$

where, of course, the quantified variables are to be given the exclusive interpretation. There will remain an obligation to define the new predicable '$H(—, —)$', but there is no reason to suppose that this cannot be done.

§ 4. We need not confine ourselves to a posteriori arguments to show that it is possible to define a three-place predicable which will allow us to dispense with a two-place 'identity' predicable in arithmetical equations. There is an a priori proof that such a three-place predicable is necessary anyway. If we take '$4 + 5 = 9$' to be asserting a relation of identity between 9 and the sum of 4 and 5, we are faced with the question of how to interpret the phrase 'the sum of 4 and 5'. It is a definite description. Translated into Russellese, '$4 + 5 = 9$' becomes '(The n such that n = the sum of 4 and 5) = 9', and by the same token this becomes '(The n such that n = (the n such that n = the sum of 4 and 5)) = 9'. The infinite regress can only be stopped if we introduce a three-place predicable such as '$S(—, —, —)$', so that we can obtain the rendering '(The n such that $S4,5,n$) = 9'. But having got this far, there is no point in retaining the form of an identity proposition, rather than writing '$S4,5,9$'. To do otherwise would be like insisting on rewriting 'x is between y and z' on each occasion of its use as '(The w such that w is between y and z) = x'. There is no way in which we can rest with the analysis of '$4 + 5 = 9$' as an identity proposition, or avoid recognizing a three-place predicable having the form of '$S(—, —, —)$'.

§ **5.** The Wittgensteinian theory of identity, therefore, has nothing to fear from the analysis of arithmetical equations. But we have reason to press on with the analysis which was begun in § 2, because it will provide further support both for the general view advanced in this book about the role in our language of the operation of *reflection*, and for the usefulness of the exclusive interpretation of variables. The latter, which is essential if we are not to be in the ridiculous position of having an account of identity but none of difference, will contribute to the elegance, if nothing more, of our definition of numerals. The former, so I have claimed, is an operation which provides the best account of our concept of identity. I am going to argue in §§ 13–15 of this chapter that a generalized account of the reflection operator will enable us to define the successor operation, and in the following chapters this generalized account of reflection will be put to work to provide answers to questions in the philosophy of mind. Philosophers have often claimed that some key concept, be it Platonic form, Leibnizian monad, Fregean sense, or whatever, has the power to illuminate a wide range of topics; and their claim to have lighted on a truly significant feature of our thinking is backed by their view that they have obtained a master key to unlock strikingly dissimilar doors. The reader may feel that in the course of the next few pages he is being asked to consider material which has little obvious connection with *identity*; but it is the very unobviousness of the connection which, it is hoped, will in the long run be found impressive. My wish to develop an analysis of arithmetical equations which avoids construing them, not only as asserting an identity of object(s), but as asserting anything at all about numbers *as objects* is not mere Nominalist prejudice. (I must confess, however, that readers who are familiar with my previous work, *What is Existence?* will recognize that although Nominalist prejudice is not the whole story, it is at least a partial explanation.)

§ **6.** Expressions like '$4x$' and '$5y$' are obviously analogous to quantifiers. Following a suggestion of William Kneale, I call them 'quotifiers'.[4] The Latin for 'How many?' is '*Quot?*', and statements of number are all, as we have seen, answers to questions of the form 'How many things are there which φ?' One answer to this

---

[4] W. C. Kneale, 'Numbers and Numerals', *British Journal for the Philosophy of Science*, 23 (1972), pp. 191–206, and particularly p. 197.

question is 'None'. Another, somewhat less precise, is 'Not none'; and this, as Frege saw, is tantamount to saying 'There is something which φ's'. 'Affirmation of existence is in fact nothing but denial of the number nought.'[5] If 'There is nothing which φ's' is a quotified proposition, so is 'There is something which φ's'. This, however, is expressible by the familiar quantified proposition $\exists x\ (\varphi x)$. Quantifiers may therefore be regarded as a subspecies of quotifiers. 'There is nothing which φ's' may be expressed either as $\neg\ \exists x\ (\varphi x)$ or as $0x\varphi x$. So the existential quantifier can be defined as the equivalent of $\neg\ 0x$, and the universal, by the same token, as $0x\ \neg$, since $\forall x\ (\varphi x)$ will obviously be equivalent to $0x\ \neg\ (\varphi x)$. The quantifiers are simply quotifiers combined with negation.

Frege introduced quantification (though he did not use that name for it) as a special case of quotification (without, of course, using that name either). He then went on to define numbers, as objects, with the help only of quantifiers, and lost interest in the wider field of quotification. We can, if we wish, reverse the process and introduce quotifiers in terms of quantifiers. Taking $\exists x\ (\varphi x)$ as undefined, $0x\varphi x$ can be defined as equivalent to $\neg\ \exists x\ (\varphi x)$; and it will easily be seen that $1x\varphi x$, understood as 'There is at most one thing which φ's' can be defined as $\neg\ \exists x\ \exists y\ (\varphi x\ \&\ \varphi y)$. This takes for granted the Wittgensteinian understanding of quantifiers and variables where $\exists x\ \exists y\ (\varphi x\ \&\ \varphi y)$ means 'Something φ's and so does something else'. The variables are to be exclusively interpreted. $\neg\ \exists x\ \exists y\ (\varphi x\ \&\ \varphi y)$ means 'No two things φ', and this means the same as 'At most one thing φ's'. We thus get the series of definitions:

$$0x\varphi x\ =_{df}\ \neg\ \exists x\ (\varphi x)$$
$$1x\varphi x\ =_{df}\ \neg\ \exists x\ \exists y\ (\varphi x\ \&\ \varphi y)$$
$$\text{(D4)}\quad 2x\varphi x\ =_{df}\ \neg\ \exists x\ \exists y\ \exists z\ [(\varphi x\ \&\ \varphi y)\ \&\ \varphi z]$$
$$3x\varphi x\ =_{df}\ \neg\ \exists x\ \exists y\ \exists z\ \exists w\ \{[(\varphi x\ \&\ \varphi y)\ \&\ \varphi z]\ \&\ \varphi w\}$$
$$nx\varphi x\ =_{df}\ \neg\ \exists x_1\ \exists x_2,...,\exists x_{n+1}\ \{...(\varphi x_1\ \&\ \varphi x_2)\ \&\ ...$$
$$\&\ \varphi x_{n+1}\}.$$

§ 6. Given these definitions (in the last there would have to be n &s) and our previous definition (D1) of *Snmk* (or '$n + m = k$'),

<hr/>

[5] Frege, *The Foundations of Arithmetic*, § 53.

the elementary Arithmetical equation '1 + 2 = 3' comes out as

(13) $\forall\varphi \; \forall\psi \; \{\neg\exists x \; \exists y \; (\varphi x \; \& \; \varphi y) \rightarrow$
$\quad [\neg \; \exists x \; \exists y \; \exists z \; \{(\psi x \; \& \; \psi y) \; \& \; \psi z\} \rightarrow$
$\quad \neg \; \exists x \; \exists y \; \exists z \; \exists w \; \{ \; [(\varphi x \; \mathsf{v} \; \psi x) \; \& \; (\varphi y \; \mathsf{v} \; \psi y)]$
$\quad \& \; [(\varphi z \; \mathsf{v} \; \psi z) \; \& \; (\varphi w \; \mathsf{v} \; \psi w)] \}\}\}$,

and this is a truth of logic. It is quite clear that all truths of the form '*n* + *m* = *k*' reduce to logical truths of this form.

Gottlieb, however, is worried that some falsehoods of the form '*n* + *m* = *k*' come out as true, if not logically true, on this analysis. This is due to some, possibly naïve, considerations about the number of objects in the Universe. Russell was similarly worried by the consideration that $\exists x \; (x = x)$, which he took to be a contingent proposition, was deducible in the system of *Principia Mathematica*. He regarded it as equivalent to 'There is at least one object'. The logical purity of the system was felt to be endangered by this. (Wittgenstein ridicules this at *Tractatus*, 5.5352.) Gottlieb is worried by the possibility that in a universe which contains only *j* objects, every proposition of the form *Snmk*, where $n > j$, will come out true. This is because Gottlieb's own analysis of *Snmk* begins 'If there are *n* objects which φ', where 'if' is taken as material implication (as I have taken it by representing it as → in (D1)). On this understanding of 'if', all propositions which begin in this way are true when it is false, for every φ, that there are *n* objects which φ. Gottlieb, therefore, takes elaborate steps to relativize his theorems to universes which have the requisite number of objects.

On my definition, propositions of the form *nxφx* create a difficulty which occurs at a different point. I interpret *nxφx* as meaning 'There are at most *n* things which φ', and this is equivalent to 'It is not the case that there are at least $n+1$ things which φ'. The definition of *Snmk* (D1) accordingly makes it equivalent to 'There is no φ or ψ such that both there are at most *n* things which φ and at most *m* things which ψ and at least $k + 1$ things which either φ or ψ'. (This is because the *definiens* of (D1) is equivalent to $\neg \; \exists\varphi \; \exists\psi \; \{nx\varphi x \; \& \; [my\psi y \; \& \; \neg \; kz \; (\varphi z \; \mathsf{v} \; \psi z)]\}$, and $\neg \; kz \; (\varphi z \; \& \; \psi z)$ means 'It is not the case that there are at most *k* things which either φ or ψ', i.e., 'There are at least $k+1$ things which either φ or ψ'.) Any proposition of the form *Snmk*, therefore, is true if there is no φ or ψ such that there are at least

$k+1$ things which either φ or ψ. And *this*, it may be urged, is true in a universe which contains less than $k + 1$ objects. In such a universe, then, every proposition of the form *Snmk* will be true, regardless of the values given to *n* and *m*. If there are less than 10 objects, not only will $5 + 4 = 9$ be true, but so will $3 + 2 = 9$ and $75 + 428 = 9$.

The possibility we are envisaging is that

(14) $\neg \exists \varphi \, \exists \psi \, \neg \, kz(\varphi z \lor \psi z)$

is true. And this will be true if $\neg \exists \varphi \, (\neg \, kz\varphi z)$, i.e.,

(15) There is no φ such that at least $k + 1$ things φ

is envisaged as actually true. We are asked, that is to say, to envisage the possibility, for some k, that there aren't $k + 1$ of *anything*. But how could this be true? Any piece of string consists of $k + 1$ pieces of string whose length is $n/(k + 1)$ cm., where n cm. is the length of the original piece. We may thus substitute for φ 'is a piece of string $n/(k + 1)$ cm. long', for any k we need, and (15) is false. If there is a minimum length for pieces of string, try lines. Only an Atomist would wish to dispute that there are $k + 1$ lines $1/(k + 1)$ units in length in a line one unit in length, for any k. This indeed was Aristotle's way of securing all the numbers he wanted. There were no actual infinities, but the infinite divisibility of all extended things made it impossible for the mathematician ever to run short. No doubt a Logicist of the primitive observance will be unwilling to leave his theory of arithmetical truth open to attack from any physical or metaphysical quarter: he will not wish to be at risk from Atomism. Reliance on the infinite divisibility of matter or space will be unwelcome. Even so, it seems hard to imagine how an opponent could upset his theory by discovering that some proposition of the form (15) is true. How could it ever be established that there were not $k+1$ instances of *anything*, for any given substitution for k?

It is, no doubt, a matter of fact how many instances there are of φ, for any given φ—i.e., once we have decided what to count. But the decision what to count, colours, chimes, insects, species, tunes, recipes, numbers, or whatever, is very much our decision. If a person wishes to be an idealist, he will be well advised to begin with an idealist account of the *ways* in which we classify objects, the predicables that we allow ourselves to use to provide substitution instances of φ. It is difficult for the idealist to convince us that it is up to us to determine whether the world corresponds to the way we think about it. He has less difficulty in persuading us that the world does not dictate that we should think about it in this way rather than that. There seems little chance of our discovering a hard rock of fact in the form of there being some number k, such that there just is no predicable φ, such that there are $k+1$ things which are φ. We can always invent new predicables, i.e. form new concepts. Where there are no hard factual rocks, there is no chance of our theory being shipwrecked on them.

The naïvety of Gottlieb's worry, and of Russell's, stems from their failure to appreciate that *object* is, in Wittgenstein's terminology, a formal concept. Objects, unlike elephants or typing errors, are not the sort of things one can count. There is something comical about philosophers experiencing alarm at the thought that they might one day discover that there are only n objects in the Universe, and that they are faced with truth of every proposition of the form $n + m = k$. The absurdity lies in their failure to ask themselves what sort of fact the fact of there being this finite number of 'objects' could be.

§ 8. The theory itself I have described just now as a Logicist theory. Frege, the original Logicist, was also a Realist, in the sense of 'Platonist'. Gottlieb's theory and my adaptation of it have the advantage, as I see it, of being at once Logicist and Nominalist. It is logicist in that it reduces all true propositions of the form '$n + m = k$' to logical truths, as '$1 + 2 = 3$' is shown to be equivalent to (13). Vastly more is needed before the Logicist programme can be said to have succeeded, but this is a start. It is also a start for a Nominalist account of Arithmetic. '$1 + 2 = 3$' seems to state a relationship between three objects, the numbers One, Two, and Three. The logical structure of the proposition seems to be that the three proper names which name these objects are attached to the three-place first-level predicable '--- and ...... make ---'. (D1), on the other hand, allows us to see '$S1,2,3$' as an abbreviation for what is stated by inserting '1', '2', and '3', intended as quotifiers, in the gaps of the formula

(16) $\forall\varphi \, \forall\psi \, \{(-)x\varphi x \rightarrow [(-)y\psi y \rightarrow (-)z \, (\varphi z \vee \psi z)]\}$.

Quotifiers, like quantifiers, are to be regarded as second-level predicables. (16), which is the expansion of '$S(-, -, -)$', is an expression for a function whose arguments are quotifiers. It is therefore a function of third level, and since its value for appropriate arguments is a proposition, it is classifiable as a third-level predicable. We have, therefore, the typical Nominalist analysis, showing the true syntactical category of expressions which seem to be names as something other than names, and simultaneously revealing as illusory some supposed first-level predicable. Thus if 'Blueness inheres in hyacinths' is taken to be merely a 'blown-up' version of 'Hyacinths are blue', 'blueness' is revealed as only posturing as a name, its work being done more perspicuously by the first-level predicable '--- are blue', and the ostensible two-place predicable '--- inheres in ......' vanishes as so much unwanted padding. Again, 'Thirty-one is the number of the days in July' seems to be asserting a relation—that of identity (!)—between something whose name is 'Thirty-one' and something which is designated by the definite description 'the number of days in July'. Frege enabled us to see 'days in July' as a concept expression (*Begriffswort*) and 'Thirty-one is the number of ......' as merely a blown-up version of the quotifier 'There are thirty-one ......', which is evidently a second-level predicable.

It is with propositions like 'Four and five make nine', as I have said, that Arithmetic begins. It begins, that is, precisely at the place where numbers take on the appearance of objects which stand in certain relations to each other, or which possess certain properties ('Five is prime'). So long as we stick to statements of number (i.e., answers to 'How many?' questions), numbers do not seem like objects. The word 'two' in 'There are two watches in that drawer' does not even look like a name—a noun; it looks more like an adjective. 'There are two watches in that drawer' is on a par with 'There are many watches in that drawer', and I doubt if anyone has ever treated 'many' as the name of an object. But addition and subtraction, multiplication and division—these operations seem to require numbers as objects to operate on. And the propositions which state the results of such operations, e.g., '$1 + 2 = 3$', seem to be formed by attaching names to three-place predicables of first level. The philosopher of mathematics asks 'What are numbers?', and by that he means 'What are these things which we add and subtract, multiply and divide, call odd or even, relate to each other as double to half or square to square-root?' It is the arrival in human language of predicables like '--- and ...... make ---',

'--- times ...... is ---', etc., which prompts ideas of mathematical realism. We should never have 'believed in' numbers if we had not found ourselves apparently talking about them.

§ 9. The analysis provided by the definitions (D1) and (D4) saves us from the prima facie Realist commitments of propositions like '4 + 5 = 9'. This, however, will not take us far. Subtraction is partially definable: '$n - m = k$' can be represented as $Smkn$ as long as k is a positive number. But for multiplication we need a richer vocabulary. Even in the case of addition, where more than three numbers are involved, we need more apparatus than $Snmk$ can provide. How are we to represent '4 + 5 = 6 + 3'?

'4 + 5 = 9' is dealt with as a three-term relation which has no affinity whatsoever to identity propositions like 'My mother-in-law is my Russian teacher'. Propositions like this, as we have seen, are canonically representable with the help of quantifier and variables, by sentences like 'For some x, both x bore my wife and x teaches me Russian'. In languages which have an identity operator the form of these propositions can be expressed by $\exists x\ \Xi u\ [\varphi u\ \&\ \psi u]\ x$ or by Der Ref Conj $\varphi\psi$. Arithmetical equations involving more than three numbers require expression in exactly this way. '4 + 5 = 6 + 3' can be expressed as

(17) $\exists n\ (S4,5,n\ \&\ S6,3,n)$,

which is equivalent to $\exists n\ \Xi u\ [S4,5,u\ \&\ S6,3,u]\ n$ or Der Ref Inv inv Inv inv Inv Conj $SS6,3,4,5$.

§ 10. Let us stay for the moment with (17). I have been using n, m, and k for some time as what Quine would call 'schematic letters' for numerals. They were used thus in the definition (D1). With (17) I have moved to using n as a bound variable. Quine would insist that this was a momentous decision involving me in 'ontological commitment' to the objects which are the values of this variable, namely the natural numbers. Quine's views about ontological commitment, however, seem to me to be confused and misguided.[6] Gottlieb is also willing to use variables like n the way I use them, and to bind them with quantifiers; but he thinks that the way for someone to defend this practice, while remaining a

---

[6] See my criticisms of Quine in *What is Existence?*, chs. VI–VIII.

Nominalist, is to regard the quantification involved as 'substitutional'. Again, I think this view misguided; and in the places just cited I have called in question the importance of the distinction between 'substitutional' and 'objectual' quantification. I do agree with Gottlieb, however, that if we are to use bound variables we must have a way of indicating their 'substitution class', that is to say, the category of constants which can significantly be substituted for the variables in instantiations of the quantified propositions.

We can, of course, say that the expressions we require are, quite simply, quotifiers. (17) is true precisely because

(17$_s$) $S4,5,9$ & $S6,3,9$

is true. '9', which is the substituend in (17$_s$) for 'n' in (17), is a quotifier, and is seen to be one if we inspect the *definiens* of (17$_s$) which (D1) allows us to produce. What happens, though, if we continue the process of definition by means of (D4)? One result of using (D4) to eliminate the quotifiers from (17$_s$) is to produce an intolerably lengthy formula, and we should not at a glance, or even at several glances, be able to take it in. Let us therefore consider a simpler formula. We may follow Gottlieb and examine the proposition '$\exists n$ [nx (x is bald)]', which says, in effect, 'There is some number n such that there are at most n bald men'. Exististically quantified propositions may be regarded as equivalent to a disjunction of indefinitely many propositions which are their instantiations, if these can be found. There is no difficulty in finding such a disjunction in the case of '$\exists n$ [nx (x is bald)]'. It would be of the form '$0x$ (x is bald) $\vee$ {$1x$ (x is bald) $\vee$ [$2x$ (x is bald) . . .]}'. But what of the proposition to which this can be reduced if we replace the quotified disjuncts by their quantified *definientia*? According to the method of defining quotified propositions favoured by Gottlieb, we get this result: speaking of his equivalent of '$\exists n$ [nx (x is bald)]' he says that it

gathers together the following sentences for disjoint assertion

$\sim$ ($\exists x$) (x is bald)
($\exists y$) (y is bald & $\sim$ ($\exists x$) (x is bald & $x \neq y$))
($\exists y$) (y is bald & ($\exists z$) (z is bald & $y \neq z$ & $\sim$ ($\exists x$) (x is bald & $x \neq y$ & $x \neq z$))).

If we were to introduce substitutional variables whose substituends are expressions of ⟨this basic quantificational vocabulary⟩, how would we accomplish this? (*Ontological Economy*, p. 97.)

One sympathises with Gottlieb's distress at the untidiness of the list with which he is saddled by his equivalent of (D4). But we do not have to leave things in this disagreeable state of confusion.

§ **11.** This is where (D4) scores heavily over its rivals. One can state simply the rule for producing the *definiens* of $nx\varphi x$ for any n:

(Rnxφx)   Replace $0x\varphi x$ with $\neg \exists x (\varphi x)$; and for every $n > 0$, add n quantifiers after $\exists x$, and n open sentences formed by attaching a single variable to φ separated from each other by occurrences of '&' with appropriate bracketing, allowing no repeated occurrences of variables after φx.

Thus $3x\varphi x$ is replaced by $\neg \exists x \exists y \exists z \exists w \{\varphi x \,\&\, [\varphi y \,\&\, (\varphi z \,\&\, \varphi w)]\}$. The superiority of (D4) over Gottlieb's equivalent is obtained by two means. First, the exclusive interpretation of variables eliminates the needs for clusters of clauses of the form $x \neq y$. Secondly, the interpretation of quotified propositions as 'At most n things φ' allows the series to run on smoothly from $0x\varphi x$ without changing from negative to affirmative formulae. It also permits an economy in the definition of $Snmk$. Gottlieb's definition of S is as follows:

(S) 'Sabc' is true iff '(F)(G)(($\exists$!axF & $\exists$!bxG & ~($\exists$x)(F & G)) → $\exists$!cx(F V G))' is true (Ibid., p. 95.)

Here '$\exists$!axF' is equivalent to 'the number of F things is a': e.g., '$\exists$!2xF' would be read as 'There are just two things which are F'. '$\exists$!cx(F V G)' means 'The number of things which are either F or G is c'. With this interpretation of quotified propositions Gottlieb needs the extra clause '~($\exists$x)(F & G)', i.e., 'There is nothing which is both F and G', to rule out the possibility that some or all of the a things which F coincide with some or all of the b things which G. For instance, if there are exactly four doctors who are Presbyterians and exactly five doctors who are Welsh, it by no means follows that there are exactly nine who are either Presbyterian or Welsh. All the Presbyterian doctors may turn out to be Welsh, so that there are only five doctors who are either Presbyterian or Welsh. To get an adequate definition of 'S' with quotifiers interpreted in this way we have to add a clause requiring substitutes for 'F' and 'G' to be contraries. The same would be necessary if '$\exists$!nxF' were read as 'There are at least *n* things which are F', etc. I call this latter reading the 'minimalist' interpretation of quotifiers, and mine, with *nxφx* read as 'There are at most *n* things which *φ*', the 'maximalist' interpretation. The maximalist interpretation does not need the clause requiring substitutes for F and G, or *φ* and *ψ*, to be contraries. Even if four of the five Welsh doctors are Presbyterian, it still follows that at most nine doctors are either Welsh or Presbyterians. The point is that if the Presbyterians are no more than four, and the Welsh no more than five, there cannot be more than nine who are either Welsh or Presbyterian, although of course, there can be fewer than this. (The whole can indeed be true if there are none of either sort.) So not only is (D4) more elegant than Gottlieb's equivalent, but (D1) is more economical than his (S).

§ 12. The rule allowing us to replace quotified propositions by quantified propositions (R*nxφx*) might be adapted to tell us how to provide a quantified substitution instance for a proposition containing a quotifier variable like *n*. Such a substitution rule would be

(S*nxφx*) A substitution instance of *nxφx* is obtained by negating a quantified proposition formed by existentially quantifying the variables (interpreted exclusively) in an open sentence formed by conjoining *n* + 1 open sentences obtained by attaching each of *n* + 1 distinct variables to a separate occurrence of *φ*.

This way of providing substitution instances of formulae containing a variable quotifier may be compared with definitions in use. We cannot provide a list of expressions, or a category of expressions simply substitutable for *n*, but we can provide a categorization of whole formulae substitutable for whole formulae in which *n* occurs.

§ 13. For those who, like Frege, disapprove of contextual definition or definition in use, we can do better than this. Just as quantifiers can bind variables of categories other than that of names,[7] so reflection can be applied to expressions of categories other than names. Let us use 'Ref$_0$' to do the job previously done

---

[7] For a defence of this practice see my *What is Existence?*, chs. VI–VIII.

by 'Ref' *tout court*, and 'Ref$_n$' as an operator on predicables of nth level. Then the proposition logically equivalent to φa & ψa which we previously wrote Ref Conj $\varphi\psi a$, we now write Ref$_0$ Conj $\varphi\psi a$. And the proposition equivalent to φa & φb we now write Ref$_1$ Conj φab. $\exists x\, \exists y\, (\varphi x$ & $\varphi y)$ will now be Der Der Ref$_1$ Conj φ. The maximally quotified formula $1x\varphi x$ will then be equivalent to Neg Der Der Ref$_1$ Conj φ. But $\exists x\, \exists y\, (\varphi x$ & $\varphi y)$ is equivalent to $\exists x\, [\varphi x$ & $\exists y\, (\varphi y)]$ (i.e. Der Ref$_1$ Conj Der φ), which may be read 'Something φs and so does something else', and $\exists x\, \exists y\, \exists z\, [\varphi x$ & $(\varphi y$ & $\varphi z)]$ to $\exists x\, \{\varphi x$ & $\exists y\, [\varphi y$ & $\exists z\, (\varphi z)]\}$ (Der Ref$_1$ Conj Der Der Ref$_1$ Conj Der φ). Using 'Else' to abbreviate 'Ref$_1$ Conj Der', we can rewrite (D4) thus:

$$\begin{aligned}
&0x\varphi x &&=_{\mathrm{df}} \text{Neg Der } \varphi \\
\text{(D5)}\quad &1x\varphi x &&=_{\mathrm{df}} \text{Neg Der Else } \varphi \\
&2x\varphi x &&=_{\mathrm{df}} \text{Neg Der Else Else } \varphi \\
&nx\varphi x &&=_{\mathrm{df}} \text{Neg Der Else}_1 \text{ Else}_2 \dots, \text{Else}_n\, \varphi.
\end{aligned}$$

§ 14. Moreover, the same apparatus of inversion and reflection which allowed us to get rid of variables from quantified formulae will allow us to get rid of them from quotified formulae. The *definienda* of (D5) can in this way be shortened to 0φ, 1φ, 2φ, etc. Again, following Gottlieb and using the 'formal' numerals 0, $0'$, $0''$, $0'''$ to replace the Arabic numerals in quotifier position, we can make a further alteration to these shortened *definienda* of (D5), and obtain a revised definition:

$$\begin{aligned}
&0\varphi &&=_{\mathrm{df}} \text{Neg Der } \varphi \\
\text{(D6)}\quad &0'\varphi &&=_{\mathrm{df}} \text{Neg Der Else } \varphi \\
&0''\varphi &&=_{\mathrm{df}} \text{Neg Der Else Else } \varphi \\
&n\varphi &&=_{\mathrm{df}} \text{Neg Der Else}_1 \text{ Else}_2 ,\dots, \text{Else}_n\, \varphi
\end{aligned}$$

Here '0' can be regarded simply as the abbreviation of 'Neg Der', and each prime as an abbreviation of 'Else', which is itself an abbreviation for 'Ref$_1$ Conj Der'. The formal numerals will thus be nothing more than a symbolic variant for the alternative to the vocabulary of the classical predicate calculus which Quine provided in 'Variables Explained Away'. The variable quotifier, n, has as its substitution instances 0, $0'$, $0''$, etc., which can directly replace n in formulae without further adjustment, and which are themselves part of the symbolism of the variable-free predicate calculus. Gottlieb's pained question about how to accomplish the introduction of substitutional variables whose substituends are expressions of this symbolism is thus painlessly answered.

§ **15.** The introduction of 'Ref₁' allows our symbolism to approximate to the quotified sentences of natural languages in one important respect. 'There are no ducks on the pond', 'There are at least three ducks on the pond', 'There are at most five ducks on the pond' are all alike in having just one occurrence of the expression 'ducks on the pond'. If we abbreviate 'x is a duck on the pond' to φx the equivalents of these propositions will, in the style of (D4) be $\neg \exists x\,(\varphi x)$, $\exists x\,\exists y\,\exists z\,[\varphi x\ \&\ (\varphi y\ \&\ \varphi z)]$, and $\neg \exists x\,\exists y\,\exists z\,\exists w\,\exists v\,\exists u\,[\varphi x\ \&\ (\varphi y\ \&\ \{\varphi z\ \&\ [\varphi w\ \&\ (\varphi v\ \&\ \varphi u)]\})]$, respectively. The number of times φ appears increases all the time. With 0φ, $\neg\,0''\varphi$ and $0'''''\varphi$, and even with Neg Der φ, Der Else Else φ and Neg Der Else Else Else Else Else φ, one occurrence of φ is sufficient in each formula. Each quotifier is of the same syntactical category, the category of second-level one-place predicable, and takes as its argument a single one-place predicable of first level. This is a perfect match with natural languages, where 'Nothing', 'At least three things', and 'At most five things' can all combine with 'wrote *Waverley*' to form significant sentences.

§ **16.** I have been dealing with what Gottlieb saw as a difficulty involved in using a bound variable whose substituends are quotifiers. Since the difficulty proved to be illusory, we may go ahead and use such variables. As I have already indicated, they are needed in order to express, in a language without a relational expression for identity, those Arithmetical equations which involve addition and more than three numbers. '4 + 5 = 6 + 3' comes out as $\exists n\,(S4,5,n\ \&\ S6,3,n)$; '2 + 2 + 5 = 3 + 3 + 3' comes out as $\exists n\,\exists m\,\exists k\,\{S2,2,m\ \&\ [Sm5n\ \&\ (S3,3,k\ \&\ Sk3n)]\}$.

With '3 + 3 + 3' we are ready to turn to multiplication. Now that bound variables in the category of quotifiers are available we can define multiplication recursively.[8] In order to eliminate the need for '=', we write, instead of '$n \times m = k$', '$Pnmk$'. The recursive definition of this is given by the following schemata:

(D7) $\quad \begin{aligned} P0mn &=_{\text{df}} S00n \\ Pn'mk &=_{\text{df}} \exists j\,(Pnmj\ \&\ Sjmk). \end{aligned}$

----

[8] In this I borrow directly from Gottlieb.

Here we are taking advantage of the prime notation, where n' is the successor of n. But a less concise definitional schema can be given by noting the equivalence of $\exists i \, (Sn1i \ \& \ Pimk)$ and $\exists j \, (Pnmj \ \& \ Sjmk)$. Thus bound quotifier variables are again what we need to express what we could not express at the beginning of this chapter, namely, the notion 'the successor of ---'.

Again, the recursive definition of exponentiation is as follows, using $Tnmk$ to represent '$n^m = k$'.

$$(D8) \quad \begin{array}{l} Tn0m =_{df} S01m \\ Tnm'k =_{df} \exists j \, (Tnmj \ \& \ Pnjk). \end{array}$$

§ 17. Since the variables take only quotifiers as their substituends, i.e., range only over positive whole numbers, the converses of these operations, i.e., subtraction, division, and the extraction of roots, are available only when the result is a positive whole number. Thus Inv Inv $Snmk$ for '$n - m = k$' is all right if '9' is substituted for 'n' and '5' for 'm', but not vice versa; Inv Inv $Pnmk$ for '$n \div m = k$' is all right if '10' is substituted for 'n' and '2' for 'm', but not vice versa; inv Inv $Tnmk$ for $^m\sqrt{n} = k$ is all right if '16' is substituted for 'n' and '2' for 'm', but not vice versa. We have as yet no way of defining negative, rational, and real numbers.

For any two natural numbers, there is a natural number which is their sum. We can represent this with the help of 'S' by

$$\forall n \ \forall m \ \exists k \, (Snmk).$$

From this we can deduce

$$\forall n \ \forall m \ \exists k \, (Pnmk) \text{ and } \forall n \ \forall m \ \exists k \, (Tnmk).$$

But we cannot similarly affirm

$$\forall n \ \forall m \ \exists k \, (Snkm), \ \forall n \ \forall m \ \exists k \, (Pnkm), \text{ or}$$
$$\forall n \ \forall m \ \exists k \, (Tknm).$$

That is to say, it is not guaranteed that, for any two natural numbers taken in a given order, there is a natural number which is their difference, their ratio or, for one of them n, the nth root of the other, m. $\forall n \ \forall m \ \exists k \, (Snmk)$, from which $\forall n \ \forall m \ \exists k \, (Pnmk)$ and $\forall n \ \forall m \ \exists k \, (Tnmk)$ may be derived, can be thought of as an axiom for Arithmetic. It implies Peano's axiom $\forall n \ \exists k \, (Hnk)$, since, for any number, n, there is a number k which is equal to $n + 1$. To get the arithmetic of the rational and real numbers going it would be necessary to add $\forall n \ \forall m \ \exists k \, (Snkm)$, $\forall n \ \forall m \ \exists k$

(*Pnkm*), and ∀*n* ∀*m* ∃*k* (*Tknm*) as additional axioms. But whereas the Nominalist analysis I have given yields ∀*n* ∀*m* ∃*k* (*Snmk*) as a truth of logic, it will in no way guarantee the truth of ∀*n* ∀*m* ∃*k* (*Snkm*), ∀*n* ∀*m* ∃*k* (*Pnkm*), and ∀*n* ∀*m* ∃*k* (*Tknm*). The crux of the matter is that the third-level predicable, (16), which provided a sense for *Snmk*, and, derivatively, for *Pnmk* and *Tnmk*, will not serve as a fruitful analysis of the converses of these operations.

This is what we should expect. What produced the appearance of a set of strange objects called 'natural numbers' was the use of predicables like '--- and ...... make ---' which have the appearance of first-level predicables. We saw in § 7 that '*S*(—, —, —)', which serves as the abbreviation of this apparent first-level predicable, can be regarded more intelligibly as the abbreviation of (16), which is a predicable of third level. Once introduced into the range of human concepts, the operations *sum*, *product*, and *power* acquire their own momentum. What holds good for them is expected to hold good also for their converses. Just as the definite description, 'the number obtained by multiplying six by five', can be relied on to identify a number, so it is assumed that a number will be identified by the definite description, 'the number obtained by dividing six by five'. With '*Wx*' representing '*x* is greater than one', ∃*n* (*P*6,5,*n* & *Wn*) & ¬ ∃*m* ∃*k* (*P*6,5,*m* & *P*6,5,*k*) is Wittgenstein's version of the Russellian analysis of 'The number obtained by multiplying six by five is greater than one', and the truth of that is guaranteed by the availability of ∀*n* ∀*m* ∃*k* (*Pnmk*) as an axiom. By the same token, the proposition 'The number obtained by dividing six by five is greater than one' comes out as ∃*n* (*P*5,*n*,6 & *Wn*) & ¬ ∃*m* ∃*k* (*P*5,*m*,6 & *P*5,*k*,6). In this case, however, we do not have an axiom ∀*n* ∀*m* ∃*k* (*Pnmk*) to guarantee its truth.

The truth of ∀*n* ∀*m* ∃*k* (*Pnmk*) is ensured by the fact that we can always produce larger numbers by adding primes to 0, or, what is the same thing, 'Elses' to 'Neg Der'. All this was obtained by the analysis of '*S*' in terms of quotifiers and truth functions. The only way in which we could similarly ensure the truth of ∀*n* ∀*m* ∃*k* (*Snkm*), ∀*n* ∀*m* ∃*k* (*Pnkm*), and ∀*n* ∀*m* ∃*k* (*Tknm*) would be by finding alternative, more sophisticated analyses of '*S*'. For instance, the distinction between positive and negative numbers seems to be an abstraction from situations such as those involving credit and debit: if the cooker I sold you was worth a hundred pounds, while the lawn-mower you sold me was worth only ninety, then I owe you minus ten pounds. A variant of '*Snmk*', '*S'nmk*', might be defined in terms of a three-place predicable, φ, which abbreviates '--- is a pound's worth of chalk which ...... has bought from ---', ψ, an abbreviation for '--- is a pound's worth of cheese which ...... has bought from ---', χ, an abbreviation for '--- is a pound which ...... pays to ---', and 'O', which stands for 'It is legally obligatory that ---'. We then get:

(D9) $S'n,m,k =_{df} \forall y\ \forall z\ \{n\#x\ (\varphi xyz) \rightarrow [m\#x\ (\psi xyz) \rightarrow$
$O\ (k\#x\ (\chi xyz))]\}$.

The meaning of this in ordinary English is 'If someone has bought n pounds' worth of chalk from someone else, and the former has bought m pounds' worth of cheese from the latter, then the former has a legal obligation to pay the latter k pounds'. Note that an arbitrary pair of distinct commodities has to be specified in order to rule out the possibility that the second antecedent's truth conditions are wholly or partly satisfied by the first. Note also that we can no longer make use of the maximalist interpretation of numerals. In reckoning my debts I need to know, not how many pounds' worth of chalk *at most* I bought from you, but *exactly* how many. We have to make use of $n\#x\varphi x$, whose definition is given by (D3).

The substitution of a negative number for n, m, or k in the *definiendum* would be represented by adding the prefix 'inv' to one or more of the predicables φ, ψ, or χ in the *definiens*. Thus:

(D9–Neg) $S'n,-m,-k =_{df} \forall x\ \forall y\ \{n\#x\ (\varphi xyz) \rightarrow$
$[m\#x\ (\text{inv } \psi xyz) \rightarrow O\ (k\#x\ (\text{inv } \chi xyz))]\}$,

an instantiation of which is 'If Mary has bought seventy pounds' worth of chalk from Jane, then if Jane has bought ninety pounds' worth of cheese from Mary, Mary is twenty pounds in credit'. (Propositions of the form (D9–Neg) would be false if m was equal to or less than n.) Other interpretations could be given of φxyz and ψxyz in terms of movement in two directions along a line, rising and falling of temperature, acceleration and deceleration of a moving object, etc. '*S'nmk*' is supposed to capture the logical structure which all these have in common.

This provision for negative numbers was intended to allow us to affirm $\forall n\ \forall m\ \exists k\ (S'nmk)$ as readily as we affirm $\forall n\ \forall m\ \exists k$

(*Snmk*). To obtain this result it will be necessary to allow 3#, 7#, −2#, −4#, etc., to figure as substituends for *n*, *m*, and *k* in our formulae. This may revive Gottlieb's worries about the difficulty of producing a tidy version of the substitution rule for these variables. Instead of Neg Der, Neg Der Else, Neg Der Else Else, etc., we shall have to accommodate Ref₁ Conj Der Neg Der Else, Ref₁ Conj Der Neg Der Else Inv, and the like. And with the advent of rational and real numbers even more ragged substitution rules might be needed. But mere untidiness is a price I would be very willing to pay for deliverance from the army of abstract objects.

I have nothing but sketchy proposals to make here; and where rational and real numbers are concerned, I rely on Gottlieb's analyses.[9] But I remain convinced that the way to make negative, rational, and real numbers intelligible is not to construct dubious abstract objects such as sets, ordered pairs, etc., but to look again at the operations of addition, multiplication, and exponentiation in so far as they operate on these apparent objects. Realism thrives by concentrating on abstract objects: the urge to Realism is quietened by redirecting attention to the things we find ourselves apparently saying about such objects.

§ 18. Whatever the result of this reappraisal of the arithmetical operations, it will not, I believe, require the reintroduction of identity as a two-place first-level predicable. In Arithmetic, which is extensional, identity will be shown by identity of sign, difference by difference of sign. But this requires that there be, in the case of numbers, a contrast analogous to the contrast between names and definite descriptions. 'Thirty-three' must be distinguished in this way from 'the product of three and eleven'. We must even distinguish it from 'The successor of thirty-two', if this is thought of as having the same sense as 'The sum of thirty-two and one'. The quotifiers provided in the series (D5) and (D6) are

---

[9] To take account of multiplying negative numbers, (D9) and (D9–Neg) would have to be supplemented by the following adaptation of (D7): in addition to '$P0n0$' and '$Pn'mk \leftrightarrow \exists j\,(Pn, m, j\ \&\ S'j, m, k)$', we shall need '$P-0, n, 0$' and '$P-n', m, -k \leftrightarrow \exists j\,(P-n, m, j\ \&\ S'j, -m, -k)$'. With these axioms, '$P-1, -2, 2$' comes out appropriately true, since we have '$P-0, -2, 0$' and '$S0, -(-2), 2$'. We can equate '$-(-n)$' with 'n', because '$nx\,(\text{inv inv } \varphi xyz)$' is clearly equivalent to '$nx\,(\varphi xyz)$'. For Gottlieb's suggestions for the rational and real numbers, see *Ontological Economy*, ch. VII.

canonical symbols for the natural numbers. Neither '$(\imath n)(P11,3,n)$'
nor '$(\imath n)(S32,1,n)$' is to be regarded as a canonical symbol. Like
Russell we regard them as incomplete symbols.

With every extension of the concept of number there will have
to be an extension for the range of canonical symbols for numbers,
or, what is the same thing, substituends for the number variables,
n, m, k, etc. We have seen how '$-33\#$' and the like need to be
accommodated in this way. When it comes to rational numbers,
the symbols for fractions expressed in lowest terms will be the
canonical symbols. Thus $\frac{1}{3}$ will be canonical; but 'the number
obtained by dividing five by fifteen', and, for that matter, 'the
number obtained by dividing one by three', whose symbolical
expressions in Russellese are $(\imath n)(Pn,15,5)$ and $(\imath m)(Pm,3,1)$, will
be definite descriptions and incomplete symbols.

'The number obtained by dividing five by fifteen is different
from the number obtained by dividing eleven by forty-four' will be
written

$$\exists n\ \exists m\ (Pn,15,5\ \&\ Pm,44,11)$$

(We may discharge the clauses securing the uniqueness of the
results of division, as of addition, subtraction and multiplication,
of any two numbers, since they are all necessarily true.) This will
be true because we have the instantiation

$$P\tfrac{1}{3},15,5\ \&\ P\tfrac{1}{4},44,11$$

which is true. If we counted

$$P\tfrac{5}{15},33,11\ \&\ P\tfrac{11}{33},15,5,$$

as an instantiation of

$$\exists n\ \exists m\ (Pn,33,11\ \&\ Pm,15,5)$$

we should have to regard the proposition 'The number obtained by
dividing 33 by 11 is different from the number obtained by dividing
15 by 5' as true. In consequence, '$\frac{11}{33} = \frac{5}{15}$' would be false, but
this is just the sort of proposition which we should wish to call a
true statement of identity in this field. To prevent this result we
shall have to disallow expressions of fractions otherwise than in
their lowest terms, like '$\frac{11}{33}$' and '$\frac{5}{15}$', as substituends for n and m
in quantified propositions of this sort, and permit only one symbol,
'$\frac{1}{3}$' as the canonical expression of this fraction. Expressions like
'$\frac{11}{33}$' and '$\frac{5}{15}$' will be mere abbreviations of $(\imath n)(Pn,33,11)$ and
$(\imath m)(Pm,15,5)$, etc.

If further extensions of the concept of number are responsive to the same treatment, we shall be entitled to say that any identity propositions involving numbers will be subject to the sort of analysis which this book is proposing for other varieties of identity proposition. In this analysis identity of number will show itself by identity of numerical variable, difference of numbers by difference of variables. I do not foresee the Arithmetic of the rational or real numbers emerging as the Waterloo for the Wittgensteinian theory of identity. But there is an element of blind faith is this statement.

THE IDENTITY OF EVENTS

§ 1. Aristotle made a distinction between 'numerical' and 'specific' identity which has passed almost into common speech. Certainly, the ambiguity he was concerned to pin down is a feature of everyday language. Your wife comes home from a meeting of the Women's Institute in a state of fury. 'She was wearing the same dress I bought at County Clothes last week!', she shouts, referring to the visiting speaker. Now it is just possible that your house was burgled two days ago, and that amongst the objects missing is the dress your wife bought at 'County Clothes' last week. Are we to suppose that the burglar is the visiting speaker's son, or that the visiting speaker is a fence? An unlikely scenario. A much more probable interpretation is that your wife and the visiting speaker have both bought dresses of the same model, tokens of the same type. Her next remark makes it clear that this *is* what she means: 'Thank Goodness I didn't put *mine* on to go to the WI'. If she had done that, the state of affairs produced would have been even more likely to provoke her to a state of fury than the theft of the particular token dress she bought last week. Wearing the same dress as the visiting speaker, in this sense, is a well-known category of disaster.

Since the second interpretation of the cry of distress is correct, we must recognize that your wife's cry amounts to a claim only of 'specific' identity. Why 'only'? Is specific identity a weaker, watered-down variety of identity, unworthy of philosophical attention? Is it so called only in what Butler referred to as the 'loose and popular', as opposed to the 'strict and philosophical', sense of identity?[1] Did Aristotle lose his grip on the concept of

---

[1] Cf. R. M. Chisholm, 'The Loose and Popular and the Strict and Philosophical Senses of Identity', in N. S. Care and R. H. Grimm (eds.), *Perception and Personal Identity*, Cleveland, Ohio: Case Western University Press, 1969. Butler's distinction is made in his dissertation 'Of Personal Identity', which is probably most accessible

identity, showing, in his first treatment of it in the *Topics*, a proper appreciation of Leibniz's Law, but then falling from grace[2] and introducing senses of 'same' in which it differs in meaning from 'identical', lapsing in his later writings into a notion of 'specific' identity, which confuses identity with similarity?[3]

I do not believe that this 'down-grading' of specific identity is the least bit justified. 'She was wearing the same dress as the one I bought last week' can be analysed in either of the following ways:

(18A) For some dress x, both I bought x (and no other dress) last week and she was wearing x

and

(18B) For some φ, both the dress I bought last week φ's and the dress the visiting speaker was wearing φ's.

In the last case some pretty tight restrictions are needed on substitutions for φ. A substitution for φ will be truly predicable of each of a pair of dresses only if each is a token of the same type, in a sense of 'token' and 'type' which has to be explained in terms of 'models' and processes of manufacture of dresses which are neither too 'up-market' nor too 'down-market'. But φ is nonetheless a genuine predicative variable.

The idea that 'identical' means something different from 'same' is wholly mistaken. It may on occasion be used for emphasis. When the stress in the spoken sentence is desired to fall on the word expressing identity, 'same' may be found too slight a word for the purpose. 'She was wearing the *same* dress I bought at County Clothes last week' sounds wrong: 'She was wearing the *identical* dress I bought at County Clothes last week' is what is needed. But this can still be interpreted as meaning what (18B) sets out rather than what (18A) sets out. 'Identical' may in some way be stronger than 'same', but that doesn't tie it to numerical as opposed to specific identity.

as reprinted in J. Perry (ed.), *Personal Identity*, University of California Press, 1975, pp. 100–1.

[2] Cf. P. T. Geach's view of Aristotle's beliefs about subject and predicate: 'Aristotle, like Adam, began right, but soon wandered into a wrong path, with disastrous consequences for his posterity'. From 'A History of the Corruptions of Logic', Geach's inaugural lecture at Leeds, repr. in *Logic Matters*, Oxford: Basil Blackwell, 1972, p. 44.

[3] This is a view put forward by N. P. White, in 'Aristotle on Sameness and Oneness', *Philosophical Review*, 80 (1971), pp. 177–97.

§ 2. Both (18A) and (18B) involve the repeated use of a variable bound by the existential quantifier. (18A) could be analysed as being of the form $\exists x \ (\varphi x \ \& \ \psi x)$, or, avoiding variables, $\text{Der}_0 \ \text{Ref}_0$ Conj $\varphi\psi$. If we allow ourselves to give dresses names, and substitute 'Ethel' for 'the dress I bought last week' and 'Bessie' for 'the dress the visiting speaker was wearing', (18B) will then be of the form $\exists\varphi \ (\varphi a \ \& \ \varphi b)$, or $\text{Der}_1 \ \text{Ref}_1$ Conj ab[4] ('For some φ, both φ Ethel and φ Bessie'). 'Ref$_0$' and 'Ref$_1$' made their original appearance in the last chapter. 'Der$_0$' and 'Der$_1$' have only raised their ugly heads in this paragraph. 'Der$_0$' does the same job as $\exists x$, an existential quantifier suitable for binding name variables. 'Der$_1$' does the same job as $\exists\varphi$, namely binding predicative variables. If 'Der$_0$' is a second-level predicable, 'Der$_1$' is third-level predicable. 'Der' and $\exists$ do not in themselves belong to any syntactical category. This is true of the quantifiers even before we introduce higher-order quantification. Using Geach's notation for designating syntactical categories,[5] $\exists x$ in $\exists x \ (\varphi x)$ is of the category :s:sn—it forms a proposition from a one-place predicable of first level. But $\exists x$ in $\exists x \ (\psi xx)$ is of the category :s::snn (or :s:s(2n))—it forms a proposition from a two-place predicable of first level. Since $\exists x$ is capable of combining with first-level predicables of any number of places to produce a complete proposition, there is no limit to the

---

[4] The rule for the use of 'Ref$_0$' is that a repeated occurrence of an individual (nominal) variable or name at the end of a sentence can be deleted and 'Ref$_0$' simultaneously placed in front of the sentence. As we have seen, this requires possibly iterated applications of the inversion operators to position the repeated names or variables at the end of a sentence. The same mechanism could be used for 'Ref$_1$', but the result would be so far removed from ordinary language that it would be difficult to obtain a quick understanding of what was taking place. Thus (18B), unamended, is of the form $\exists\varphi \ (\imath x \psi x \varphi x \ \& \ \imath y \chi y \varphi y)$. Three predicative expressions are involved in the matrix of this quantified formula, and if the repeated variable were deleted and 'Ref$_1$' prefixed to the remaining sub-formula we should obtain Ref$_1$ Conj $\imath x \psi x \varphi x \imath y \chi yy$. This, however, would correspond, not to the matrix we started with, but to Conj $\imath x \psi x \varphi x \imath y \chi y \chi y$, since reflection operated on repeated elements occurring at the end of a formula. To avoid this, major and minor inversion are required to convert Conj $\imath x \psi x \varphi x \imath y \chi y \chi y \varphi y$ to Inv$_1$ inv$_1$ Inv$_1$ Conj $\imath x \chi x \psi x \imath y \varphi y \varphi y$, and the formula using reflection would thus be Ref$_1$ Inv$_1$ inv$_1$ Inv$_1$ Conj $\imath x \chi x \psi x \imath y \chi yy$. The whole quantified formula $\exists\varphi \ (\imath x \psi x \varphi x \ \& \ \imath y \chi y \varphi y)$ would thus come out as Der$_1$ Ref$_1$ Inv$_1$ inv$_1$ Inv$_1$ Conj $\imath x \chi x \psi x \imath y \chi y \varphi y$. I leave it to the reader, should he perhaps become intoxicated by the idea of a variable-free notation, to reduce (or rather expand) this formula, via the Russellian Theory of Descriptions, to the pure language of Quine's 'Variables Explained Away'.

[5] P. T. Geach, 'A Program for Syntax', in D. Davidson and G. Harman (eds.), *Semantics for Natural Languages*, 2nd edn., Dordrecht and Boston, Mass.: Reidel, 1972, pp. 483–97.

number of syntactical categories to which it could be said to belong. In this respect 'Der$_0$' is more circumscribed than $\exists x$: it only forms a proposition from a one-place predicable of first level. It is thus of the form :s:sn. Nor will 'Der$_1$', as $\exists \varphi$ will, need on occasion to be categorized as ::s:s:sn:s:sn or as :s:s::snn, and so on. Equipped with its subscript, 'Der' is categorially better behaved than $\exists$, even when $\exists$ is attached to a determinate category of variable.

'Ref' too escapes from the categorial net in this way, and needs subscripts in order to be tied down. Ref$_0$ is of the category ::sn::snn—it makes a one-place predicable of first level out of a two-place predicable of first level. Ref$_1$ is of the category ::snn:sn::snn:sn:sn—it makes a one-place predicable of second level out of a two-place predicable of second level.

We should not be surprised that 'Der' and 'Ref' transcend the categories[6] in this way. As we saw in Chapter IV, they do the work of variables, and variables can come in every category. One of the functions of variables that I did not mention in Chapter IV is to indicate the category of expression whose substitution will provide instantiation of a quantified proposition. Thus the presence of x in '$\exists x$ (x is coming to dinner)' shows that 'Susan is coming to dinner' is an instantiation of it, and the presence of p in '$\forall p$ ($p \rightarrow$ The Headmaster knows that p)' shows that 'If Jones was absent, the Headmaster knows that Jones was absent' is an instantiation of *it*. This function of variables cannot be performed by 'Ref' and 'Der' without some modification of the kind I have provided by subscripts. In themselves, however, 'Ref' and 'Der'[7] do not belong to one category rather than another. Identity, like existence, transcends the categories.

We can, therefore, cheerfully produce identity propositions about colours, shapes, textures, thoughts, and numbers as well as about objects. Where φ_c is a variable having colour predicates as its substitution instances 'For some φ_c, both φ_c the dress and φ_c the accessories' means the same as 'The colour of the accessories is the same as that of the dress' (or 'The accessories are self-coloured'). Similarly 'For some φ_s, both φ_s the window and φ_s the door' means 'The shape of the window is the same as the shape of the door', 'For some φ_t, both φ_t the petals and φ_t the leaves' means

---

[6] As the medievals said of the 'transcendentalia': *ens, verum, unum et bonum.*

[7] And, for that matter, 'Inv'. We might write $\neg \ \forall x \ \forall \varphi \ \forall \psi \ [(\varphi x \rightarrow \psi x) \rightarrow (\psi x \rightarrow \varphi x)]$ thus: Der$_0$ Der$_1$ Der$_1$ Ref$_0$ Ref$_0$ Ref$_0$ Ref$_1$ Ref$_1$ Inv$_1$ Conj Imp Neg Imp.

'The texture of the petals is the same as that of the leaves', 'For some p, both John is thinking that p and Mary is thinking that p' means 'Mary's thought is the same as John's', and 'For some n, both nx (x is a girl) and ny (y is a boy)'[8] means 'The number of girls is the same as the number of boys.

§ 3. How do events fit into this system? Recent philosophers have shown considerable interest in the identity of events. By no means all of these philosophers have been aware of any difficulties involved in saying such things as 'The lightning flash was the same as a massive discharge of electricity in the atmosphere' or 'The tickle Bill felt was the firing of certain neurones in his cerebral cortex'. Donald Davidson is an exception. He is under the misapprehension that all identity propositions must be about objects ('No identity without entity'),[9] and that if we are going to allow ourselves to say that event A is the same as event B, we shall have to reckon events as objects ('admit events to our ontology'). However, I have just been producing reasons for thinking this is an unnecessary worry. Davidson's justification of his 'ontological commitment' to events can, I believe, be left on one side. Identity is relevant to innumerable categories other than objects.

Davidson evidently feels a need to justify talk about the identity of events. He appeals to intuition to prove that there is a such a thing as event-identity.

We can easily frame identity statements about individual events; examples (true or false) might be:

The death of Scott = the death of the author of *Waverley*.

The assassination of the Archduke Ferdinand = the event that started the First World War.

The eruption of Vesuvius = the cause of the destruction of Pompeii.

(*Essays on Actions and Events*, Oxford: Clarendon Press, 1980, p. 210.)

The first of these examples has little to do with event identity. It is a trivial consequence of Scott's being the author of *Waverley*. With '=' instead of an English phrase, we do not even know how the verb is supposed to be tensed. It might represent a remark of George IV to the effect that when Scott dies it *will* be the death of

---

[8] For an explanation of quotifiers like 'nx' and 'ny' see ch. vii, § 3.

[9] D. Davidson, *Essays on Actions and Events*, Oxford: Clarendon Press, 1980, p. 164.

the author of *Waverley*. So we cannot even take it as saying that Scott *is* dead. It tells us nothing more than the fact that Scott wrote *Waverley*.

The remaining examples are more interesting, but still in a certain way unsatisfactory. They are analogous to the propositions about objects which in Chapter II were said to be of the form (K). Just as 'Scott was the author of *Waverley*' can be paraphrased by 'Scott wrote *Waverley* and no two people wrote *Waverley*', so 'The eruption of Vesuvius in AD 79 = the cause of the destruction of Pompeii' can be paraphrased by 'The eruption of Vesuvius in AD 79 caused the destruction of Pompeii and no two things caused the destruction of Pompeii'. The denial that two people wrote *Waverley* strikes one as superfluous, since it is so unusual for two people to co-author a novel that we hardly need to be told in any particular case that this is *not* what happened. The denial that two things caused the destruction of Pompeii will be thought by some to be even more superfluous, on the grounds that it would be self-contradictory to affirm that two things caused anything at all. Be that as it may, propositions of this form seem to have little to do with identity as such. The first clause in each case seems to be of the simplest subject predicate form: 'Scott wrote *Waverley*', 'Vesuvius's eruption caused the destruction of Pompeii'. If any relation is involved, it is not the alleged relation of identity. According to Russell's doctrine, the negation of identity is required for the second clause; but we have followed Wittgenstein in maintaining that it is not needed even there. Exactly the same doubts can be raised about the second of Davidson's examples: it seems to say that the assassination of the Archduke started the First World War and that no two events started it.

Expressions like 'the event that started the First World War' and 'the cause of the destruction of Pompeii' are obviously definite descriptions. (I shall be giving reasons in § 7 below for not regarding 'the assassination of the Archduke' or 'the eruption of Vesuvius' in this light.) Davidson's examples fit comfortably the first Russellian pattern for representing identity propositions, those which contain one definite description. This is the type of proposition which in Chapter II was given, first the Russellian analysis formalized by (F), and later the Wittgensteinian analysis formalized by (K). It is the type of proposition described by Geach as one in which the definite description is 'used predicatively or attributively'.[10] It is a mistake to think that the 'is' in 'Smith is the man who broke the bank at Monte Carlo' is a copula of identity; rather, Geach holds, the predicable '--- is *the* man who broke the bank at Monte Carlo' is analysable as '--- is *a* man who broke the bank at Monte Carlo and only --- is a man who broke the bank at Monte Carlo'. In Polish, Geach tells us, a definite description in such a case would 'bear a predicative inflection, even if it came first in the sentence' (as e.g. in 'The King of France at that time was Louis XV'). If this is right, Davidson's second and third examples are not identity propositions at all.

When *is* an identity proposition an identity proposition? Geach rejects examples like 'Scott is the author of *Waverley*' with the remark that it is 'quite wrong' to take the 'is' in such propositions as a copula of identity. This presupposes that there is such a thing as a copula of identity, but that it occurs elsewhere, not in these propositions. If not in these propositions, which I have argued have the form exhibited by (K), it must occur in propositions which have the form exhibited by (L), since these are the only possible forms for usable, informative identity propositions to take. But '--- is ......' or '--- is the same as ......', as a two-place predicable, does not occur in (L) either. What does occur in (L) is a repeated variable bound by a quantifier, which, in the vocabulary developed in Chapters III and IV, would require the Xi-operator or 'Ref' for its expression. These, I have argued, are the perspicuous forms for an expression of identity to take. Where they are present, implicitly or explicitly, the concept of identity is in use. They are present in propositions which contain *two* definite descriptions, those whose Wittgensteinian analysis is given by (L). They are not present in propositions which contain only one definite description, those whose Wittgensteinian analysis is given by (K).

§ 4. Can we find clear examples of propositions containing two definite descriptions of an event, whose analysis would require something closer to (L) than to (K)? What about this?

> (19) The event Henrietta reported was the event which caused the vase to be broken.

Let us suppose that Henrietta reported the neighbours' cat jumping through the window and that it was the cat's jumping

[10] *Reference and Generality*, pp. 74, 150.

through the window which caused the vase to be broken. With φx read as 'Henrietta reported x' and ψx as 'x caused the vase to be broken', (19) seems to be represented accurately by (L). What the first conjunct of (L) represents can, and in certain cases should, be analysed as having the form $\exists x \; \Xi u \; [\varphi u \; \& \; \psi u] \; x$ or $\mathrm{Der}_0 \; \mathrm{Ref}_0$ $\mathrm{Conj} \; \varphi\psi$; so the concept of identity is certainly involved here.

The remarks just made seem to imply that event-identity is simply a species of the genus object-identity. Do we then have to follow Davidson and agree that the concept of identity is involved here only if events are recognized as a type of objects? Was it correct to use individual variables or the zero subscript for 'Ref' in the characterization of the logical form of (19)? Let us go back to the instantiation of (19) suggested earlier:

(20) Henrietta reported the neighbours' cat jumping through the window and the neighbours' cat's jumping through the window caused the vase to be broken.

It is easy to rephrase this:

(20A) Henrietta reported that the neighbours' cat jumped through the window and the vase was broken because the neighbours' cat jumped through the window.

An existential generalization of this is

(19A) For some p, both Henrietta reported that p and the vase was broken because p.

(19) no doubt presupposes that no two events were reported (on the relevant occasion) by Henrietta, and that just one thing caused the vase to break. If we added all this to (19A) we should have a proposition of the form

(19L) $[\exists p \; (\delta_1 p \; \& \; \delta_2 p) \; \& \; \neg \; \exists q \; \exists r \; (\delta_1 q \; \& \; \delta_1 r)]$
$\& \; \neg \; \exists s \; \exists t \; (\delta_2 s \; \& \; \delta_2 t)$.

Here p, q, r, s, t are propositional variables and δ_1 and δ_2 are variables of category :ss (their substitution instances form propositions out of propositions). (19L), I maintain, gives a clearer picture than we have yet had of the logical form of propositions like (19), genuine propositions of event identity. If we were to represent the first conjunct of (19L) in the variable-free notation with identity explicitly symbolized by the reflection operator, that operator would have to be indexed by a subscript appropriate for the category of propositions, or some narrower category of event-stating propositions. What that category is, or what the subscript is that should be allotted to it, I do not wish to decide;[11] but it is clear that the zero subscript is *not* appropriate. With δ_1 and δ_2 understood in the way I have indicated, $\text{Der}_0 \text{ Ref}_0 \text{ Conj } \delta_1 \delta_2$ would be actually ill-formed.

§ 5. We seem to have come to a clear understanding of propositions which state event identity, by noting both their similarities to, and their differences from propositions which state object identity. But why did we have to invent (19) in order to achieve this classification? (19) was imported in order to have an identity proposition containing *two* definite descriptions of events. Davidson's examples contained the definite descriptions 'the event which started the First World War' and 'the cause of the destruction of Pompeii'. But they also contained the phrases 'The assassination of the Archduke Ferdinand' and 'The eruption of Vesuvius in AD 79'. Why the insistence that Davidson's (relevant) examples contained only *one* definite description of an event apiece?

We may begin at an intuitive and superficial level. Definite descriptions can be regimented to the very limited extent of rephrasing them with the help of the circumlocution 'the x such that ...... x ......'. Thus 'the author of *Waverley*' can be expanded to 'the x such that x wrote *Waverley*', and 'the birthplace of Boscovich' to 'the x such that Boscovich was born in x'. Even if we use (with Davidson) a special category of variable for events, we can rewrite 'the cause of the destruction of Pompeii' as 'the e such that e caused the destruction of Pompeii'. Davidson's other example is almost in this form already: 'the e such that e started the First World War'. This operation, however, cannot plausibly be carried out in the case of 'The assassination of the Archduke ⟨Franz-⟩Ferdinand'. 'The e such that e = the assassination of the archduke' is clearly a cheat. It depends, for a start, on taking '=' as a two-place predicable. The other expressions we looked at had words standing for genuine relations in the position: 'the e such that e caused ......', 'the e such that e started ......'. If identity is admitted as a relation which can enter into the deep structure of a definite description, *any* expression could be forced into the

---

[11] If we take seriously the categorization of propositions as no-place predicables, the correct subscript is '1'.

definite description mould: 'Scott' could reappear as 'the x such that x = Scott'. And a vicious regress lies in wait: why stop at 'the e such that e = the assassination of the archduke' and not proceed to 'the e such that e = the e such that e = the assassination of the archduke'. We had better hold back from the first move and resist the temptation to twist 'the assassination of the archduke' into the 'the e such that e ......' form. The same reluctance to accept this 'definite description form' is exhibited by 'the eruption of Vesuvius in AD 79'.

§ 6. This so far intuitive and undeveloped feeling about certain designations of events is not simply a point Davidson has missed: it is an outright rejection of a point on which he insists. In his seminal paper 'The Logical Form of Action Sentences', Davidson proposes that

verbs of action—verbs that say 'what someone did'—should be construed as containing a place, for singular terms or variables, that they do not appear to. For example, we would normally suppose that 'Shem kicked Shaun' consisted in two names and a two-place predicate. I suggest, though, that we think of 'kicked' as a *three*-place predicate, and that the sentence to [*sic*] be given in this form:

(17) $(\exists x)$(kicked (Shem, Shaun, x)).

(Ibid., p. 118.)

By the time Davidson wrote his paper 'Causal Relations' he had instituted the practice of using e as a variable appropriate for the category of events, and was combining it with the definite description operator:

To do justice to 'Jack's fall caused the breaking of Jack's crown' what we need is something like 'The one and only falling down of Jack caused the one and only breaking of his crown by Jack'; in some symbols of the trade, '$(\imath e)F$(Jack, e) caused the $(\imath e)B$(Jack's crown, e)'. (Ibid., p. 155.)

The rule seems to be to take any sentence which would normally be thought to report an event, e.g., 'Jack fell', and to convert whatever predicable it contains from an n to an $(n+1)$-place predicable, to fill the extra argument place with an event variable and bind this with the definite description operator. Thus '--- fell' becomes '--- fell ......', a relational predicable which relates Jack . . . to what? This is the mystery about Davidson's jargon. We understand 'The x such that Joan married x' because we already understand the expression '--- married ......' as a two-place predicable that could relate Joan to, say, Harold. We can understand 'The p such that the policeman said that p' (i.e., 'What the policeman said') because we can understand '--- said that ......' as a 'relator'[12] which links a name to a proposition, e.g., 'The door was unlocked'. But how are we to understand 'The e such that Jack fell e'? What constant could provide a substitution for e here, or for x in '$(\exists x)(\text{kicked (Shem, Shaun, } x))$'? How are we to understand the variables if we have no idea what could function as a substituend for them? And how are we to make sense of 'kicked' as a three-place predicable, or to interpret 'F' in Davidson's formula '$(\imath e)\, F\,(\text{Jack, } e)$'.

In one place Davidson gives what seems to be intended as an answer to this question:

Take as an example 'Sebastian strolled': this may be construed along lines suggested by 'Sebastian took a stroll'. 'There is an x such that x is a stroll and Sebastian took x' is more ornate than necessary, since there is nothing an agent can do with a stroll except take it; thus we may capture all there is with 'There is an x such that Sebastian strolled x'. (Ibid. p. 167.)

This suggests that 'Jack fell e' or 'Sebastian strolled x' are to be understood by analogy with 'Margaret danced a dance' or 'Joseph dreamed a dream' or 'Henry hit a six'. The accusatives are internal accusatives. But we get into trouble if we take such accusatives as specifying terms of genuine relations, as external accusatives do. 'Bonzo fights only what he hates; Bonzo has fought many cats; *ergo* Bonzo hates cats' is a valid argument. Not so 'Bonzo fights only what he hates; Bonzo has fought many fights; *ergo* Bonzo hates fights'. The internal accusative in 'Fight the good fight', etc., has sometimes been called an adverbial accusative. With less resonance, but without change of meaning, we could say 'Fight well'. To dance a waltz is to dance in a particular way, namely to waltz. Instead of forming a new, specific, verb to take the place of the generic 'dance', we add an internal accusative. We do not have a verb 'to gavotte' as we have the verb 'to waltz'; but if we had, it would mean no more and no less than 'to dance a gavotte'. In the same way, we have a specific verb 'to itch', which means no more

---

[12] To use Timothy Potts's useful label. See M. Dummett, *Frege: The Philosophy of Language*, London: Duckworth, 1973, p. 269.

and no less than 'to feel an itch', but lack (in English) a corresponding specific verb to match 'to feel a pain'. In all these cases the appearance of a relation, of a genuine two-place predicable, is an illusion. So it is in 'Sebastian took a stroll', and this can lend no plausibility to the neologisms 'There is an x such that Sebastian strolled x' and '($\imath e$) F (Jack, e)'.

§ 7. I believe that the use of the definite article in phrases like 'The eruption of Vesuvius in AD 79' and 'The assassination of the Archduke Franz-Ferdinand' has misled Davidson into thinking that what we have here are definite descriptions. What we have in fact are what I call 'direct nominalizations' of propositions like 'Vesuvius erupted in AD 79' and 'The Archduke Franz-Ferdinand was assassinated'. Such nominalizations are constructed by replacing the main verb of the proposition by the corresponding verbal noun or gerund and putting the subject or the object of the proposition into the genitive case: 'Vesuvius's eruption' or 'the assassination of the Archduke'. In other contexts the word 'of', or the genitive case, can signify or help to signify a relation— paradigmatically that of possession. In the phrase 'the pen of my aunt' the 'of' is synonymous to 'belonging to', whereas 'my' is equivalent to 'of me', where the 'of' has no independent meaning, but is part of the relational expression 'aunt of'. In the case of direct nominalizations, however, the genitive, which grammarians used to call a 'subjective' or 'objective genitive', does not signify any relation at all. It is simply a part of the transformation which converts a proposition into a noun phrase. The fact that the genitive does not correspond to, or even contribute to a correspondence with, a relation on a par with 'cause of' or 'start of' is a further reason for refusing to treat direct nominalizations as definite descriptions.

Davidson is worried that the converse transformation from phrase designating an event ('the eruption of Vesuvius in AD 79') to proposition reporting it ('Vesuvius erupted in AD 79') may involve a loss of uniqueness: perhaps Vesuvius erupted several times in AD 79. However, the difficulty is, in my view, a feature, not of the propositional form as such, but of the aorist tense or of the way in which the time is specified. 'Doris capsized the canoe yesterday' is, as Davidson says, 'no less true . . . if she capsized it a dozen times than if she capsized it once'; but 'Doris capsized the canoe at 11.17 a.m. yesterday' is fully determinate, and so is 'Vesuvius *was erupting* in May of AD 79'. Davidson's problems are to be solved by taking a closer look at the logic of tenses and the distinction between 'time within which' and 'time at which', rather than by squeezing all talk about events into alleged definite descriptions.

A genuine definite description is replaceable by the expression taking its place in the proposition which, in Prior's terminology, would provide 'the verifier' of the proposition containing it. Thus 'the author of *Waverley* was Scotch' is verified by 'Scott alone wrote *Waverley* and Scott was Scotch'. (20) is in this sense the verifier of (19). What 'the x such that x wrote *Waverley*' designates indirectly[13] 'Scott' designates directly. Similarly, what 'the event Henrietta reported' (or '(ɹe) reported (Henrietta, e)') designates indirectly, 'the neighbours' cat jumping through the window' designates directly. Definite descriptions, if they can be said to designate at all, designate indirectly; and if an expression designates indirectly that must be by way of contrast with some other expression whose mode of designation is direct. But what more direct way could there be of designating the cat's jumping through the window than by the phrase 'the cat's jumping through the window'? Where definite descriptions of events are indirect designations of them, direct nominalizations are, as their name indicates, direct.

Here is a further mark of a direct designator: an expression which merits this description enables us to reconstruct the proposition which would report the event designated. Easily understood grammatical rules make it possible to pass from 'the assassination of the Archduke Franz-Ferdinand' to 'The Archduke Franz-Ferdinand was assassinated'. (No need to worry in this case about the possibility of its happening several times.) No such rules allow us to set out the proposition which reports the event indirectly designated by the phrase 'the event which started the First World War'. Definite descriptions of events, like definite descriptions of persons or other objects, do not in virtue of their meaning provide us with an answer to the question 'What event?' or 'Which person do you mean?' If someone speaks of the author of *Waverley*, I can intelligibly ask 'Who are you referring to?' and

---

[13] For the terminology of 'verifiers' and 'indirect designation', see A. N. Prior, *Objects of Thought*, Oxford: Clarendon Press, 1971, p. 160.

be told 'Scott'. If someone speaks of the cause of the destruction of Pompeii, I can once more ask 'Why was Pompeii destroyed?' and be told 'Because Vesuvius erupted in AD 79'. But if the event is referred to by a direct nominalization there is no such question to ask. I already know how to report the event that is being spoken of.

§ 8. We may compare direct nominalizations with Kripke's 'rigid designators', which I glanced at at the end of Chapter II. Non-rigid designators are those which in different possible worlds designate different objects. There are possible worlds in which 'the inventor of bifocals' does not designate Benjamin Franklin. In the same way non-rigid designators of events are those which in different possible worlds designate different events. 'The cause of the vase being broken' could easily have been other than the neighbours' cat jumping through the window: possible worlds in which this is so do not have to be very different from this one. Again, it is not logically necessary that the words 'the event which started the First World War', given the meaning that they have, should refer to the assassination of the Archduke, or that the words 'the cause of the destruction of Pompeii' should refer to the eruption of Vesuvius. Pompeii might have been destroyed by a tidal wave, and the First World War might have been started by the assassination of a Grand Duke in Lithuania rather than by that of an Archduke in Bosnia-Herzegovina. But it is difficult to see how the words 'the neighbours' cat jumping through the window' could refer to another event than that to which they do refer without suffering a change in their meaning—or, rather, we could not suppose the event referred to to be different unless the objects referred to were different: the neighbours might of course have had a different cat. This distraction can be removed. (It is an irrelevance similar to that of Davidson's first example.) 'The event which caused Jack to break his crown' is a non-rigid designation of Jack's falling down: there are possible worlds in which Jack's crown is broken as a result of some other disaster. We can see this by noticing that different 'namely-riders' can be added to 'the event which caused Jack to break his crown': as well as 'namely, his falling down' we can say 'namely, Bill's hitting him over the head with a stick' or 'namely, Jill's throwing the rolling pin at him'. But 'Jack's falling down' does not attract namely-riders in this way. My whole contention is that the notion of event-identity is obscure, and it does not become any less obscure when it is 'trans-world' identity which we are considering. But it appears unlikely that 'Jack's falling down in Banbury at 4 o'clock on Christmas Day 1984' could refer to any other event than that to which it does refer (supposing that Jack does fall down at that time in that place). Those direct nominalizations which themselves contain only rigid designators of the objects figuring in the events they designate must, it seems, themselves be rigid designators of these events.

Not all definite descriptions in Kripke's view are non-rigid designators. 'The square of six' designates the number it does in every possible world. It may nevertheless be said to designate indirectly what 'thirty-six' designates directly. So the terms 'rigid designator' and 'direct designator' are not co-extensive. Proper names, however, which are the paradigm of direct designators, are all, for Kripke, rigid designators. What proper names are for objects, direct nominalizations are for events. It seems that direct designators must all be rigid, even if the converse is false.

Kripke's view, as I recalled in Chapter II, is that where both terms of an identity proposition are rigid designators the proposition is, if true, necessarily true. Thus he agrees with Russell in holding that 'Scott is the same as Sir Walter', where both 'Scott' and 'Sir Walter' are being used as proper names, is necessarily true. What analogue of this can be found in the case of propositions which state event identities? Davidson's examples and my own (19) all have non-rigid designators on at least one side of the identity sign. It might well be wondered what could count as a true identity proposition with a rigid designator in each of the argument positions. An overt tautology might count: 'Jack's falling down was the same event as Jack's falling down' would be analogous to 'Scott is the same as Scott'. A proposition where one of the words on the left-hand side of the identity sign is replaced on the right-hand side by a synonym might also count: 'Jack's falling down was the same event as Jack's tumbling down' would go into the same category as 'Scott is the same as Sir Walter'. On Russell's view, and on the view propounded above in Chapter VI, different proper names of the same object are synonymous.

§ 9. Kripke, of course, has more interesting targets to shoot at. The so-called 'Identity Theorists' had held that events described in purely mental terms like 'the pain Bill felt five minutes ago' and events described in purely physical terms like 'the firing of the C-fibres in Bill's cerebral cortex five minutes ago' might be discovered, a posteriori and as a matter of contingent fact, to be identical. Kripke argues that designators like 'the pain Bill felt five minutes ago' and 'the firing of Bill's C-fibres' are rigid. Each designates the same event in any possible world in which it designates any event at all. If, then, they designate the same event as each other in this world, they cannot designate different events from each other in any possible world. In that case, the identity proposition 'The pain Bill felt five minutes ago was the same event as the firing of the C-fibres in Bill's cerebral cortex five minutes ago' must, if true at all, be necessarily true. The Identity Theorists maintain, with great emphasis, that such propositions are not necessarily true. Kripke is therefore able to construct an *ad hominem* argument to show that their claims are false.

I think we can do better than that. If Wittgenstein is right about identity propositions, it is not just false but senseless to assert an identity proposition which contains a direct nominalization on each side of the identity sign. Propositions like Davidson's second and third examples, which have a direct nominalization on one side only of the identity sign, make perfectly good sense, but, as we have seen, are not in fact identity propositions at all. They are analogous to propositions whose form is given by (K) of Chapter II, which contains no expression whatsoever of the concept of identity. Propositions like my (19) which contain definite descriptions on either side of the identity sign are analogous to those whose form is given by (L). They do employ the concept of identity and can be expressed in a way which gives explicit indication of that concept by some logically perspicuous sign like $\equiv$ or 'Ref'. But they do this only because they are also existential generalizations, because their perspicuous expression also requires an operator like $\exists$ or 'Der'. Containing indirect designators they must be capable of significant replacement by propositions containing the corresponding direct designators, as 'The author of *Waverley* is the same as the author of *Marmion*' is replaceable by 'Scott wrote *Waverley* and Scott wrote *Marmion*'. A genuine identity proposition of this sort is an existential proposition which must *salva congruitate* be exchangeable for an instantiating proposition—what Prior would call a 'verifier'. Thus (20) could be seen as the existential instantiation of (19). But what would count as the existential instantiation of 'The pain which Bill felt five minutes ago was the same event as the firing of the C-fibres in Bill's cerebral cortex five minutes ago'? What event *was* it that was felt by Bill as a pain and observed on the electro-encephalograph as a firing of C-fibres? Without identity as a relation the propositions of the Identity Theorists are all, as Wittgenstein would say, 'pseudo-propositions'.

§ **10.** Even with identity as a relation, in the way envisaged in the eirenic parts of Chapter V, things are no better for the Identity Theorists. Identity there was explained extensionally, in terms of the set of pairs of objects which satisfy this two-place predicable. These pairs are just those which consist of an object taken twice over. If *this* is our understanding of '--- is the same as ......', it is after all important that events should be objects of a kind. 'Ontological commitment' to events would be necessary for this interpretation of event identity. I think there would be pressing Nominalist objections to such a commitment. But for now I am happy to waive these objections. Suppose that 'The pain Bill felt five minutes ago was the same as the firing of Bill's C-fibres five minutes ago' is true because just one object is named twice over in the sentence. Understood extensionally in this way it says exactly what is said by 'The pain Bill felt five minutes ago was the same as the pain Bill felt five minutes ago'. In so far as a proposition is construed as a two-place predicate attached to two names or two occurrences of a name, what it is designed to communicate is entirely determined by the object or objects named and the meaning of the predicate. *But*, it will be said, this ignores the Fregean distinction between sense and meaning. Maybe; and maybe rightly, since I believe there are insuperable objections to Fregean doctrines about the sense of a proper name. But again, let these objections be waived. If the importance of the proposition about Bill lies in the fact that the two event-designations have the same meaning but a different sense, let this important fact be stated explicitly. There is something which can be referred to both as a pain felt by Bill five minutes ago and as the firing five minutes ago of bill's C-fibres. But what *is* this thing? We are saying, implicitly or explicitly, something which has the form $\exists x \, (\varphi x \, \& \, \psi x)$. It must be possible to make a corresponding statement of the form $(\varphi a \, \& \, \psi a)$. This event which is variously described must be nameable in some way—it is not one of the unspecifiable real numbers.[14]

§ 11. I said a little while ago that an identity proposition must be viewable as an existentially quantified proposition, one that can be expressed with the help of 'Der'. This is true if by 'identity proposition' one means a proposition whose assertion is an assertion of identity, where the content of the identity proposition is what is *said*. Thus in 'For some x, both x wrote *Waverley* and x wrote *Marmion*' what is *said* is that the author of the novel is the same as the author of the poem. In the instantiation of this, namely, 'Scott wrote *Waverley* and Scott wrote *Marmion*', what is *said* in the proposition which is its existential generalization is *shown*. And even if Wittgenstein was wrong in thinking that there is no need for a sign of identity, that the truths of identity cannot be said but can only be shown by identity of signs, he was nevertheless right in thinking that the possibility of showing the truths of identity is what is in some way fundamental. There could be no truths of the form $\exists x \, (\varphi x \,\&\, \psi x)$ if there were no truths of the form $(\varphi a \,\&\, \psi a)$. And there could be no truths of the form $\exists p \, (\delta_1 p \,\&\, \delta_2 p)$ if there were no truths of the form $(\delta_1 q \,\&\, \delta_2 q)$. The possibility of repeating a name, a proposition, or even a direct nominalization of a proposition, is what lies at the root of identity claims, whether about objects or events.

Identity of objects is thus something which it must be possible, at least, to show by the repetition of a name. If an object has more than one name it would make no difference to what was shown if one were substituted for the other: what is shown by 'Scott wrote *Waverley* and Scott wrote *Marmion*' is shown equally well by 'Sir Walter wrote *Waverley* and Sir Walter wrote *Marmion*'. In this context, as in others, different names of the same object are synonymous. Identity of events is similarly something which it must be possible, at least, to show by repetition of that which is the analogue of a name in this case, namely, the direct nominalization of an event-reporting proposition. Thus what is said by (19) is shown by (20). Just as different names will name the same object only if they are synonymous, so different direct nominalizations will designate the same event only if they are, like 'Jack's falling

---

[14] See W. V. Quine, 'Existence and Quantification', in his *Ontological Relativity and Other Essays*, New York: Columbia University Press, 1969, pp. 91–113.

down' and 'Jack's tumbling down', synonymous. No one pretends
that the nominalizations beloved of Identity Theorists are synonymous. It is impossible to make out how the repetition of any of
them could show what the Identity Theorists claim to be saying.
But what cannot be shown in this way certainly cannot be said.
The Identity Theorists had better be silent.

£ 12. Perhaps there is room here for the same eirenic attitude that
I tried to display in Chapter V. The Identity Theorists do not yet
have to keep total silence. What I hope to have shown is that the
'nothing-buttery' involved in saying such things as 'Bill's pain is the
same as (nothing but) the firing of C-fibres in Bill's cerebral cortex'
cannot be construed on the lines of straightforward identity
propositions. That is to say, it is no use appealing to propositions
like (19), let alone to the examples given by Davidson, to assure
ourselves that we know what the Identity Theorists mean. They
may mean something, but that has yet to be established. Their
claim is on a par with time-honoured philosophical theses, like
those of Atomists, ancient and seventeenth-century, about 'secondary qualities': 'Greenness *is* the power possessed by certain objects
in virtue of the number, size, shape, arrangement, and motion of
the minute insensible particles of which they are composed to
cause certain sensations in a perceiver'. This is not to be made
intelligible by comparison with propositions like 'Greenness is the
property which indicates the presence of chlorophyll in plants' or
'The colour of my leg splint is the colour of the skin of unhealthy
Caucasians'. The first is not a genuine identity proposition at all,
and what is *said* by the second could be *shown* by a proposition in
which a word like 'pinkish' was repeated. Locke's nothing-buttery
could not be 'shown' in this way, any more than the claims of the
Identity Theorists. I am not saying, or am no longer saying, that it
cannot in any way be shown or said; but I am suggesting to Identity
Theorists and other advocates of Reductionism that what they
mean is in question, as well as the truth of what they say. It is not
enough, in fact it will not do at all, to profess simply to be making
contingent, a posteriori, assertions of identity. We await an
alternative account of what they intend.

PERSONAL IDENTITY

§ 1. Nothing has been said so far about criteria of identity. It hardly seemed necessary to discuss what criteria we would employ in coming to the conclusion that the town where Edna spent her holiday last year was the birthplace of Boscovich, or that the sum of four and five is the same as the square of three. With personal identity it is otherwise. Ever since Locke's famous chapter 'Of Identity and Diversity' was written,[1] it has been necessary to debate the sort of criteria which would be needed if we were to determine whether the person Edna got friendly with during her holiday last year was in fact Boscovich. Are the criteria 'mentalistic', thus allowing Boscovich to be reincarnated in time to have met Edna; or are they 'corporeal', so that exhuming Boscovich's corpse and certifying its remoteness from the Adriatic at the time of Edna's visit would settle the matter negatively?

Few have set out the issues more clearly than Bernard Williams in his paper 'The Self and the Future'.[2] Two men, A and B, are told that they are both to be subjected to an operation which may be thought of as the total transfer of information from A's brain to B's and vice versa, and which will result in the person who, to outward appearance at least, is A ('the A-body person') seeming to remember all that B had previously remembered ever having done or experienced, in his having all of B's character traits, likes and dislikes, prejudices, etc., and thus seeming, by every mentalistic criterion, to be B. This person will simultaneously lose all the memories of A's actions and experiences and all the mental characteristrics whose loss is not already implied by the acquisition of B's characteristics. The B-body person suffers the inverse

---

[1] John Locke, *Essay concerning Human Understanding*, Book II, ch. XXVII; repr. in J. Perry (ed.), *Personal Identity*, Berkeley, Los Angeles and London: University of California Press, 1975.

[2] *Philosophical Review*, 79 (1970); repr. in Perry (ed.), *Personal Identity*.

change. Williams gives, successively, two descriptions of these events, one which disposes us to regard the A-body person after the operation as being the same person as B was before the operation, and one which disposes us to regard the A-body person as being, all along the line, A. If we accept Williams's first account of what happens we are taking the mentalistic criteria of personal identity as paramount; if we accept the second account we take the corporeal criteria to be paramount.

§ 2. Criteria of each of these kinds consist of features whose presence is empirically verifiable. By bestowing primacy on the mentalistic criteria we in no way make the concept of personal identity a non-empirical concept. Identity as such, of course, is a non empirical-concept, in the way that existence is, as such, a non-empirical concept. The judgement that *there is* a rational square root of thirty-six and the judgement that *there was* a cat who jumped through the window both employ the concept of existence, but the one requires empirical verification and the other does not. Just so, the concept of identity is involved in the judgement that the sum of six and thirty is the same as the square of six, and the very same concept is involved in the judgement that the event which Henrietta reported is the same as the event which caused the vase to break. The former judgement will not, the latter will, require empirical criteria for its verification. If personal identity is a concept which requires empirical criteria for its application, this will be a fact about the concept of a person, not a fact about the concept of identity.

Richard Swinburne has claimed that the meaning of 'same person' transcends the criteria for the application of the concept it expresses.[3] He holds that both sets of criteria, the mental and the physical, are used in applying the concept, and that one or the other may be required if a person is to learn the concept. Once he has learned it, however, he will have a grasp of its meaning which permits him to make judgements which do not rest on either set of criteria. Swinburne's view seems to imply that there is a non-empirical element in the concept of personal identity, an extra

---

[3] R. G. Swinburne, 'Personal Identity', *Proceedings of the Aristotelian Society*, 74 (1973–4), pp. 231–48; id., 'Persons and Personal Identity', in H. D. Lewis (ed.), *Contemporary British Philosophy* (Fourth Series), London: George Allen and Unwin, 1979, pp. 221–38.

factor that goes beyond the emirical criteria we use in connection with it. He does not, however, have anything positive to tell us about what this extra factor might be.

§ 3. This deficiency can, I believe, be remedied. To do so, it will help to continue Williams's tale of the A-body and the B-body person. Before the operation, each is told that one of them, at a date soon after the operation, will be given a large sum of money, while the other will be tortured. Clearly each of A and B will have reason, either to look forward with eager anticipation, or to view the future with dread, according to whether he thinks that he is the one who will be given money or the one who will be tortured. Given that both know that the money will be given to the A-body person and the torments to the B-body person, hope and fear will be present in accordance with each man's belief as to which person he will be when the different treatments are meted out. Let us suppose that A belongs to the school of Locke and uses mentalistic criteria to judge questions of personal identity. He will therefore believe that he will be the B-body person, and will have every reason to fear for the future. B, on the other hand, we may suppose to be a follower of Butler and Reid,[4] and to use corporeal criteria to judge such questions. He too, in that case, will believe that he will be the B-body person, and will be in exactly the same state of fear as A.

Each of the subjects believes that he himself will be the B-body person. The reflexive pronoun 'himself' which occurs here might tempt us to use some of the apparatus of earlier chapters to express the facts about this belief. Taking a as the name of A, and reading $\delta\varphi xy$ as 'x believes that y will be the B-body person', the fact about A could in that case be stated by $\delta\varphi aa$, and therefore by $\Xi u \, [\delta\varphi uu] \, a$ or $\mathrm{Ref_0} \, \delta\varphi a$.

But this would be wrong. Suppose that A is amnesiac. He is then told the story about A and B in just the same way as other people are told it; the only thing he is not told is that *he* is A. Being in fact A, and not having shed his general philosophical beliefs about personal identity, despite his loss of his particular beliefs about his own identity, he subscribes to Locke's view about these matters, and therefore thinks that A will be the B-body person. So $\delta\varphi aa$ will

---

[4] See passages printed in Perry (ed.), *Personal Identity*.

be true, along with $\varXi u$ [$\delta\varphi uu$] a and Ref_0 $\delta\varphi a$; but it will not be true of A in the intended sense that he believes that he himself will be the B-body person. He is blissfully unaware of his own involvement in the affair, which he views from a perspective of judicious philosophical detachment. In particular *he does not fear being tortured.*

When we said that each of the subjects believes that he himself will be the B-body person, we were evidently using 'himself' in a way which goes beyond the logical concept of reflection. In Chapter IV I argued that 'same' and 'self' express the same concept, that the reflexive pronoun is only the manifestation in a restricted area (that of atomic as opposed to molecular propositions) of a feature of language that has much wider application and a wide variety of alternative expressions. This position has now to be qualified in a more precise way than was possible earlier. There are two concepts of 'self'. They are indeed connected—closely connected, as we shall see. But the topic-neutral, category-transcending concept expressible by 'Ref' captures only part of what is often meant by 'myself', 'yourself', 'herself', 'himself', 'ourselves', 'yourselves', and, on some occasions of their use, of 'themselves' and 'itself' (cf. 'The child is concerned about itself'). When philosophers talk grandly about The Self, they always mean more than can be expressed by 'Ref'. The French, who have to make do with *Le Soi* and *Le Moi*, do not need to be worried about this.

The use of 'himself', etc., with which I am now concerned has been interestingly explored by Hector-Neri Castañeda.[5] Castañeda employs an argument to show the indispensability of the 'he' of self-consciousness and the use of 'himself' which we need to track down. His argument belongs to the same genre as that which I used in Chapter III. Just as in Chapter III I tried to show that (6A) was not entailed by (2A), that propositions of the form $\delta\mathrm{Ref}\,\varphi a$ could be false even when propositions of the form $\delta\varphi aa$ were true, so Castañeda shows that propositions of the form 'Paul thinks that he himself φs' can be false, even though corresponding propositions of the form 'Paul thinks that φa' are true, where 'Paul' and a

---

[5] H.-N. Castañeda, ' "He": A Study in the Logic of Self-Consciousness', *Ratio*, 8 (1966), pp. 130–57; see also id., 'On the Phenomeno-Logic of the I', *Proceedings of the XIVth International Congress of Philosophy*, 3 (Vienna, 1969), which has useful bibliographical references.

designate the same man. The use of the pronoun he is interested in, which he signalizes by an asterisk thus: 'he*', cannot be equated with any other device for indicating the object of Paul's thought. Definite descriptions cannot be substituted for 'he*', whether they are given primary or secondary occurrence.

David, after he had committed adultery with Bathsheba and had her husband Uriah the Hittite killed in battle, was reproached for this wickedness by Nathan the prophet. Nathan told the king a parable of a rich and powerful man who stole from a poor neighbour the ewe lamb which was his only and loved possession. David, full of righteous indignation, exclaimed 'The man who did this thing deserves to die', only to be told 'Thou art the man!'[6] Before the denouement occurred, David could be described as thinking that the man who had committed the crime deserved to die. The definite description could be taken as having either primary or secondary occurrence in this case: it would still be true that David thought that the man who had committed the crime deserved to die, though false that David thought that he* deserved to die. If the views about proper names expressed above in Chapter VI are correct, it would be true to say that David thought that David deserved to die—a proposition of the form $\delta\varphi aa$. David still did not think that he* himself deserved to die. We may even suppose that he was told that it was David, the king, who had done these things; so that he was prepared to say, expressing his sincere belief, 'King David deserves to die'. Even in this case it is possible to have resort to the assumption of amnesia to make it false to say that he thought that he* himself deserved to die. Tricks with mirrors or drugs can even be devised to make it possible for David to point to himself and say 'That man deserves to die', and not even then believe that he* deserves to die himself. No way of specifying the object (subject?) of David's thought can replace *salva veritate* what we may call the 'Castañeda Reflexive Pronoun' (CRP).[7]

§ 4. The CRP, then is indispensable. But what is it? It is the oratio obliqua counterpart of the first person pronoun in oratio recta.

[6] See above, ch. I, § 4 n. 6.
[7] Elizabeth Anscombe has pointed out that Ancient Greek possesses a special pronoun to do the job of CRP, the so-called 'indirect reflexive'. (See 'The First Person' in S. Guttenplan, *Mind and Language*, Oxford, 1975.)

What David could not say until he had been told 'Thou art the man' was 'I deserve to die'. A language which had no *oratio obliqua*, which, as Geach envisaged in *Mental Acts*,[8] used the form '*x* says in his heart "*p*" ' instead of '*x* has the thought that *p*', could dispense with the CRP. Russian, I understand, does not modify tenses when it shifts from oratio recta to oratio obliqua: it does not have to move from 'He said in his heart "All men *are* liars" ' to 'He thought that all men *were* liars'. I am told that Sanskrit similarly avoids the change from first person to third person, so that the Sanskrit equivalent of 'Louis XIV thought that the State was me' will do to report his saying in his heart '*L'Etat c'est Moi*'. As it is, were Madame de Maintenon to say 'The King thinks that the State is me', we should have to suppose that it was she, and not her husband, who was suffering from *la folie de grandeur*.

§ 5. We are interested in the CRP because we are trying to track down the non-empirical element in the concept of personal identity. Light may be thrown on this from consideration of a peculiar feature of its oratio recta counterpart, a feature which claims made in the first person sometimes possess, and which Sydney Shoemaker has called 'immunity to error through misidentification'.[9] I announce: 'I have got pins and needles in my left arm'. I may be telling a lie. That would not of course mean that I was in error. I may have misidentified my sensation, perhaps through failure to have grasped what people mean by 'pins and needles'. I may have mistaken my left arm for my right; or I may have no left arm—the case discussed by Descartes in the Sixth Meditation. But it can hardly be the case that while someone has pins and needles in his right arm, and is aware of the fact and makes his announcement on the basis of it, he mistakes the identity of the sufferer. I shall not enlarge on the sort of reasons I might have for judging another person to have pins and needles in his right arm; but whatever they are, reasons of this kind are

---

[8] London: Routledge and Kegan Paul, 2nd edn., 1971, § 18. Adam Morton has presented the following as a problem for me: 'John thinks that Sally thinks that he* is handsome'. I suggest 'John says in his heart "Sally says in her heart of me '--- is handsome' " '. So '*x* says in his heart "*φ*" of *y*' is needed as well as '*x* says in his heart "*p*" '.

[9] 'Persons and their Pasts', *American Philosophical Quarterly*, 7 (1970), p. 269, repr. in S. Shoemaker, *Identity, Cause and Mind*, Cambridge University Press, 1984.

irrelevant to *my* claim that *I* have this sensation. I do not have to rely on cues of memory or information from my friends in order to determine whether I am attributing pins and needles to the right person when I say that it is I who have them. I do not, in this case, employ *criteria* of identity. And in this sense, there is no empirical information which I require in order to be able to judge that the pins and needles are mine. I discover empirically, perhaps, that the pins and needles are *there*. It is not a further empirical discovery that the 'owner' of the sensation is myself. An empirical concept is required if I am to judge of anyone, myself included, that he has pins and needles. If there is a further question of establishing who it is who has pins and needles, this will probably need a further empirical concept or set of concepts: *the red-headed boy*, perhaps, or *the girl with the fox-terrier*. But my ability to ascribe to people the sensation of pins and needles already provides me with all I need for ascribing the sensation to myself. As Strawson says, to possess such a concept I must be both an other-ascriber and a self-ascriber.[10] No *further* empirical skill has to be called upon.

§ 6. The denial that we have an empirical concept expressible by 'I' or 'my' does not imply that we have no concept of the self at all. We should not think that because we have no need of criteria to ascribe experiences to ourselves, we therefore make no such ascription. When someone says 'I have pins and needles in my arm' he may be speaking the truth. It would make sense to say that he is speaking the truth precisely because it makes sense to say that he is lying. If he *is* speaking the truth, it follows that *someone* has pins and needles in his arm. 'I have pins and needles in my arm' is subject to existential generalization.[11] Wittgenstein's remark that 'the verbal expression of pain replaces crying'[12] does not mean that 'I am in pain' has no more significance than 'Ouch!'. 'Ouch!' cannot be existentially generalized. There is no reason therefore to deny that an assertion is made by someone who says 'I have pins and needles in my arm'. The conceptual content of this assertion is

---

[10] P. F. Strawson, *Individuals*, London: Methuen, 1959, p. 108.

[11] Cf. the first paragraph of Sydney Shoemaker's paper 'Self-Reference and Self-Awareness', *Journal of Philosophy*, 65/19 (Oct. 1968), pp. 555–67, repr. *Identity, Cause and Mind*, pp. 6–18.

[12] *Philosophical Investigations*, Oxford: Basil Blackwell, 1953, I, § 244.

not fully determined by the predicate expression used. The words 'I' and 'my' play a significant role in its determination. They express some concept, and if this concept is not an empirical concept—if it is nearer to what Kant had in mind when he talked of 'the Transcendental Ego', what sort of concept is it?

§ 7. We turned our attention to the first-person pronoun after noticing that the CRP was its *oratio recta* counterpart. But, in fact, I believe, illumination is to be sought by returning to the CRP. The meaning of the words 'I deserve to die', uttered by King David, is only to be grasped fully by examining the meaning of the sentence

(21) David thought that he* deserved to die.

This thesis about the order of understanding of 'I' and 'he*' has already been put forward by Roderick M. Chisholm,[13] but Chisholm's reasons for propounding it are quite different from mine. Mine can only emerge after a good deal of discussion of the logical form of (21).

The first thing to notice about this proposition is that it does not seem at first sight to be of the form δ*pa* (using the symbol δ as δ' was used in § 9 of Ch. VI). The words 'he* deserved to die' do not by themselves constitute a proposition. They are not, therefore, substitutable without transformation for *p* in δ*pa*. Like many other pronouns, the CRP cannot, it seems, provide by itself the subject for a proposition; sometimes we have to know what a pronoun's antecedent is before we are able to judge whether the proposition in which it occurs is true or false. Thus in 'Hitler despised Chamberlain after he abandoned Czechoslovakia', the words in the subordinate clause can only be assessed as a proposition if we know whether the name to be substituted for 'he' is 'Hitler' or 'Chamberlain'. But this sort of substitution is not always possible. It is not possible, for instance, in 'Any politician is despised if he is seen to be a coward'. Nor is it possible in (21). Substituting 'David' for 'he*' in this proposition yields

(22) David thought that David deserved to die,

---

[13] 'The Indirect Reflexive', in C. Diamond and J. Teichman (eds.), *Intention and Intentionality: Essays in Honour of G. E. M. Anscombe*, Brighton: Harvester Press, 1979.

a proposition which, as we have seen, may well be true when (21) is false. What David is said by (21) to have thought cannot be expressed by the complete proposition 'David deserved to die'.

Even if it could, even if (21) and (22) expressed the same proposition, this proposition would not be of the form δpa.[14] (21) and (22) each say that David thought something, but the 'something' cannot be specified by producing a proposition. What was argued in Chapter VI with respect to 'Queen Mary thought that George VI made a good king', holds good for (22). Nevertheless, if the Duchess of Gloucester had agreed with Queen Mary, there is a form of words which either of them could have used to express their judgement about George VI. Queen Mary could have said to the Duchess 'Bertie made a good king', and obtained the reply, 'I quite agree'; but it could just as well have been the other way round. Equally, if (22) were true though (21) was not, an amnesiac David who had forgotten his own name could have echoed Nathan's 'David deserves to die' with 'Yes, David deserves to die'. But if (21) were true, though David could express his thought by using the words 'I deserve to die', Nathan would not be expressing agreement with David if he too said 'I deserve to die'. There is no form of words which can be used both by David and by others to express agreement with what David is said to think in (21), in so far as this differs from what he is said to think in (22). This seems to be a reason for saying that what David is said to think in (21) is even less able to be identified by specifying a proposition than what he is said to think in (22).

§ 8. The difference between (21) and (22) is hard to state. Even if we deny that (22) is of the form δpa, we can say that the proposition 'David deserves to die' specifies what has to be true if, in thinking what in (22) David is said to think, he is thinking something true. But exactly the same proposition will serve to specify what has to be true if, in thinking what in (21) he is said to think, he is thinking something true: if David does deserve to die, then when he thinks that he* deserves to die he is quite right, just as much as when he thinks that David deserves to die. The difference between (21) and (22) cannot be stated by giving the conditions for the truth of what in each of these propositions David is said to think.

[14] See above, ch. VI, § 9.

§ 9. So the difference between (21) and (22) is very unlike the difference between, say, (22) and 'David thought that Saul deserved to die'. How then do we explain the difference between the thought involved in (21) and the thought involved in (22)? The particular to which the thinker is related is the same in both. The predicable '--- deserves to die' occurs in both. What is it that is present in one but absent in the other?

Note first that (21) entails (22). That (22) does not entail (21) is what I established, following Castañeda, in the last two paragraphs of § 3 of this chapter. Castañeda thought that he had also shown that propositions like (21) do not entail propositions like (22), but his arguments involve confusion between opaque and transparent interpretations of the latter.[15] Of course, if David thinks that he* deserves to die, it does not follow that he thinks that someone called 'David' deserves to die. It does not follow that he uses any proper name or description to think of himself. But it cannot be denied that it is of himself that he is thinking: it is true of that man, David, that David thinks of him that he deserves to die. Here, if nowhere else,[16] we have a thought which is *de re*. The *res* is guaranteed because it coincides with the *cogitans*.

§ 10. To get a clear view of the logical structure of (21), we should turn our attention next to the sentence which is obtained by omitting Castañeda's asterisk, namely

(23) David thought that he deserved to die.

(23) is to be understood in this way: there is, as we have seen, a two-place predicable which occurs in (22) with 'David' occupying both its argument-places, and this predicable occurs also in 'David thought that Saul deserved to die' and in 'David thought that Goliath deserved to die' with 'David' occupying just one of its

---

[15] In ' "He": a Study in the Logic of Self-consciousness', pp. 134 f., Castañeda argues that 'The Editor of *Soul* knows that he* is a millionaire' does not entail 'The Editor of *Soul* knows that the Editor of *Soul* is a millionaire' on the grounds that he may not know that he has been appointed to the editorship. This requires that the definite description on its second appearance have secondary occurrence. Castañeda says 'the same considerations apply to any name'; but the distinction between primary and secondary occurrence does not apply to names. (See my *What is Existence?*, ch. IX.)

[16] This seems to be precisely what Chisholm, in the article previously cited, holds: that *nowhere else* do we have a thought which is *de re*. He thus sets about defining 'he*' by means of *de re* thinking, and 'I' by means of 'he*'

argument-places. But there is another predicable discernible in (22), which occurs also in 'Saul thought that Saul deserved to die' and in 'Judas thought that Judas deserved to die'. Frege would have used an expression like 'ξ thought that ξ deserved to die' to indicate this predicable, and '--- thought that he deserved to die', where 'he' is not the CRP, expresses it in ordinary English. In my own symbolism, it is of the form $\Xi u\,[\delta\varphi uu](—)$ or $\text{Ref}_0\,\delta\varphi(—)$.

Looking at (23), which is intended to be understood as being of this form (i.e., 'he' here is *not* the CRP), we can easily see that it is a mistake to look for the sense of this occurrence of 'he deserved to die', or to ask how 'he' is related in this proposition to '--- deserved to die'. In this context at least, 'he deserved to die' is not a syntactically coherent string. (23) is built up in this way: the one-place predicable '--- deserved to die' is produced by making the predicable 'die' subject to the predicable-forming operator 'deserved to'; this one-place predicable is operated on by the predicable-forming operator 'thought that' to produce the two-place predicable '--- thought that ...... deserved to die'. This two-place predicable is now made subject to the reflection operator, here expressed by 'he', to yield the one-place predicable '--- thought that he deserved to die' which is then attached to the name 'David'. The role of 'he' can only be appreciated when it is seen as operating on the complex two-place predicable '--- thought that ...... deserved to die'. The one-place predicable '--- deserved to die' is a mere fragment of this complex two-place predicable and cannot by itself have any relation with the reflection operator, here realized by 'he'.

§ 11. What then are the differences between (21), on the one hand, and (22) and (23) on the other? We have just noticed the reasons for denying that 'he deserved to die' in (23) is a syntactically coherent string. Reasons for denying that 'David deserved to die' as it occurs in (22) is a coherent string can be gathered from the arguments in Chapter VI (§ 9) about analogous cases. But these reasons do not seem to apply to 'he* deserved to die' in (21). The CRP is not simply an expression of the concept of reflection, as 'he' is in (23). Nor is it 'purely referential' (in Quine's terminology),[17] as the occurrence of 'David' is in (22). Given that 'thought that' in (22) is understood transparently, there is no

---

[17] See W. V. Quine, 'Reference and Modality' in his *From a Logical Point of View*, 2nd edn., New York: Harper and Row, 1961, p. 140.

information provided by (22) about the mode of presentation by which David thinks of himself: substitution for 'David' of another name for David would not affect its truth value. Not so with (21). This gives us to understand that David's thought about himself was mediated by the first person pronoun. Other ways of thinking of himself would suffice for the truth of (22), but not for the truth of (21). The 'I' for which the 'he*' of (21) goes proxy is part of the content of David's thought.

(21) represents David as having the thought, or 'saying in his heart', 'I deserve to die'. Whatever else this is, it must surely in some sense be a syntactically coherent string. If 'he* deserved to die' in (21) is its proxy, it seems that it too will be a syntactically coherent string. There can be no doubt that, again in some sense, the predicable '--- deserved to die' occurs in it as a logical unit. What then is the relation of 'he*' to this predicable? How is the coherent string 'he* deserved to die' formed from the predicable and the CRP? It is impossible to construe 'he*' as argument to '--- deserved to die' as function. The only syntactical category of expressions which can provide arguments in this way to first-level predicables is that of proper name, and 'he*' is not a proper name. If '--- deserved to die' were being predicated of some object in this context, so as to form an atomic proposition, it would not matter how that object was named. But it clearly does matter that we have here 'he*' and not 'David'. If it cannot be by way of supplying 'he*' as argument to '--- deserved to die' as function, could it by way of supplying '--- deserved to die' as argument to a higher-level function represented by 'he* ---'? In that case, the CRP could be thought of as another operator forming a predicable out of a predicable. Let us then add to our symbolism Castañeda's asterisk, which we can use as a predicate-modifier analogous to Quine's 'Ref' or 'Der'. Thus, if φ is taken to represent 'deserves to die', δ 'thinks that' and a 'David', 'Der φ' will stand for 'someone deserves to die', '*φ' for 'he* deserves to die', 'Ref $\delta\varphi a$' for (23), and δ*φa for (21). Is 'he* deserved to die', then, like 'Someone deserved to die', a complete proposition? Does '*', like 'Der', form a no-place predicable, i.e. a proposition, from a one-place predicable, e.g., '--- deserves to die'?

§ 12. Let us assume, for the moment, that it does. Let us further assume that it is only a feature of the surface grammar of languages like English that the oratio obliqua version of the proposition which could be expressed in oratio recta by 'David said in his heart "I deserve to die" ' requires replacement of 'I' by 'he' (and, what need not trouble us at the moment, replacement of 'deserve' by 'deserved'). We can imagine a dialect of English in which a single word, say 'self', does both the job done by 'I' and that done by 'he*' (in Castañedese). Thus David could be represented as saying out loud 'Self deserves to die', and his doing so would be reported by 'David said that self deserved to die'. The asterisk, in the role assigned to it in the last paragraph, may be considered as an abbreviation of 'self' in this idiom.

§ 13. The two assumptions of the last paragraph, taken together, entail that 'Self deserves to die', or 'I deserve to die', which is the same thing, is a complete proposition. This view of the matter is, of course, much controverted. Frege, for one, would have denied that the words 'I deserve to die', taken by themselves, express a complete thought, something capable of being true or false. Before the complete thought is available, facts about the time of utterance and the identity of the utterer have to be obtained.[18] But when these words *are* uttered, an associated sentence can always be found which will say something true, regardless of the time of its utterance or the identity of the person who utters it. When at a given time a utters a sentence of the form $*\varphi$, the fact that he does so at that time implies the truth of a corresponding proposition of the form $\delta*\varphi a$, where δ goes proxy for 'says at time t that'. Thus David's uttering (at time t) the words 'I deserve to die' makes true a proposition expressible by the words 'David says (at time t) that he* deserves to die'. And we do not need to be told who said *this* or when it was said in order to determine *its* truth value.

The truth of 'David said that he* deserved to die' entails that of 'David said that David deserved to die', which in turn entails that of 'David said that he (non-Castañeda) deserved to die'. The inference pattern here is the same as that which allows the entailments, already noted, of (22) by (21) and (23) by (22). We may formalize this by saying that $\delta*\varphi a$ entails $\delta\varphi aa$, which entails Ref $\delta\varphi a$, and that $\delta*\varphi a$ accordingly entails Ref $\delta\varphi a$. The concept of *self* expressible by '*' is distinct, as we have seen, from the concept

[18] G. Frege, 'The Thought', in P. F. Strawson (ed.), *Philosophical Logic*, Oxford: Oxford University Press, 1967, p. 24.

of *self* (or *same*) expresible by 'Ref'; but the two are not unconnected. 'Ref' enters essentially into the explanation of '*'.

§ 14. The last section was devoted to establishing that when David uttered the words 'I deserve to die', whether or not these words by themselves constitute a proposition, he thereby made true the corresponding propositions of the form $\delta^*\varphi a$, $\delta\varphi aa$ and Ref $\delta\varphi a$. It has already been pointed out that if David uttered the words 'I deserve to die', what he said was true if and only if David deserved to die. Taking φa and $^*\varphi$ as dummy sentences we may put it this way: it is the truth value of φa which determines whether or not, in saying $^*\varphi$, a says something true. But it does not follow that $^*\varphi$ means the same as φa. It would be possible for a to say that $^*\varphi$ and at the same time deny that φa; and yet it would still be φa's truth value which would determine the truth value of what he intends to assert. Even if 'I deserve to die' is not in itself a proposition, David's act of saying 'I deserve to die' makes 'David says that he* deserves to die' true, and it would be entirely in order to add 'and what he says is true' to this proposition. 'I deserve to die' is as it were a fragment of a proposition which can be completed in virtue of the fact that the fragment has been uttered. The truth of the completed proposition makes clear what David wishes to assert.

§ 15. Philosophers are familiar with the Wittgensteinian claim that the first person pronoun is not a name or a 'referring expression'. Even if there is an assertion which someone who says, e.g., 'I deserve to die' intends to make, the word 'I' does not *tell* us what this assertion is about. Since the utterance of a predicable without a name to indicate what the predicable is being predicated of does not amount to an atomic proposition, Wittgensteinians deny that a form of words like 'I deserve to die' is such a proposition; and they have not investigated the possibility of its being a molecular one. They have, however, tended to conclude from this that someone who says 'I deserve to die' is not intending to assert a proposition at all. They may be right to deny that 'I deserve to die' is the proposition he intends to assert. They are wrong to deny that there is such a proposition, and wrong to deny that the utterance of 'I' helps to specify its subject. It is the fact that 'I' has been prefixed to 'deserve to die' which makes it true that the utterer has said that he* deserves to die. The fact that he has done so entails, if David is the speaker, that David has said that David deserves to die. We know, even if David does not, the proposition which would make what David has said true: it is whatever proposition predicates the predicable in question of the person who has uttered the word 'I'. This is what David intended to assert, and indeed asserted, although he himself may not know what proposition it was that he asserted.

'I am worried'—to change the example—is not a complete proposition; but if Sarah says 'I am worried' she thereby asserts that she* is worried. That entails that she asserts that Sarah is worried, since 'asserts that' here is intended to be interpreted transparently, i.e. 'Sarah' is being *used* as a proper name, not *mentioned*. So even if 'I am worried' is not a proposition, the person who says it does assert a proposition, namely, the proposition that Sarah is worried, given that that person is Sarah. The clue to understanding this lies in a shift from looking at *what is said* to *the saying of it*, from looking at the content of the speech act to the speech act itself. The speech act that Sarah performs when she says 'I am worried' is one of assertion. But, contrary to what happens in most cases of assertion the identity of the proposition asserted is not determined by the words spoken. Rather, it is the words spoken, together with the fact that they are spoken by a particular person at a particular time, which determines what it is that is asserted. Since in saying 'I am worried' Sarah has made it true that Sarah has asserted that she* is worried, and has thus made it true that she has asserted that Sarah is worried, she has indeed asserted this. How could I make it true that I have asserted something unless I had asserted it? It remains the case that the proposition asserted is not completely specified by the words 'I am worried'.

§ 16. In § 11 we looked at various apparent similarities between $*\varphi$ and Derφ. These were syntactical. But important differences, semantic ones, emerge when we come to consider the logical relations of $*\varphi$ and Der φ to other propositions. Der φ's meaning is fixed primarily by existential generalization, the fact that it is entailed by every proposition of the form φa. $*\varphi$ has its meaning determined, partly at least, by the corresponding proposition of the form Ref $\delta\varphi a$, where δ is to be read as '--- says that ......'. As I have already indicated, this is not an entailment relation. It is not what the speaker says when he says something of the form $*\varphi$, but the fact that he says it, that entails the corresponding proposition of the form Ref $\delta\varphi a$. If David says 'I deserve to die', the fact that he says it, the fact that David says that he* deserves to die, entails the fact that David says that David deserves to die, which itself entails the fact that David says of himself (*not* the CRP) that he (still not the CRP) deserves to die. This is one of the principal features which gives 'I' the meaning it has. The reason for a person's saying 'I deserve to die' is to allow others to conclude *from the fact that he says it* that that person has said that *he deserves to die, and thence to conclude that that person has said that that person deserves to die. He also, of course, in the normal case intends his hearers to take it that what he says is true of himself is true of him, *that the person he in fact is does deserve to die*. But this is not something he says, and his saying what he does is compatible with his not even knowing that it is the case, since he may not know that he is the person he in fact is. *What he says* when he uses the word 'I' does nothing to establish who it is he is speaking of: it is *the fact that he says it* which gives the predicable he is using a subject. This is a reason for saying that 'he*' is, as it were, logically prior to 'I': 'I' gets its meaning from the consequences that can be drawn from the fact of its use; and the fact of its use is precisely what is stated by a proposition which has the form '*a* says that he* ......'.

The analysis that has just been given applies to indexical expressions in general, not just to 'I'. It is not the words 'We saw a goldfinch here yesterday' that identify the place and time of the sighting of the goldfinch, but the fact that the words were uttered at Alfred's Tower on 1 June 1985. Nothing that has been said so far is special to indexical methods of indicating *personal* identity. There *are* special features which 'I' and the CRP possess which other indicators and quasi-indicators lack, and these will be explained later in this chapter. But all alike get their meaning partly from the consequences that can be drawn from the fact of their use.

§ 17. In the last few paragraphs I have been concentrating upon viva voce utterances of the word 'I'. What of the case where David thinks, rather than says, that he* deserves to die? It is plausible, perhaps, to see spoken uses of 'I' as deriving their meaning from their ability to allow a hearer to conclude that the speaker is saying the he* ......; but when someone thinks to himself that he* ......, there is no hearer, and the purposes of communication cannot be appealed to directly to establish what it is that he means. It is, of course, true that when Descartes thinks a thought expressible by the words 'I am thinking' he thereby makes it true that he is thinking that he* is thinking. But is his having this thought something which has to be understood in terms of an intention on his part to make this true? In Descartes' case the answer may be 'Yes'. His making it true that he is thinking that he* is thinking makes it true that he is thinking, and therefore that what he is thinking is true. It is this self-validating feature of his performance which is important to him.[19] But suppose someone has the thought 'I am facing the door'. Is it reasonable, even partially, to explain what it is that he is thinking by invoking the fact that in thinking it he makes it true that he is thinking that he* is facing the door?

Sed contra, when it comes to demonstrating that indexicals, such as the first person, are essential, it is to propositions like 'John thinks that he* is making a mess' that philosophers have turned.[20] John Perry showed that such propositions play a role in the explanation of actions and of behaviour which no other propositions can play. Viewed in itself, what is said by 'I am making a mess' may be expressible in other ways. Propositions containing 'indicators', as Castañeda calls them, have truth conditions which can be given, with reference to context of utterance, by propositions without indicators. Propositions containing quasi-indicators,[21] the oratio obliqua equivalents of indicators in oratio recta, on the other hand, have truth-conditions which are incapable of being given by propositions which lack them. We may compare Prior's proof that tenses are ineliminable. What is said by 'That's now over', which employs the indexical language of tenses and indicators (McTaggart's A-series), can perhaps be said in untensed, non-indexical language, e.g., by 'Prior's first utterance on 24 June 1967 is later than the end of the 1967 examination season in Manchester'

[19] This is why Descartes has so much more success with '*Cogito*' than with '*Sum*'. Since Kant philosophers have doubted whether 'exist' is a genuine predicate: since Wittgenstein they have doubted whether 'I' is a genuine subject. Not much is left of the indubitable proposition 'I exist'!

[20] J. Perry, 'The Problem of the Essential Indexical', *Noûs*, 13 (1979), pp. 3–21.

[21] For this terminology see H.-N. Castañeda, 'Indicators and Quasi-Indicators', in *American Philosophical Quarterly*, 4 (1967), pp. 85–100.

(McTaggart's B-series). What is said by 'Arthur was thankful that it was then over', on the other hand, depends essentially on tenses and quasi-indicators for its expression. Here too the oratio obliqua occurrences of indexical expressions (Castañeda's 'quasi-indicators') seem to take precedence over oratio recta occurrences. The explanatory value of 'he*' seems greater than that of 'I'.

Nor is it altogether absurd to give a general explanation of the use that the concept of the first person has in silent thought in terms of the use of 'I' in spoken language, even though a particular unspoken use of 'I' may not perform the function of a spoken use. It may be asked whether a being incapable of using first-person linguistic expressions on any occasion for purposes of communication could intelligibly be credited with first-person thoughts. The dog may scratch, but is it reasonable to attribute to him the thought 'I am itching'? The availability of 'I', whose original purpose, on this view, is to enable a hearer to note that the person uttering it is saying something about himself (not, here, himself*), may facilitate a multitude of utterances *in petto* by a thinker who is willing, if not anxious, to keep them to himself.

§ **18.** There is, however, more to it than that. In § 3 of this Chapter, I remarked that the word 'self' was used to express two distinct concepts: the concept which in earlier chapters '$\exists$' and 'Ref' were employed clearly to express, and the concept I have referred to as the CRP. Since then it has begun to look as though the distinction between these two concepts is about to vanish. The CRP gets its meaning, I have been arguing, from the fact that its use makes a proposition of the form Ref$\delta\varphi a$ true. I called utterances of the form *φ 'fragments of propositions': perhaps the propositions of which they are fragments just *are* propositions of the form Ref $\delta\varphi a$, and the fragments in question are themselves of the form 'Ref$(-)\varphi(-)$', the substitutions for δ and a being inferable from the circumstances of utterance. It looks as though the introduction of a special Castañeda-type reflexive '*' was unnecessary, the ordinary topic-neutral reflexive 'Ref', being adequate for the purpose. But this cannot be the whole story. Although David's utterance of 'I deserve to die' makes (22) true, and therefore also the corresponding proposition of the form Ref $\delta\varphi a$, the truth of a proposition of the form Ref $\delta\varphi a$, does not entail that a has uttered a sentence of the form $*\varphi$. $\delta*\varphi a$ implies Ref $\delta\varphi a$, but not vice versa.

Ref $\delta\varphi a$ and $\delta\varphi aa$ are, on the other hand, mutually implicative, and $\delta\varphi aa$, as well as containing the predicable $\delta\varphi\xi\xi$, contains the predicable $\delta\varphi\xi\zeta$.[22] Propositions of this form, e.g., $\delta\varphi ba$ ('David thinks that Nathan deserves to die'), will in general be true because the subject has picked out the object by name, or by pointing, or by some other method, and said or thought of him that he φs. $\delta\varphi ba$ will be true only if a has some means of identifying b. $\delta\varphi aa$ too may be true because a has some such means, whether or not by using his name 'a', of picking himself out, without prejudice to the correct answer to the question whether he realizes that the person he picks out is himself. But $\delta\varphi aa$ may also be true without a having any means of picking out who it is that he is speaking or thinking of, or without a employing such means in the act of speech or judgement which makes $\delta\varphi aa$ true. Thus, 'David says that David deserves to die' can be true in virtue of the fact that David utters the words 'David deserves to die' and in this way uses a means available to him and to others of identifying the person of whom he says that he deserves to die, namely, a proper name. But it can also be true in virtue of the fact that he utters the words 'I deserve to die', and in doing so does not use any means, even if such are available to him, of identifying the person he is talking about. He may not indeed have any such means of identification: he may not know who he is. He knows, if he reflects on the matter, that he* has said that someone deserves to die; and he knows that someone has said that he* deserves to die. More he need not know. What he has said does nothing to indicate who it is he is talking about. The function of 'I' is not to tell us, in this case, that David is talking about David, but to make it true by virtue of the fact of David's utterance of it that he is talking about David. The difference between 'David says that David deserves to die' and 'David says that he* deserves to die', and hence between Ref $\delta\varphi a$ and $\delta*\varphi a$, is that the first is compatible with David's having *said*, by using a name or some other identifying device, who the person is who, in his view, deserves to die, while the second makes clear that David did not, on this occasion, make use of any such device.

---

[22] The letters ξ and ζ serve only as indicators of the number of argument places of the predicate in question. The distinction between inclusive and exclusive interpretations of variables applies only to bound variables.

We can give the truth-conditions of 'David says that he* deserves to die' in this way: it is true if, and only if, David says that David deserves to die without what he says, as opposed to his saying it, identifying the person of whom he says that he deserves to die.

It will be illuminating at this point to compare 'he*' with another quasi-indicator 'then*'. Consider the proposition

(24) Jones remarked at noon that it was then* time for the meeting to begin.

What Jones actually said was 'It is now time for the meeting to begin'. Just as 'he*' is the oratio obliqua proxy for 'I', so 'then*' is the oratio obliqua proxy for 'now'. (21) entails

(25) If David was right, David deserved to die,

and in the same way (24) entails

(26) If Jones was right, noon was the time for the meeting to begin.

That is to say, the truth value of the thought attributed to David by (21) is that of 'David deserved to die', and the truth value of the remark attributed to Jones by (24) is that of 'Noon was the time for the meeting to begin'. But just as nothing in the content of David's thought actually identifies David, so nothing in what Jones actually said identifies noon as the time when the meeting was to begin. David could well not have realized that he was David, and Jones could have thought, wrongly, that it was eleven o'clock when he was speaking (and if he was also wrong about the time of the meeting, his actual remark could still have been correct).

I supposed in the last paragraph that what Jones actually said was 'It is *now* time for the meeting to begin', but he might just as well have said simply 'It is time for the meeting to begin'. Prior argued convincingly for a redundancy theory of the present: 'It is now the case that p', like 'It is true that p', says nothing more nor less than that p.[23] Someone who says 'It's hot' indicates *when* the temperature is high by omitting any indication of time such as would be necessary if he wanted to say that it was going to be hot tomorrow. The present tense is, as it were, the zero case of time indication. And the same significance assigned to simplicity allows

---

[23] Cf. A. N. Prior, *Papers on Time and Tense*, Oxford: Clarendon Press, 1968, pp. 21 f.

us to say 'It's hot' *tout court*, meaning that it's hot *here*, as opposed to, say, in Scarborough. But if Sheila in Cannes on Easter Monday said that it was then* hot there* (by simply uttering the words 'It's hot'), we know that the truth of her remark depends on its having been hot in Cannes on Easter Monday, not from what she said, but from the fact of her having said it *then* and *there*.

Quasi-indicators like 'he*', 'then*', and 'there*' were contrasted by Castañeda with *indicators* like 'I', 'now', and 'here'. But the indicators in fact fail to indicate without the help of the quasi-indicators: the sentence 'I feel hot here now' does not by itself indicate person, place, or time; only if we know enough to enable us to report its utterance by ourselves saying 'Sheila said in Cannes on Easter Monday that she* felt hot there* then*', can we fully identify the thought (in Frege's sense) that is being expressed.

Just as there is a difference between 'David said that he deserved to die (Ref $\delta\varphi a$)' and 'David said that he* deserved to die ($\delta^*\varphi a$)', so there is a difference between 'Sheila said on Easter Monday that it was then hot' and 'Sheila said on Easter Monday that it was then* hot'. The first is compatible with Sheila's having said (rather implausibly) 'It is hot on Easter Monday'. The second indicates that she did not, on this occasion, make use of any dating device, that she just said 'It's hot'.[24]

We have seen that the truth conditions for 'David says that he* deserves to die' include the clause that nothing David says, as opposed to the fact of his saying it, identifies the person of whom he says that he deserves to die. In the same way, 'Sheila said on Easter Monday that it was then* hot' includes among its truth-conditions the clause that Sheila could have said what she did without any of the things she said, as opposed to the fact of her saying them, indicating the time of which she was speaking.

---

[24] It may be objected that even without the use of 'now' the present tense of 'It *is* hot' is a positive time indication. This may be true of English as a natural language. But Prior described a possible dialect of English in which the central core of every proposition is in the 'present' tense, so that 'It will be hot' becomes 'It will be that (it is hot)' and 'It was hot' becomes 'It was the case that (it is hot)', etc. Here the core sentence is, as it were, the unmodified, zero case of tense. And the fact that this is a possible language, reflecting tense-logic, which contrasts *Fp* and *Pp* with simple *p*, shows that what Sheila is said to say by 'Sheila said on Easter Monday that it was then* hot' is something *sayable* without any time indication. Logic has to do with what languages are possible, not what are actual.

§ **19.** This way of setting out the difference between Ref $\delta\varphi a$ and $\delta^*\varphi a$ relies on the addition of a negative clause to the truth conditions of the first in order to obtain the truth conditions of the second. Am I, therefore, committed to the view that the total explanation of the concept of *self* can be given by the account of the relation between Ref $\delta\varphi a$ and $\delta^*\varphi a$ together with this denial of the use of a method of identification? When I say that I deserve to die, is my doing so achieved by my failure to say who it is who deserves to die? How would this differ from saying that *someone* deserves to die?

This last question can be answered swiftly. $\delta[\exists x\,(\varphi xa)]$ ('David says that there is someone who deserves to die') does not entail $\exists x\,[\delta(\varphi xa)]$ ('There is someone of whom David says that he deserves to die'), but $\delta^*\varphi a$, like $\delta\varphi aa$, *does* entail $\exists x\,[\delta(\varphi xa)]$. Saying that I deserve to die, therefore, is more than saying that someone deserves to die, but is less than saying who it is who deserves to die.

We have, as it were, indicated the logical space into which $\delta^*\varphi a$ must fit, but surely there must be something more positive to say about what goes into this space? There is. It is to be found by turning our attention from the question 'What is Sarah talking about when she says such things as "I am worried"?' to the question 'Which are the most significant, for our purpose, of the things that Sarah says about herself?' I have in mind such statements of Sarah's as: that she* is thirsty, that she* is sitting down, that she* has a ringing in her ears, that she* is facing the door. Familiar territory. We were concerned earlier with the absence, in some cases, of any need for criteria in judging the identity of the person to whom one is ascribing predicates when one ascribes them to oneself. The point now to be recalled is the absence, in some cases, of the need for criteria in ascribing the predicates themselves. I can sensibly ask you how you know Sarah is sitting down. Possible answers: she has told you (over the telephone) that she is; you can see her; you cannot hear her any longer pacing up and down the room above you. But I cannot, except in very unusual circumstances, sensibly ask Sarah how she knows she* is sitting down. There is an epistemological asymmetry between the first-person and the other-person ascription of certain predicates. And this epistemological fact is what we must look to for a positive account of $\delta^*\varphi a$.

This epistemological asymmetry is one that has been much talked about since Strawson's discussion of it in *Individuals*.[25] I think, however, that there is another asymmetry, this time a logical or syntactical one, which is not explicit in Strawson's argument. Strawson contrasts the 'philosophical solipsist', who uses the concept of *self* to assert that no one other than himself has experiences, with the 'true solipsist', who has no use for the concept of *self*, who is just not in the business of *ascribing* experiences. Such a one might have a vocabulary which treated 'pain' as an impersonal verb. Instead of saying 'I am in pain', he would say 'It is paining', with no more thought of ascribing pain to anything than of ascribing rain to anything when he says 'It is raining'. Perhaps children learn to use 'It hurts' in this fashion.

Now 'It is raining' *is* a complete proposition, and if Billy has the thought that it is raining we can report this by using a proposition of the form δpa.[26] If Billy says in his heart 'It hurts', or 'It is paining', we can presumably report this fact too by asserting a proposition of the form δpa. However, if this were the whole story, we should soon run afoul of Wittgensteinian considerations about private languages. Billy's impersonal use of 'It hurts' is warranted only by *his* pain. He has no way of assessing for correctness anyone else's use of 'It hurts'. When his friend Emma says 'It hurts', he will, as like as not, find it inappropriate to say 'It hurts' himself. Grown-ups may on occasion ask him 'Does it hurt?' and judge his affirmative answer sincere, and on other occasions may chide him for telling fibs when he says 'It hurts'. In this way, through others' assessment of his use of the sentence, he may indirectly check the correctness of his own use. Already, however, the simple impersonal verb is being shown to be dependent on a more complex subject–predicate sentence; for when his mother judges Billy's cry 'It hurts' to be appropriate it is because *she* feels the judgement 'Billy is in pain' to be in order. Billy could, if he were more than usually precocious, use 'I am in pain', as if it were a one-word sentence, to replace 'It hurts'. But as soon as he has realized that the same predicable occurs in 'Billy is in pain' or 'Mummy is in pain' as occurs in 'I am in pain', he has abandoned his solipsism and become an ascriber of experiences, at once a self-ascriber and an other-ascriber.

[25] P. F. Strawson, *Individuals*, London: Methuen, 1958, ch. 3.
[26] See ch. VI, § 9, on Queen Mary's thinking that it is hot.

This growth in sophistication does not, however, require that he learn any new technique for judging 'I am in pain' appropriate. He continues to say 'I am in pain' on occasions of the same type as he used to when it functioned as a one-word sentence, or when he used to say 'It hurts'. No new empirical criteria are required. What he has learned is that a single concept can function impersonally in what is in effect a subjectless sentence, and also predicatively in a subject–predicate sentence to ascribe a property to an object. In 'Mummy is in pain' the words '--- is in pain' constitute a one-place predicable: in 'I am in pain' this same predicable is converted (or allowed to revert) into a no-place predicable, that is to say, a proposition, but not one formed by attaching a one-place predicable to a name. The first person pronoun (and the change from 'is' to 'am') resembles the quantifiers in that it converts a one-place predicable into a proposition, but the proposition thus obtained plays the same role as an impersonal verb. $*\varphi$ is an atomic proposition where Derφ is molecular. The asymmetry between first-person and third-person uses of 'in pain' is thus logical as well as epistemological: in the first-person use we have a simple, i.e. non-complex, no-place predicable, in the third-person use a one-place predicable needing completion by a name. From the epistemological point of view, these predicables—what Strawson called 'P-predicates'—straddle two uses, one consisting in their being ascribed on the basis of observable criteria, and one in their being ascribed not on this basis. In a similar way, from the logical point of view, they straddle two syntactical categories, that of one-place predicable of first level and that of simple no-place predicable of first level. And it is, of course, the epistemological fact which explains the logical phenomenon.

If 'I am in pain' is a simple no-place predicable, what grounds are there for remaining in doubt over whether or not it is a proposition, and how can it be denied that propositions of the form $\delta^*\varphi a$ are also of the form δpa? If 'Billy says that he* is in pain' means no more than 'Billy says that it hurts', why should it be treated differently from 'Queen Mary thought that it was hot' (see above ch. vi, § 9)?

There are, I think, two reasons why it should. First we may note that sentences like 'I am in pain' are not common property as bearers of truth and falsity. What I mean may become clear if I explain how first-person pronouns differ from other indexical expressions. As has already been remarked, the expressions, 'here', 'now', 'this', 'that', 'you', etc., like 'I', cause the sentences which contain them to express judgements that have different truth values in different contexts: we cannot decide whether what has been said by such a sentence is true until we know who said it, where, when, and to whom. But in every case except that of the first person it is possible for different people at a given time, in a given place, addressing a given audience, to use the same sentence to say the same thing. If Dick says 'It's hot here' or 'It rained yesterday', Tom can reply 'Yes, it *is* hot here' or 'It did rain yesterday', and both can say to Harry 'You ought to get your hair cut'. Locally, and for the duration of a specious present, such sentences are as closely tied to the facts they state as are eternal sentences like 'Six sixes are thirty-six'. Not so 'I ought to get my hair cut'. If Dick and Tom each say this, and act on it, the barber will have twice the number of customers he would have had if Harry had acted on the others' advice to *him*. 'It rained yesterday', though not always true, can, when it is true, be used by all of us in our village to state a common fact. Its currency may be restricted in space and time, but within these limits it is common currency, passing from person to person without necessary revaluation. 'I am in pain', on the other hand, has to be exchanged every time it passes an inter-personal frontier: 'I am feeling sick' provokes the response 'Are you?' Where the first person is concerned there is no communication without conjugation.

The second reason why sentences containing the first person pronoun fail to achieve the status of propositions is that on one interpretation of their ambivalent predicable they are incomplete. In so far as 'I am worried' can be regarded as a no-place predicable, the sentence may be a complete proposition, albeit incapable of expressing the same thought when uttered by different people. But in so far as '--- (am) worried'[27] is a one-place predicable it needs a name to be subordinated to it, or itself to be subordinated to some operator, before it will yield a complete proposition. 'I' is not a name. 'I', or 'self', or '*' is, on the other hand, a linguistic device which has strong ties with 'same', or 'self'

---

[27] I bracket the word 'am', because, although its presence is necessary to make a verb phrase out of the adjective 'worried', its restriction to the first person deprives the phrase of its ability to express what is common to ascriptions of worry to more than one person.

(in the other sense), or 'Ref'. The only way in which the same one-place predicable can be discerned in 'William is worried' and 'I am worried' is via a recognition that if Sarah says 'I am worried' she says of herself what she says of William if she says 'William is worried'. And she manages to say this of herself only in virtue of the fact that in saying 'I am worried' she has made it true that Sarah has said that she is worried (understood as being of the form Ref $\delta\varphi a$, not $\delta^*\varphi a$). And 'she is worried' here is no more a proposition than 'he deserved to die' in (23). *Qua* no-place predicable, a sentence of the form $*\varphi$ is a proposition of a sort. *Qua* containing φ as one-place predicable, such a sentence is not a proposition of any sort, but gets its meaning from the fact that its utterance makes a proposition of the form Ref $\delta\varphi a$ true. But here the realization of the form $*\varphi$ does not function even as a syntactically coherent string, let alone as a proposition. Sentences which can be formalized with the help of '*', however, could not have the meaning they do unless some of them, at least, were capable of both these interpretations. The natural language variants 'he* is in pain' and 'I am in pain' reflect these two aspects: 'he* is in pain' seems intuitively incomplete, 'I am in pain' has more claim to be regarded as a proposition. But neither can be understood without the other, and the two roles are interdependent. Nor would we have this logically ambiguous concept, if we did not also have the epistemically asymmetrical 'P-predicates' to which Strawson drew attention.

§ **20.** Is there anything more that can be said in explanation of the fact that there are in natural languages two expressions, 'I' and 'he*', the first person and the CRP, which I hold to be expressions of a single concept? (Of course, English does not discriminate between 'he*' and 'he', and indeed 'he', 'she', etc., are made to do many other jobs in addition to serving as the CRP. Greek, perhaps, is more discriminating—see above, § 3, n. 7.) The main difference between 'I' and 'he*' in my view is this: the CRP is always used within the scope of a verb of propositional attitude which has its own subject. In the simplest cases, e.g., 'Sarah said that she* was worried', it has as its antecedent the subject of a verb of saying which is the main verb of the proposition where the CRP occurs in a subordinate clause. (In more complicated cases, e.g., 'Sarah remembered that she* had said that she* was worried', the relation between pronoun and antecedent is indirect, via another occurrence of the pronoun. There are other possibilities.) The first person pronoun, on the other hand, does not have an antecedent in the sentence in which it occurs. However, the fact of its use can be stated in a proposition obtained by substituting the CRP for it and embedding the sentence thus obtained in the context '*a* says that ---', where *a* is the person who has said 'I ......'. Since the first person pronoun does not have an antecedent in the sentence in which it occurs, it can be regarded as having widest scope in that sentence. That is why, if Madame de Maintenon says 'Louis says that *he is the State', her use of '*he' refers to Louis XIV, whereas if she says 'Louis says that I am the State' her use of 'I' refers to herself. However deeply embedded in the context in which it occurs, 'I' will escape from that context, because the point of its use is to allow the hearer to conclude, from the fact of its use by *a*, a corresponding truth of the form '*a* says that ...... *he ......', where '*he' has '*a*' as its antecedent. The antecedent of 'I', so to speak, is always outside the sentence in which it occurs. It can never refer back to an antecedent within that sentence so as to have scope narrower than the sentence itself.[28] Since the difference between the first person singular and the CRP is seen to be a difference of scope, and in the logical notations I am employing, scope-distinctions are always expressible by left–right ordering, this justifies the decision not to have different symbols for 'I' and 'he*'. '*' will serve to express them both. Thus, with φx read as '*x* deserves to die', and *a* as 'David' and 'δ' as '--- thought that ......', (21) is equivalent to $\delta * \varphi a$, whereas 'I deserve to die' is equivalent to $*\varphi$. Where * occurs without a δ-type operator (any verb of propositional attitude) to the left of it, it represents 'I' or some other case of the first person pronoun; where a verb of propositional

---

[28] This account of the distinction between 'I' and 'he*' in terms of scope, can be extended to explain the relations between 'now' and 'then*', 'here' and 'there*', etc., relations which Castañeda discusses at some length in his paper 'Indicators and Quasi-Indicators', *American Philosophical Quarterly*, vol. 4 (1967). It is this feature of our use of 'here' which explains the difference between its raining here and its raining where I am, noted by Simon Blackburn in 'Thought Without Representation', *Proceedings of the Aristotelian Society*, 60 (1986), pp. 160 ff. 'It might rain here without raining where I am' has the sense of 'For some τ, both I am τ, and it could be the case that both it is raining τ and for some σ, both I am σ and it is not raining σ', where τ and σ go proxy for locative expressions, e.g., 'there' or 'in Manchester'. 'Where I am' can have, as it were, primary or secondary occurrence: 'here' can only have primary occurrence.

attitude in the third person *does* occur to the left of *, it represents
'he*' or some other CRP.

§ 21. This rationale of the first person provides an explanation of
'immunity to error through misidentification'. The person who
says 'I deserve to die' does not, in using these words, express some
identification he has made of the person who he is saying deserves
to die. He cannot therefore err through misidentifying this person.
Although what he says does not identify the person he is speaking
about, *his saying what he does* may serve to identify this person.
Any person who hears him will at least be able to identify the
person who has been said to be deserving of death as the person
who has been speaking, even if no more interesting identification
is available to him. And, of course, it is the purpose of the use of
'I' that the hearer should be able to identify the speaker as the
subject of what is said. Whilst misidentification is not a possibility
for the speaker (not, that is, in virtue of what he says), it *is* a
possibility for the hearer: he may think it was the third person
from the right who spoke when in fact it was the fourth person
from the right. Misidentification is impossible in the one case,
because no identification has occurred; where identification occurs
misidentification is usually possible—but not always.

§ 22. When Sarah says 'I am worried' she does not say who is
worried; she does not imply anything of the form 'The person who
is worried is the same as ......'. There is no identification and *a
fortiori* no use of the concept of identity. It has been claimed
already that where the concept of identity is used to *say* something, repetition of some element in a proposition could be used to
show this. Sarah's remark contains no repetition. But suppose she
made a remark which did contain repetition. Suppose she said
'I don't know where the car keys are and I am worried'. In the
notation I have introduced the form of this is given by $(*\varphi \ \& \ *\psi)$.
Could there be in this case error through misidentification? There
can be no such error if someone says something of the form $*\varphi$.
Error of this sort could hardly creep in when one simply conjoins
two such sentences. Is it possible to suppose that Sarah would lose
her immunity to error through misidentification if, instead of
saying 'I don't know where the car keys are and I'm worried',

she were to say, 'I don't know where the car keys are and am worried'?[29]

The difference between these two sentences is analogous to that between (2) and (6) of Chapter III. There the importance of the difference lay in the fact that (6), but not (2), involved the concept of identity, although the concept was expressed by the misleading device of deleting a proper name rather than by inserting some new symbol. But (6) was seen to be equivalent to a proposition formed by attaching to the name 'Dubrovnik' the predicable (6B*), which does contain a verbal expression of the concept of identity. In the same way, the concept of identity has to become explicit if we express the form of sentences like 'I don't know where the car keys are and am worried' with the help of *. We need, in this variable-free free notation to which * belongs, first to use reflection to convert the two-place predicable $(\varphi(—) \,\&\, \psi(—))$ into a one-place predicable. Then the resulting Ref $(\varphi \,\&\, \psi(—))$ can be made argument to *, yielding *Ref $(\varphi \,\&\, \psi)$. Since 'Ref' is a perspicuous expression of the concept of identity, we shall have here an identity claim, an identification. What is being claimed is that a person who does not know where her car keys are is the same as a person who is worried. Is it possible that while Sarah's remark 'I don't know where the car keys are and I'm worried' is immune to error through misidentification, the alternative remark 'I don't know where the car keys are and am worried' is not so immune?

§ 23. If the move from $(*\varphi \,\&\, *\psi)$ to *Ref $(\varphi \,\&\, \psi)$ is questioned—and I don't think it should be!—then the case should be considered where the two-place predicable is already present in the primitive expression of the first-personal claim. To go back to Bernard Williams's story, suppose that A says 'I know that I'm afraid I'm going to be tortured'. Taking him at his word, we say 'A knows that he* is afraid that he* is going to be tortured'. Using a as the name of A and reading δ as 'knows that' and β as 'is afraid that' and φ as 'is going to be tortured', this proposition can be written $\delta^*\beta^*\varphi a$. Here again nothing that A has said constitutes an

---

[29] If someone objects that the use of 'am' in the second of these sentences already involves the use of the first person, try putting the whole sentence into the past tense: 'I didn't know where the car keys were and was worried'.

identification of the person whom he says he knows is afraid of torture or of the person whom he says he is afraid is going to be tortured; it is his saying it, rather than what he says that can help people identify who it is he is talking about. Where there is no attempt at identification there can be no misidentification. But if we suppose that $\delta^*\beta^*\varphi a$ entails δ^* Ref $\beta\varphi a$, there is an attempt at an internal identification, so to speak. A implicitly identifies a person who, it is feared, is going to be tortured with a person who fears that someone is going to be tortured.[30] Although there is identification here, it surely makes no sense to suppose that there could be misidentification. How could the person whom A knows is afraid that someone is going to be tortured, namely himself, be other than the person whose torture he knows is feared, namely himself?

The tie between '*' and 'Ref' is here very close. There is no difficulty in supposing that $\delta^*\beta^*\varphi a$ entails δ^* Ref $\beta\varphi a$. We are already familiar with the entailment of Ref $\delta\varphi a$ by $\delta^*\varphi a$, and this entailment must be appreciated by anyone who possesses the concept of the CRP. No one could think of someone that he was afraid that he* was going to be tortured without thinking that he was afraid that he (not CRP) was going to be tortured. But it is possible to think of someone that he is afraid that he (not CRP) is going to be tortured without thinking of him that he is afraid that he* is going to be tortured. ($\delta\beta^*\varphi ba$ entails δ Ref $\beta\varphi ba$, but δ Ref $\beta\varphi ba$ does not entail $\delta\beta^*\varphi ba$.) This could happen if Matthew thought that Mark was afraid that Luke was going to be tortured when Matthew, but not Mark, was aware that Mark and Luke were the same person. We could even, by some weird supposition of split personalities on the scale of Miss Beauchamp, envisage Matthew, Mark, and Luke all being the same person without any of them (!) realizing it, so that Ref δ Ref $\beta\varphi a$ or Ref $\delta\beta^*\varphi a$ could be true without $\delta^*\beta^*\varphi a$ being true. What we could not suppose was that Matthew might know that he* was afraid that he (not the CRP) was going to be tortured without knowing that he* was afraid that he* was going to be tortured (i.e., not only do we have, as already argued, the entailment of δ^* Ref $\beta\varphi a$ by $\delta^*\beta^*\varphi a$, but also that of $\delta^*\beta^*\varphi a$ by δ^* Ref $\beta\varphi a$). That is, Matthew could not be in a position to say in his heart 'I am someone to whom the

---

[30] Cf. the argument of McTaggart in *Hastings Encyclopaedia of Religion and Ethics*, s.v. 'Personality'.

reflexive predicable "ξ fears that ξ is going to be tortured" applies', without also being in a position to say in his heart 'I am afraid that I am going to be tortured'. Reduplication of the CRP and attachment of the CRP to a reflexive predicable go hand in hand: you cannot have one without the other. That is why the concept of personal identity, whose essence in my view is expressed by the reflection operator, is implicit in any repeated use of the CRP.

When A judges that he* is afraid that he* is going to be tortured, his judgement is immune to error through misidentification. This is because he employs no criteria in determining who it is who is afraid, or who it is that he is afraid for. *His* fear and *his* pain are precisely those which he is aware of without need to establish their subject. But his ability to recognize a truth expressible by a sentence whose form is $*\beta^*\varphi$ is *ipso facto* an ability to recognize a truth expressible by a sentence whose form is $* \text{Ref } \beta\varphi$. If he has no need of criteria for applying the concept of *self* (the first person) he has no need in this context of criteria for applying the concept of *same*. The appropriate relativization of *same* here is, of course, *same person*. It is the concept of personal identity which he is capable of using without reference to empirical criteria. It follows that no set of empirical criteria (e.g., psychological or biological continuity or connectedness) can exhaust the concept of personal identity.

This is what gives substance to Swinburne's claim that the criteria for personal identity are not to be confused with what we mean by '--- is the same person as ......'. They cannot constitute its meaning, because on occasion we use the concept of personal identity without having to have recourse to criteria. If David comes to realize that he hates himself, he knows straight off that the person who is hated is the same as the person who hates. It would be absurd to say: 'You know who it is who is doing the hating and who it is who is hated, but how do you know they are the same?' The concept here is the same as would be involved if I were to say that I had seen someone absorbed in his own book. In the latter case it would make perfectly good sense for someone to ask me how I knew that the person who was absorbed in reading was the same as the person who wrote the book. So the concept of personal identity is one where it is sometimes appropriate to ask for criteria and sometimes not. The criteria therefore cannot exhaust the meaning.

§ 24. The concept of *self* which is expressed by the CRP is not the same as that concept of *self* or *same* which is expressed by reflection or the Xi-operator. It is, as they are not, intimately connected with the concept of the Ego, the first person. On the face of it, it seems odd that the same word 'self' should on occasion be a way of expressing the topic-neutral concept of identity (cf. 'There is a number whose square is itself') and on other occasions be tied to topic-specific psychological theories (cf. 'She has a very poor self-image'). What has '=' to do with 'me'? What I have been saying will, I hope, do something to explain this connection. The use of the first person is to be understood only in terms of the Castañeda reflexive pronoun, the CRP. That is why * could serve to express them both. When Sarah says 'I am worried', the point of her remark lies in our being able to state the fact that she does so in the words 'Sarah says that she* is worried'. From this we can deduce that Sarah says that Sarah is worried and that, for some *x*, *x* says that *x* is worried. And here we have exactly the same conceptual apparatus as we needed to express the fact that my mother-in-law is the same as my physiotherapist. If worried Sarah bore my wife *and* gives me physiotherapy, this identity proposition does not need '=' to express it, but can be got over by 'For some *x*, both *x* bore my wife and *x* gives me physiotherapy'. The self-same structure is apparent both in the type of proposition which is needed to explain the sense of the first person and in the paraphrases which solve the paradox of identity. For some *x*, both *x* reveals the secret of the Ego and *x* explains how identity propositions can be both informative and true.

X

IDENTITY, BEING, AND TRUTH

§ 1. From 'Susan comes to dinner on Fridays' I can infer that there *is* a person who comes to dinner on Fridays. From 'Sarah bore my wife and Sarah gives me physiotherapy' I may infer that my mother-in-law is *the same* as my physiotherapist. From 'Percy says that the door was locked and the door was locked' I may infer that what Percy says is *true*. The inference in each case is from a singular proposition (or the analogue of a singular proposition) to its existential generalization. It can thus be said of the concepts of being, identity, and truth that the rationale of each of them is that it provides us with the means of expressing existential generalizations of things which on occasion we may wish to say with greater specificity. We need these expressions of these concepts in natural languages because natural languages lack the resources afforded in more formal dialects by the devices of quantification and variables. Armed with such devices I can say 'For some x, x comes to dinner on Fridays' without having recourse to the word 'be', I can say 'For some x, both x bore my wife and x gives me physiotherapy' without having recourse to the word 'same', and I can say 'For some p, both Percy says that p and p' without having recourse to the word 'true'. The concepts of being, identity, and truth are, therefore, in a sense one concept, because what these three words are used in English to express can be expressed in the language of Logic by the apparatus of quantifier and variable.

§ 2. Is it right, however, to claim that the apparatus of quantifier and variable gives expression to a single concept? How do you count concepts? What is the criterion of identity for the concept of a concept? Perplexing questions! Enough has been said, perhaps, in the course of this book, and in the earlier members of the trilogy, to display the facts on which any answers to these questions would be based. And it is the facts that matter, not the answers to scholastic questions involving terms of art.

So much for what the concepts of being, identity, and truth (if we are to continue to speak of concepts) have in common. What distinguishes them? A principal aim of Chapter IV of this book was to disentangle two elements which go together in the classical symbolism of quantification and variables: these two elements were derelativization and reflection. The inference from 'Susan comes to dinner on Fridays' to 'There is a person who comes to dinner on Fridays' could be described equally well as existential generalization or as derelativization. The conclusion could be said to be either of the form $\exists x \, (\varphi x)$ or of the form Der φ. Not so the inference from 'Sarah bore my wife and Sarah gives me physiotherapy' to 'My mother-in-law is the same as my physiotherapist'. Derelativization could only get us to 'Someone bore my wife and someone gives me physiotherapy', which is not of the form $\exists x \, (\varphi x \, \& \, \psi x)$, as is the conclusion of the existential generalization. To get a variable-free equivalent of this, we have first to subject the two-place predicable '--- bore my wife and --- gives me physiotherapy' to reflection, so as to produce a one-place predicable of the form 'Ref Conj $\varphi\psi(—)$', namely '--- bore my wife and gives me physiotherapy'. Only then can we proceed to a proposition of the form 'Der Ref Conj $\varphi\psi$' which gives us what we need. So if we choose to count reflection and derelativization as different concepts, being and identity also will have to count as different.

§ 3. Is the difference between being and identity the difference between derelativization, on the one hand, and derelativization combined with reflection, on the other? Or is the concept of reflection by itself the counterpart of, indeed identical with, the concept of identity? I have spoken in previous chapters as though reflection alone provided an expression of the concept. Was this the best way of looking at the matter?

We can, I think, usefully consider a progression here. Take the propositions:

(27) Sarah bore my wife and Sarah gives me physiotherapy

(28) Sarah bore my wife and (the same person) gives me physiotherapy

(29) Someone bore my wife and (the same person) gives me physiotherapy

(30) My mother-in-law is the same as my physiotherapist.

Only the last two are equivalent in meaning (and that in virtue of the assumption that only one person gives me physiotherapy). Only the last employs the prima-facie two-place predicable '--- is the same as ......'. If the concept of identity is conceived as being expressed by whatever will express what we seek to express with this misleading 'relational' expression, only the combined resources of reflection and derelativization will suffice to express identity. If, however, it is the occurrence of the word 'same', in whatever context, which signalizes the presence of the concept of identity, it may be supposed present in (28) as well as in (29) and (30).

§ 4. Wittgenstein believed that all that was needed to express identity of object was identity of sign. Identity of sign is present in (27). The argument of Chapter III is supposed to have shown that identity of sign is not sufficient in all contexts to express identity of object, and the crucial step that is needed in order to supply what is lacking was seen to be the step from (2) and (2A) to (6) and (6A). The move from (2) to (6) is exactly the same as the move from (27) to (28). Wittgenstein does not, I think, explicitly use his contrast between 'saying' and 'showing' to make his point about identity, although he does say 'identity of object I express by identity of sign'. Disagreeing, as I do, with his view about the need for a sign of identity, I would not accept the (at least implicit) Wittgensteinian thesis that identity is something which can be shown but cannot be said. It can, of course, be shown; and propositions like (27) which contain a repeated element do precisely this. I have also argued that any fact about identity must be something which can be shown in this way. The inability of the Identity Theorists to show what they are attempting to say is a sign of the incoherence of their claims. But where truths of identity can be shown, what they show can also, *pace* Wittgenstein, be said. And the sign of identity which is principally employed to say this has to be a sign with the function of my Xi-operator or Quine's 'Ref'.

§ 5. Whether the existential quantifier (or 'Der') is also required depends on what counts as saying what is shown by propositions like (27). (28) contains an explicit feature (even if it takes the form of deletion) expressing the concept of identity. It does not, however, assert identity in the sense that the main purpose of the sentence is to say something of the form 'A is the same as B'. Assertions of this form, like (30), are what Wittgenstein regards as misleading; it is these which, he suggests, try to say something which cannot be said. It *can* be said, of course, and he himself indicates how it can be done. It can be done using a form of proposition exemplified by (29). And this does require the equivalent of derelativization, as well as reflection, for its expression. That is because it has to express what is expressed in (30) by definite descriptions. I shall argue towards the end of this chapter that identity as a seeming relation is foisted on us by definite descriptions as seeming names. For the reductive analysis of the definite descriptions we need the existential quantifier. For a reductive analysis of identity as a relation, therefore, we need 'Der' as well as 'Ref'.

§ 6. The symbol I have been using for the reflection operator in the last few paragraphs has been 'Ref', unadorned with subscripts. Had I been punctilious about syntactical categories, I should have said that the predicable present in (28) was of the form Ref_0 Conj $\varphi\psi(—)$, and that (29) and (30) were of the form Der_0 Ref_0 Conj $\varphi\psi$. The form of a proposition asserting event identity, however, if its depth grammar is taken to be that of (19A) rather than (19), will be Der_1 Ref_1 Conj δ_1 δ_2.[1] Here it is assumed that not only n-place predicables for $n \geq 1$, which are representable by the variables φ, ψ, etc., but no-place predicables also, i.e., propositions, which are representable by the variables p, q, etc., can be regarded expressions of first level. Quantifiers binding predicate variables, of whatever polyadicity, are accounted third-level predicates: quantifiers binding propositional variables, whose substituends are no-place predicables, should also be regarded as third-place predicates. The variable-free equivalent of $\exists p$. therefore, as well as of $\exists\varphi$, should be 'Der_1'. And, since the function of reflection is analogous to that of derelativization, where the variables it serves to replace are predicative or propositional variables, the appropriate subscript is again '1': we should write, therefore, 'Ref_1' as well as 'Der_1' in displaying the form of propositions like (19A).

[1] See ch. VIII, § 4.

This means that if we are to express propositions like 'What Percy says is true', taken as equivalent to 'For some p, both Percy says that p and p',[2] in the variable-free notation, we shall need a sentence of the form Der_1 Ref_1 Conj δ. Here the two bound propositional variables have first been reduced to one by the operation of 'Ref_1', and then the single remaining variable has been eliminated by the operation of 'Der_1'. An important difference, therefore, between the concepts of being and identity, on the one hand, and the concept of truth, on the other, is that derelativization and reflection, which represent being and identity, respectively, are operations which transcend the categories, whereas truth can be represented by the operators of derelativization and reflection only when these are restricted to the category of third-level predicable. 'There is' and 'same' can be replaced by 'Der' and 'Ref' with a variety of subscripts to suit the context: 'true' can only be replaced by a combination of 'Der_1' and 'Ref_1'.

§ 7. A corollary of the thesis that truth can be represented by a categorially restricted use of derelativization and reflection is the thesis that correspondence can be represented by a similar use of reflection. To say that what Percy says is true is to say that Percy's remark corresponds with the facts. Geoffrey Warnock argued that correspondence in this context must fall short of identity, that what *is* the case cannot be exactly the same as what Percy *says* is the case.[3] I criticized Warnock's argument in Chapter V of my *What is Truth?* by insisting that it is precisely because the same proposition occurs after 'Percy says' and again after 'and' in 'Percy says that the door was locked and the door was locked' that we can give 'For some p, both Percy says that p and p' as the existential generalization of this, and thus conclude that what Percy says is true. Correspondence with the facts is *shown* by taking the identical proposition which gives the content of Percy's assertion

---

[2] Strictly speaking, this is compatible with Percy's saying more than one thing, only one of which is true, so that the uniqueness of 'what Percy says' is not captured. This is why, in ch. III of my *What is Truth?*, I used, not the existential quantifier, but the definite description operator, to symbolize 'What Percy says is true': with Jp abbreviating 'Percy says that p', we can in this way represent 'What Percy says is true' by $\imath pJpp$. The full equivalent of this in the variable-free notation would be Conj Der_1 Ref_1 Conj J Neg Der_1 Der_1 Ref_1 Conj J.

[3] Geoffrey Warnock, 'Truth: or Bristol Revisited', *Proceedings of the Aristotelian Society*, Supplementary Volume 47 (1973).

and repeating it as the second conjunct of our conjunctive proposition—a conjunct which is provided simply by the naked, unqualified repetition of the same proposition. What is *shown* by this repetition can be *said* by the use of a repeated variable bound by a quantifier, or by reflection and derelativization. It is reflection here which corresponds to correspondence. The tedious perplexities which have teased philosophers attempting to expound a correspondence theory of truth can be banished by the reflection that correspondence *is* reflection. It is a concept with which we are by now, I hope, intimately familiar: it is not merely analogous to sameness, it is the same as it.

§ **8.** In *What is Truth?*[4] I argued that natural languages have need of the word 'true' and its synonyms because they lack the equivalent of propositional variables which can be bound by quantifiers. (They lack also, of course, reflection and derelativization operators which can be used over the whole range of syntactical categories). Natural languages possess, in the form of pronouns, an equivalent of the bound individual variables of logical notation. They lack a corresponding vocabulary of prosentences.[5] Quite as important as this lack, however, is a positive feature of natural languages, their possession of locutions having the form of definite descriptions. These locutions are easily regarded, as they were even by such a great logician as Frege, as a species of proper name. There are, no doubt, many partial explanations of the tendency so to regard them,[6] but one explanation is to be found in the fact that a definite description yields a proposition when attached to a one-place predicable of first level—just as a name does. A similar syntactical analogy constitutes a perennial temptation to regard expressions like 'some man', 'every orchestra', or 'an arbitrary number' as names or 'denoting phrases'. Definite descriptions, in fact, like these other expressions, should most often be regarded as second level predicables. Expressions of this category, like proper names, do indeed yield propositions when attached to first-level

---

[4] See, particularly, pp. 46 ff.

[5] This 'prosentential' account of truth had been adumbrated by Prior, and was developed in considerable detail by Dorothy L. Grover, Joseph L. Camp, Jr., and Nuel D. Belnap, Jr., in 'A Prosentential Theory of Truth', *Philosophical Studies*, 27 (1975).

[6] Some of these explanations I have tried to set out in ch. IV of *What is Truth?*. For definite descriptions as second-level predicables, see pp. 32 ff.

predicables; but this similarity is a bad reason for lumping them all together in the category of names. Looking more closely, we have to recognize that definite descriptions, again like expressions formed from 'some', 'every', etc., are not always even second-level predicables. They are sometimes third-level predicables. 'What the postman brought', like 'every sausage', is a second-level predicable, but 'What every great general is' and 'Something every schoolboy knows' are third-level predicables. Such expressions, if paraphrased with the help of the operators of reflection and derelativization, will require, not Ref_0' and 'Der_0', but 'Ref_1' and 'Der_1'. This is, as we have seen, true in particular of 'What Percy says'.

These distinctions of level, however, are not apparent in the surface grammar of natural languages. Such languages lack prosentences, and *a fortiori* lack subscripts of the kind I have introduced. On the surface, expressions like 'What Percy says' and 'What Jane has always wanted to be' are on a par with 'What the postman brought' and 'The pen of my aunt'. We find it easy to suppose that they all refer to objects, albeit outlandish objects like properties and propositions. Even those, like Quine, who have recognized that quantifiers are necessary for the interpretation of propositions containing definite descriptions have thought that 'higher order quantification' such as is involved in the introduction of third-level predicables, brought with it 'ontological commitment' to a whole range of undesirable objects.

Moreover an expression like 'What Percy says', no less than an expression like 'What the postman brought', requires completion in a natural language by a predicative expression. 'What the postman brought' may be represented in semi-logical jargon by 'For some x, the postman brought x and nothing but x, and x' where the sentence may be continued by 'is on the mantlepiece' or 'is a letter from the Inspector of Taxes'. Similarly 'What Percy says' may be represented by 'For some p, Percy says that p and nothing else, and p', where words like 'I have always believed that' or 'it may be the case that' can be inserted before the final p. In the case of the string of words beginning with 'For some x', something *has* to be added after the final x if we are to have a complete proposition. In the case of the string of words beginning with 'For some p', something *may* be inserted immediately before the final p; but we *can* leave them alone and still have a complete proposition. Their equivalent, however, 'What Percy says' can no more stand as a complete proposition than 'What the postman brought'. To get a complete proposition, equivalent in sense to 'For some p, Percy says that p and nothing else, and p', we have to add to 'What Percy says' the words 'is true'. 'What Percy says', like 'What the postman brought', has the appearance of naming an object; and if someone introduces this pseudo-object in this way we want to know what it is he wishes to say of it: is it foolish, or not the case, or actually true?

§ 9. The adjective 'true', then, is dragged into the language on the coat-tails of definite descriptions. As we saw when looking at the propositions of elementary arithmetic in Chapter VII, pseudo-objects and pseudo-predicables live by taking in one another's washing. As long as we say only such things as 'The king's carriage is drawn by four horses', we are not tempted to hypostatize the number four. But as soon as we start saying of four that it and five make nine, as soon as '(—) + (—) = (—)' starts masquerading as a three-place predicable of first level, we find ourselves 'ontologically committed' to numbers. It is not, as Quine thought, by quantifying over them that we embrace them as entities, but by seemingly saying things about them. And the converse is true: where we seem to have entities, foisted upon us by the way our language uses definite descriptions, we find a need to say something about them. Something has got to be said about what Percy says, if only that it is true. Where the ordinary-language equivalent of a third-level predicable has given us propositions, truth has to be invented as a property of these propositions.

Just so, when the idiom of definite descriptions presents me with objects in the shape of my mother-in-law or my physiotherapist, it becomes an open question whether these objects (this object) are (is) related to each other (itself) in a certain way, namely, by way of identity. Just as pseudo-objects collect pseudo-properties, so when two or three of them (or the same one twice) are gathered together they collect pseudo-relations. Russell's reductive analysis of definite descriptions, in getting rid of the pseudo-objects gets rid simultaneously of the pseudo-relation of identity. When we realize that we can say 'For some p, both Percy says that p and nothing else, and p', we find that truth as a property evaporates; it is redundant; we have no need of this hypothesis. Similarly, when we can say 'For some x, x bore my wife and x alone gives me physiotherapy', we have no more need of the relation of identity: it is already there with the repetition of the bound variable. Ockham's razor is ready to hand. 'I do not write "$(\exists x,y).f(x,y).x = y$", but "$(\exists x).f(x,x)$".'[7] The illusion that '--- is true' is a one-place predicable and the illusion that '--- is the same as ......' is a two-place predicable are both created by the same surface structure of natural languages which make definite descriptions look like logical subjects. Russell made much of the logical fictions created by construing the grammatical subjects of sentences containing definite descriptions as genuine logical subjects. He left it to his successors to dispel the illusions produced by construing the grammatical predicates of such sentences as genuine logical predicates.

§ 10. There has been much use in these pages of logical symbolism, borrowed, dug up, or newly contrived. Many readers, no doubt, will have been irritated by this, even if they have stayed long enough with the book to allow it to grate on their nerves. I do not believe it has all been self-indulgence; but I should like to end by making my point about being, identity, and truth without benefit of symbols. The inferences with which I began this chapter can be seen to be valid as soon as we grasp the meaning of the English sentences which are their premises and conclusions. Moreover, we can see the analogy between them: as 'There is a person who comes to dinner on Fridays' is to 'Susan comes to dinner on Fridays', so 'My mother-in-law is the same as my physiotherapist' is to 'Sarah bore my wife and Sarah (alone) gives me physiotherapy' and 'What Percy says is true' to 'Percy says that the door was locked and the door was locked'. We can express this analogy in technical terms, if we wish, by saying that the first member of each pair is an existential generalization of the second; but without any technicality we can see that the relationship of first to second in each case is the same. The proposition inferred is in each case weaker than the proposition from which it is inferred. (The entailments are not mutual.) It seems difficult to suppose that new one-place predicables signifying being and truth, in the first and third cases, and a new two-place predicable signifying identity, in the second case—predicables standing for genuine properties or

---

[7] Wittgenstein, *Tractatus*, 5.532.

relations—could be introduced into the discourse by this weakening process of inference. Susan, Sarah, and the door's being locked have dropped out of the discussion in the course of the derivations: it is difficult to see how any new substantive concepts could be supposed to have been brought in. The meaning of the conclusions is, I maintain, given in terms of the rules which allow them to be drawn from their respective premises. Their analysis is important only as a means to making these rules explicit. The analogy between the three inferences points to a large degree of overlap between the three concepts of being, identity, and truth. The area covered by this overlap has always been the scene of great activity on the part of practitioners of Metaphysics. I hope that the logical geography of this area is somewhat better known as the result of the maps I have been attempting to draw. The methods of projection used have not, I trust, appeared to produce unacceptable distortion.

EXPRESSIONS GIVEN A LABEL
IN THE TEXT

(α) $\exists x \{\varphi x \ \& \ [\forall y \ (\varphi y \rightarrow x = y) \ \& \ x = a]\}$

(β) $\exists x \ (\varphi x \ \& \ a = x) \leftrightarrow \varphi a$

(γ) $\varphi a \ \& \ \forall y \ (\varphi y \rightarrow a = y)$.

(A) $\exists x \ [(\varphi x \ \& \ \psi x) \ \& \ \forall y \ (\varphi y \rightarrow x = y)]$

(B) $\exists x \ (\varphi x) \ \& \ \{\forall y \ \forall z \ [(\varphi y \ \& \ \varphi z) \rightarrow y = z]$
  $\& \ \forall w \ (\varphi w \rightarrow \psi w)\}$

(C) $\exists x \ \forall y \ [(\varphi y \leftrightarrow x = y) \ \& \ \psi x]$

(D) $\exists x \ (\varphi x \ \& \ \psi x) \ \& \ \neg \ \exists y \ \exists z \ [(\varphi y \ \& \ \varphi z) \ \& \ y \neq z]$

(E) $\exists x \ (\varphi x \ \& \ a = x) \ \& \ \neg \ \exists y \ \exists z \ [(\varphi y \ \& \ \varphi z) \ \& \ y \neq z]$

(F) $\varphi a \ \& \ \neg \ \exists x \ \exists y \ [(\varphi x \ \& \ \varphi y) \ \& \ x \neq y]$

(G) $\exists x \ (\varphi x \ \& \ (\imath v)(\psi v) = x) \ \& \ \neg \ \exists y \ \exists z \ [(\varphi y \ \& \ \varphi z) \ \& \ y \neq z]$

(H) $\varphi \ ((\imath v)(\psi v)) \ \& \ \neg \ \exists y \ \exists z \ [(\varphi y \ \& \ \varphi z) \ \& \ y \neq z]$

(I) $\exists x \ (\psi x \ \& \ \varphi x) \ \& \ \{ \ \neg \ \exists w \ \exists v \ [(\psi w \ \& \ \psi v) \ \& \ w \neq v]$
  $\& \ \neg \ \exists y \ \exists z \ [(\varphi y \ \& \ \varphi z) \ \& \ y \neq z]\}$

(J) $\exists x \ (\varphi x \ \& \ \psi x) \ \& \ \{\neg \ \exists y \ \exists z \ [(\varphi y \ \& \ \varphi z) \ \& \ y \neq z]$
  $\& \ \neg \ \exists w \ \exists v \ [(\psi w \ \& \ \psi v) \ \& \ w \neq v]\}$

(K) $\varphi a \ \& \ \neg \ \exists x \ \exists y \ (\varphi x \ \& \ \varphi y)$

(L) $\exists x \ (\varphi x \ \& \ \psi x) \ \& \ [\neg \ \exists y \ \exists z \ (\varphi y \ \& \ \varphi z)$
  $\& \ \neg \ \exists w \ \exists v \ (\psi w \ \& \ \psi v)]$

(i) The φer is different from the ψer

(ii) The φer is the same as the ψer

(δ) $(\exists x) \ (x \neq y_1 \ \& \ x \neq y_2 \ \& \ldots x \neq y_k \ \& \ K)$

(ε) $(x)(x = y_1 \ \vee \ x = y_2 \ \vee \ldots x = y_k \ \vee \ K)$

(M) $(\exists x)(y)(y \ \varepsilon \ x \equiv \varphi y)$

(N) $(\exists x)(y)(y \ \varepsilon \ x \equiv \ \sim y \ \varepsilon \ y)$

(O) $(\exists x)(x \ \varepsilon \ x \equiv \ \sim x \ \varepsilon \ x)$

(P) $(ex)(uy)(y \ \varepsilon \ x \equiv \varphi y)$

(Q) $(ex)(uy)(y \, \varepsilon \, x \equiv \, \sim y \, \varepsilon \, y)$

(R) $(ex)(x \, \varepsilon \, x \equiv \, \sim x \, \varepsilon \, x)$

(S) $(\exists x)(y)(y = x \lor y \, \varepsilon \, x \equiv \varphi y)$

(T) $(\exists x)(x = x \lor x \, \varepsilon \, x \equiv \, \sim x \, \varepsilon \, x)$

(U) $(\exists x)(y)(y \neq x \, \& \, y \neq z_1 \, \& \, y \neq z_2 \ldots y \neq z_k \, . \rightarrow$
$(y \, \varepsilon \, x \equiv \varphi y))$

(1) Boscovich was born in Ragusa and Dubrovnik is a present-day Croatian holiday resort

(2) Boscovich was born in Dubrovnik and Dubrovnik is a present-day Croatian holiday resort

(3) For some town x, both Boscovich was born in x and x is a present-day Croatian holiday resort

(4) Some town where Boscovich was born is the same town as a present-day Croatian holiday resort

(1A) Paul thinks that Boscovich was born in Ragusa and that Dubrovnik is a present-day Croatian holiday resort

(2A) Paul thinks that Boscovich was born in Dubrovnik and that Dubrovnik is a present-day Croatian holiday resort

(3A) Paul thinks that, for some town x, both Boscovich was born in x and x is a present-day Croatian holiday resort

(4A) Paul thinks that a town where Boscovich was born is the same as a present-day Croatian holiday resort

(5A) For some town x, Paul thinks that Boscovich was born in x and x is a present-day Croatian holiday resort

(6B) ...... was the birthplace of Boscovich and is a present-day Croatian holiday resort

(6A) Paul thinks that Dubrovnik was the birth-place of Boscovich and is a present-day Croatian holiday resort

(6) Dubrovnik was the birth-place of Boscovich and is a present-day Croatian holiday resort

(1B) Boscovich was born in --- and ...... is a present-day Croatian holiday resort

(6B$_1$) Boscovich was born in --- and the same town is a present-day Croatian holiday resort

(1*)˙ Ragusa was the birthplace of Boscovich and Dubrovnik is a present-day Croatian holiday resort

(1B*) --- was the birthplace of Boscovich and ...... is a present-day Croatian holiday resort

(6B*) --- was the birthplace of Boscovich and the same town is a present-day Croatian holiday resort

(6B$_2$) Ξu [Boscovich was born in u and u is a present-day Croatian holiday resort] (—)

(2A$_2$) Ξu [Paul thinks that Boscovich was born in u and that u is a present-day Croatian holiday resort] Dubrovnik

(6A$_2$) Paul thinks that (Ξu [Boscovich was born in u and u is a present-day Croatian holiday resort] Dubrovnik)

(2A$_3$) Ref δ Conj $\varphi\psi a$

(6A$_3$) δ Ref Conj $\varphi\psi a$

(3A$_3$) δ Der Ref Conj $\varphi\psi$

(6$_3$) Ref Conj $\varphi\psi a$

(3/4$_3$) Der Ref Conj $\varphi\psi$

(2$_3$) Conj $\varphi\psi aa$

(iii) For some person, x, x alone mended Locke's shoes yesterday and x alone opened Parliament the day before

(iv) For some man, y, for some man, z, y alone mended Locke's shoes yesterday and z alone opened Parliament the day before

(v) For every person, x, if x mended Locke's shoes yesterday, x opened Parliament the day before

(vi) For every man, x, if x mended Locke's shoes yesterday, x did not open Parliament the day before

(vii) Akela, and no one else, built up a strong pack in 1987, and Akela, and no one else, held a successful barbecue last week

(viii) In 1987 Akela, and no one else, built up a strong pack, and last week Akela, and no one else, held a successful barbecue

(LL1) $\forall x\ \forall y\ [\forall\varphi\ (\varphi x \leftrightarrow \varphi y) \rightarrow x = y]$

(LL1$_1$) $\neg\ \exists x\ \exists y\ [\forall\varphi\ (\varphi x \leftrightarrow \varphi y)\ \&\ x \neq y]$

(LL1$_2$) $\neg\ \exists x\ \exists y\ \forall\varphi\ (\varphi x \leftrightarrow \varphi y)$

(LL2) $\forall x\ \forall y\ [x = y \rightarrow \forall\varphi\ (\varphi x \leftrightarrow \varphi y)]$

(LL2$_1$) $a = (\imath x)(\varphi x) \rightarrow \forall \psi \, (\psi a \leftrightarrow \psi((\imath x)(\varphi x)))$

(LL2$_2$) $(\imath x)(\varphi x) = (\imath y)(\psi y) \rightarrow \forall \chi \, (\chi((\imath x)(\varphi x)) \leftrightarrow \chi \, ((\imath y)(\psi y)))$

(LL2$_{1A}$) $(F) \rightarrow [\forall \psi \, (\psi a \leftrightarrow (D))]$

(LL2$_{2A}$) $(J) \rightarrow [\forall \chi \, ((D_1) \leftrightarrow (D_2))]$

(LL2$_{1B}$) $[\varphi a \,\&\, \neg\, \exists x \, \exists y \, (\varphi x \,\&\, \varphi y)] \rightarrow \forall \psi \, \{\psi a \leftrightarrow$
$[\exists x \, (\varphi x \,\&\, \psi x) \,\&\, \neg\, \exists y \, \exists z \, (\varphi y \,\&\, \varphi z)]\}$

(LL2$_{2B}$) $\{\, [\exists x \, (\varphi x \,\&\, \psi x) \,\&\, \neg\, \exists y \, \exists z \, (\varphi y \,\&\, \varphi z)]$
$\&\, \neg\, \exists w \, \exists v \, (\psi w \,\&\, \psi v) \} \rightarrow \forall \chi \, \{\, [\exists x \, (\varphi x \,\&\, \chi x)$
$\&\, \neg\, \exists y \, \exists z \, (\varphi y \,\&\, \varphi z)] \leftrightarrow [\exists x \, (\psi x \,\&\, \chi x$
$\&\, \neg\, \exists y \, \exists z \, (\psi y \,\&\, \psi z)]\}$

(LL2$_{1C}$) $(K) \rightarrow \forall \psi \, (\psi a \leftrightarrow \imath x \varphi x \psi x)$

(LL2$_{2C}$) $(L) \rightarrow \forall \chi \, (\imath x \varphi x \chi x \leftrightarrow \imath y \psi y \chi y)$

(7A) $\imath x \varphi x \Xi u \, [\delta(\psi u \,\&\, \neg \psi u)] \, x$

(8A) $\imath x \varphi x \delta \Xi u \, [(\psi u \,\&\, \neg \psi u)] \, x$

(7A$_1$) Der Ref δ Conj ψ Neg ψ

(8A$_1$) Der δ Ref Conj ψ Neg ψ

(9A) $\delta(\psi a \,\&\, \neg \psi b)$

(10A) $\delta(\psi a \,\&\, \neg\, \psi a)$

(11A) Ref δ Conj ψ Neg ψa

(12A) δ Ref Conj ψ Neg ψa

(PISC') $\neg\, \exists p \, [\delta'(p \,\&\, \neg\, p)a]$

(PISC'') $\neg\, \exists x \, \exists \varphi \, \delta' (\varphi x \,\&\, \neg \varphi x)a$

(PISC''') $\neg\, \exists x \, \exists \varphi \, \delta' \, \Xi u \, [\varphi u \,\&\, \neg\, \varphi u] \, xa$

(LL2$_m$) If there is something of which both a and b are names, then for every φ, φa is materially equivalent to φb

(D1) $Snmk =_{\mathrm{df}} \forall \varphi \, \forall \psi \, \{nx \varphi x \rightarrow [my \psi y \rightarrow kz (\varphi z \lor \psi z)]\}$

(D2) $S\,4,5,9 =_{\mathrm{df}} \forall \varphi \, \forall \psi \, \{4x \varphi x \rightarrow [5y \psi y \rightarrow 9z \, (\varphi z \lor \psi z)]\}$

(D3) $5\#x \varphi x =_{\mathrm{df}} (5y \varphi y \,\&\, \neg\, 4y \varphi y)$

$0x \varphi x =_{\mathrm{df}} \neg\, \exists x \, (\varphi x)$
$1x \varphi x =_{\mathrm{df}} \neg\, \exists x \, \exists y \, (\varphi x \,\&\, \varphi y)$

(D4) $2x \varphi x =_{\mathrm{df}} \neg\, \exists x \, \exists y \, \exists z \, [(\varphi x \,\&\, \varphi y) \,\&\, \varphi z]$

$3x \varphi x =_{\mathrm{df}} \neg\, \exists x \, \exists y \, \exists z \, \exists w \, \{[(\varphi x \,\&\, \varphi y) \,\&\, \varphi z] \,\&\, \varphi w\}$
$nx \varphi x =_{\mathrm{df}} \neg\, \exists x_1 \, \exists x_2 ... \exists x_{n+1} \, \{...(\varphi x_1 \,\&\, \varphi x_2) \,\&\, ...$
$\&\, \varphi x_{n+1} \}$

(13) $\forall \varphi \, \forall \psi \, \{\neg \exists x \, \exists y \, (\varphi x \,\&\, \varphi y) \rightarrow$
$[\neg \, \exists x \, \exists y \, \exists z \, \{(\psi x \,\&\, \psi y) \,\&\, \psi z\}$
$\rightarrow \neg \, \exists x \, \exists y \, \exists z \, \exists w \, \{[\,(\varphi x \vee \psi x) \,\&\, (\varphi y \vee \psi y)]$
$\&\, [(\varphi z \vee \psi z) \,\&\, (\varphi w \vee \psi w)]\}\,]\}$

(14) $\neg \, \exists \varphi \, \exists \psi \, \neg \, kz \, (\varphi z \vee \psi z)$

(15) There is no φ such that at least $k + 1$ things φ

(16) $\forall \varphi \, \forall \psi \, \{(\text{—})x \varphi x \rightarrow [\,(\text{—}) \, y \psi y \rightarrow (\text{—})z \, (\varphi z \vee \psi z)]\}$

(17) $\exists n \, (S\,4,5,n \,\&\, S\,6,3,n)$

(17$_s$) $S\,4,5,9 \,\&\, S\,6,3,9$

(Rnxφx) Replace $0x\varphi x$ with $\neg \, \exists x \, (\varphi x)$; and for every $n > 0$, add n quantifiers after $\exists x$, and n open sentences formed by attaching a single variable to φ separated from each other by occurrences of '&' with appropriate bracketing, allowing no repeated occurrences of variables after φx

(S) 'Sabc' is true iff '(F)(G)(($\exists$!axF & $\exists$!bxG & ~$(\exists x)$(F & G)) $\rightarrow \exists$!cx(F V G))' is true

(Snxφx) A substitution instance of $nx\varphi x$ is obtained by negating a quantified proposition formed by existentially quantifying the variables (interpreted exclusively) in an open sentence formed by conjoining $n + 1$ open sentences obtained by attaching each of $n + 1$ distinct variables to a separate occurrence of φ

(D5)

$0x\varphi x$	$=_{\mathrm{df}}$	Neg Der φ
$1x\varphi x$	$=_{\mathrm{df}}$	Neg Der Else φ
$2x\varphi x$	$=_{\mathrm{df}}$	Neg Der Else Else φ
$nx\varphi x$	$=_{\mathrm{df}}$	Neg Der Else$_1$ Else$_2$ ...Else$_n$ φ

(D6)

0φ	$=_{\mathrm{df}}$	Neg Der φ
$0'\varphi$	$=_{\mathrm{df}}$	Neg Der Else φ
$0''\varphi$	$=_{\mathrm{df}}$	Neg Der Else Else φ
$n\varphi$	$=_{\mathrm{df}}$	Neg Der Else$_1$ Else$_2$ ...Else$_n$ φ

(D7)

$P\,0mn$	$=_{\mathrm{df}}$	$S\,00n$
$Pn'mk$	$=_{\mathrm{df}}$	$\exists j \, (Pnmj \,\&\, Sjmk)$

(D8)

$Tn\,0m$	$=_{\mathrm{df}}$	$S\,01m$
$Tnm'k$	$=_{\mathrm{df}}$	$\exists j \, (Tnmj \,\&\, Pnjk)$

(D9) $S'n,m,k =_{df} \forall y \, \forall z \, \{n\#x\,(\varphi xyz) \rightarrow [m\#x\,(\psi xyz) \rightarrow$
$\qquad \qquad O\,(k\#x\,(\chi xyz))]\}$

(D9–Neg) $S'n, -m, -k =_{df} \forall x \, \forall y \, \{n\#x\,(\varphi xyz) \rightarrow$
$\qquad [m\#x\,(\text{inv}\psi xyz) \rightarrow O\,(k\#x\,(\text{inv } \chi xyz))]\}$

(18A) For some dress x, both I bought x (and no other dress) last week and she was wearing x

(18B) For some φ, both the dress I bought last week φs and the dress the visiting speaker was wearing φs

(19) The event Henrietta reported was the event which caused the vase to be broken

(20) Henrietta reported the neighbours' cat jumping through the window and the neighbours' cat's jumping through the window caused the vase to be broken

(20A) Henrietta reported that the neighbours' cat jumped through the window and the vase was broken because the neighbours' cat jumped through the window

(19A) For some p, both Henrietta reported that p and the vase was broken because p

(19L) $\{[\exists p \, (\delta_1 p \,\&\, \delta_2 p) \,\&\, \neg \, \exists q \, \exists r \, (\delta_1 q \,\&\, \delta_1 r)]$
$\&\, \neg \, \exists s \exists t \, (\delta_2 s \,\&\, \delta_2 t)\}$

(21) David thought that he* deserved to die

(22) David thought that David deserved to die

(23) David thought that he deserved to die

(24) Jones remarked at noon that it was then* time for the meeting to begin

(25) If David was right, David deserved to die

(26) If Jones was right, noon was the time for the meeting to begin

(27) Sarah bore my wife and Sarah gives me physiotherapy

(28) Sarah bore my wife and (the same person) gives me physiotherapy

(29) Someone bore my wife and (the same person) gives me physiotherapy

(30) My mother-in-law is the same as my physiotherapist

BIBLIOGRAPHY

Anscombe, G. E. M., 'The First Person' in S. Guttenplan, *Mind and Language*, Oxford: Clarendon Press, 1975.

Butler, J., 'Of Personal Identity', in J. Perry (ed.), *Personal Identity*, University of California Press, 1975, pp. 100–1.

Castañeda, H.-N., ' "He": A Study in the Logic of Self-Consciousness', *Ratio*, 8 (1966), pp. 130–57.

——, 'Indicators and Quasi-Indicators', *American Philosophical Quarterly*, 4 (1967).

——, 'On the Phenomeno-Logic of the I', *Proceedings of the XIVth International Congress of Philosophy*, 3 (Vienna, 1969).

Chisholm, R. M., 'The Loose and Popular and the Strict and Philosophical Senses of Identity' in N. S. Care and R. H. Grimm (eds.), *Perception and Personal Identity*, Cleveland, Cleveland, Ohio: Case Western University Press, 1969.

——, 'The Indirect Reflexive', in C. Diamond and J. Teichman (eds.), *Intention and Intentionality: Essays in Honour of G. E. M. Anscombe*, Brighton: Harvester Press, 1979.

Davidson, D., *Essays on Actions and Events*, Oxford: Clarendon Press, 1980.

Dummett, M., *Frege: The Philosophy of Language*, London: Duckworth, 1973.

Evans, G., *The Varieties of Reference*, Oxford: Clarendon Press, 1982.

Flew, A. G. N., 'Selves', *Mind*, 58 (1949).

Frege, G., *The Foundations of Arithmetic*, tr. J. L. Austin, Oxford: Basil Blackwell, 1959.

——, 'The Thought', in P. F. Strawson (ed.), *Philosophical Logic*, Oxford University Press, 1967.

Geach, P. T., *Mental Acts*, 2nd edn., London: Routledge and Kegan Paul, 1971.

——, 'A Program for Syntax', in D. Davidson and G. Harman (eds.), *Semantics of Natural Language*, 2nd edn., Dordrecht and Boston, Mass.: Reidel, 1972, pp. 483–97.

——, 'A History of the Corruptions of Logic', in *Logic Matters*, Oxford: Basil Blackwell, 1972.

——, *Reference and Generality*, Ithaca and London: Cornell University Press, 3rd edn., 1980.

Gottlieb, D., *Ontological Economy*, Oxford: Clarendon Press, 1980.
Grover, D. L., Camp, J. L., Jr. and Belnap, N. D., Jr., 'A Prosentential Theory of Truth', *Philosophical Studies*, 27 (1975).
Guttenplan, S., *Mind and Language*, Oxford: Clarendon Press, 1975.
Hintikka, J., 'Identity, Variables and Impredicative Definitions', *Journal of Symbolic Logic*, 21 (1956), pp. 225–45.
——, 'Vicious Circle Principle and the Paradoxes', *Journal of Symbolic Logic*, 22 (1957), pp. 245–9.
Hume, D., *Treatise of Human Nature*, ed. Selby-Bigge, 2nd edn. revised by P. H. Nidditch, Oxford: Clarendon Press, 1985.
Kneale, W. C., 'Numbers and Numerals', *British Journal for the Philosophy of Science*, 23 (1972), pp. 191–206.
Kripke, S., 'Identity and Necessity', in M. K. Munitz (ed.), *Identity and Individuation*, New York University Press, 1971, pp. 135–64.
——, 'A Puzzle about Belief' in A. Margalit (ed.), *Meaning and Use*, Dordrecht: Reidel, 1979.
——, *Naming and Necessity*, Oxford: Basil Blackwell, 1981.
Lewis, H. D. (ed.), *Contemporary British Philosophy* (Fourth Series), London: George Allen and Unwin, 1979.
Linsky, L., *Reference and Modality*, Oxford University Press, 1971.
Locke, J., *Essay concerning Human Understanding*.
McTaggart, J. McT. E., in *Hastings Encyclopaedia of Religion and Ethics*, s.v. 'Personality'.
Marcus, R., 'Modalities and Intensional Languages', *Synthese*, 13 (1961).
Morris, T. V., *Understanding Identity Statements*, Aberdeen University Press, 1984.
Peirce, C. S., *Collected Papers*, ed. C. Hartshorne, P. Weiss, and A. W. Burks, Harvard, 1958.
Perry, J. (ed.), *Personal Identity*, Berkeley, Los Angeles, and London: University of California Press, 1975.
——, 'The Problem of the Essential Indexical', *Noûs* (1979).
Prior, A. N., 'Is the Concept of Referential Opacity Really Necessary?', *Acta Philosophica Fennica*, 16 (1963).
——, *Papers on Time and Tense*, Oxford: Clarendon Press, 1968.
——, *Objects of Thought*, ed. P. T. Geach and A. J. P. Kenny, Oxford: Clarendon Press, 1971.
Quine, W. V., 'Quantifiers and Propositional Attitudes', *Journal of Philosophy*, 53 (1956).
——, *Word and Object*, Cambridge, Mass.: MIT Press, 1960.
——, *From a Logical Point of View*, 2nd edn., New York and Evanston Ill.: Harper and Row, 1962.
——, *Ontological Relativity and Other Essays*, New York and London: Columbia University Press, 1966.

——, 'Variables Explained Away', *Proceedings of the American Philosophical Society* (1960), repr. in *Selected Logic Papers*, New York: Random House, 1966, pp. 227–35.

——, *The Ways of Paradox*, New York: Random House, 1966.

Russell, B., *Introduction to Mathematical Philosophy*, London: George Allen and Unwin, 1919.

——, *Logic and Knowledge*, ed. R. C. Marsh, London: George Allen and Unwin, 1956.

Schilpp, P. A. (ed.), *The Philosophy of Bertrand Russell*, Evanston, Ill., 1948.

Shoemaker, S., 'Self-Reference and Self-Awareness', *Journal of Philosophy*, 65/19 (Oct. 1968), pp. 555–67.

——, 'Persons and their Pasts', *American Philosophical Quarterly*, 7 (1970).

——, *Identity, Cause and Mind*, Cambridge University Press, 1984.

Smullyan, A. F., 'Modality and Description', *Journal of Symbolic Logic*, 13 (1948), pp. 31–7.

Strawson, P. F., *Individuals*, London: Methuen, 1959.

Swinburne, R. G., 'Personal Identity', *Proceedings of the Aristotelian Society*, 74 (1973–4), pp. 231–48.

——, 'Persons and Personal Identity', *Contemporary British Philosophy* (Fourth Series), ed. H. D. Lewis, London: George Allen and Unwin, 1979, pp. 221–38.

Toulmin, S. E., 'Self-knowledge and knowledge of the "Self"', in T. Mischel (ed.), *The Self: Psychological and Philosophical Studies*, Oxford: Basil Blackwell, 1977.

Warnock, G., 'Truth: or Bristol Revisited', *Proceedings of the Aristotelian Society*, Supplementary Vol. 47 (1973).

White, N. P., 'Aristotle on Sameness and Oneness', *Philosophical Review*, 80 (1971), pp. 177–97.

White, R., 'Wittgenstein on Identity', *Proceedings of the Aristotelian Society*, 78 (1977–8).

Whitehead, A. N., and Russell, B., *Principia Mathematica to *56*, Cambridge University Press, 1962.

Williams, B. A. O., 'The Self and the Future', *Philosophical Review*, 79 (1970).

Williams, C. J. F., *What is Truth?*, Cambridge University Press, 1976.

——, 'Is Identity a Relation?', *Proceedings of the Aristotelian Society*, 80 (1979–80).

——, *What is Existence?*, Oxford: Clarendon Press, 1981.

Wittgenstein, L., *Philosophical Investigations*, Oxford: Basil Blackwell, 1953.

INDEX